STOKES COUNTY, NORTH CAROLINA

WILLS

VOLUMES I - IV

1790-1864

SOUTHERN HISTORICAL PRESS
INC
Book Publishers

By
Mrs. W. O. Absher

Please direct all correspondence and orders to:

www.southernhistoricalpress.com
or
SOUTHERN HISTORICAL PRESS, Inc.
PO BOX 1267
375 West Broad Street
Greenville, SC   29601
southernhistoricalpress@gmail.com

ISBN #0-89308-557-X

Printed in the United States of America

TAPIOLA, Francis,141
TATE, Adam,033
. , Elizabeth,013,014,031
. , Francis,099 ,117
. , Owen D.,099 ,117
. , Owen,013 ,014,065
. , Rachel,013,014
. , Robert,013,014
. , Samuel,013,014
TATUM, Edward,030
. , John,006,030
. , Lettitia,144
. , Lucy,030
. , Mary,030
. , Molly,030
. , Pryor,144
. , Seth,030
. , Thomas,030
. , William,030
TAYLOR, ,025
. , Asa,149
. , Elizabeth,153
. , Ellen,153
. , Geo.,143
. , George,090 ,118,153
. , Hanner,034
. , Isaac,029
. , Josiah,060 ,090,153
. , Nancy,153
. , Fetsy,153
. , Polly,149
. , S.B.,155
. , S.H.,153
. , Sally Abington,029
. , Sally,153
. , Samuel H.,144
. , Samuel,153
. , T.B.,149
. , William,029
. , Wm.B.,148 ,149,153
TEAGUE, Benjamin,107
. , Elijah,111
. , Elizabeth,111
. , Ezekiel,073,078
. , Isaac,073 ,078,111
. , John,071
. , Martha,071
. , Susannah,107
. , William Sr.,112
. , William,071,107,111
TENNISON, Nancy,121
. , Warren,121
. , William,121
TERRY, John,034,092
. , Joseph,148
. , Wm.W.,153
TESH, Adam,023
. , Rosina,023
THOMAS, Elizabeth,141
. , H.K.,120,134
. , William,107
THOMASON, Andrew,086
. , Edy,052
. , Elizabeth,049
. , Geo.,008
. , George,031,052
. , John Jr.,008
. , John,031 ,049,052,079
. , Mary,052
. , Milly,052
. , Nancy,052
. , Pleasant,079
. , Sarah,079,101
THOMMASON, George,004
. , John Sr.,004
THOMPSON, Ephraim,053
. , John Sr.,008
. , John,035
THORNTON, Thomas,050
. , William,004 ,050
TILLEY, Aaron B.,136
. , David B.,081
. , David,100 ,104,153
. , Edmund,025 ,100,108
. , Elizabeth,136
. , Ezekial,149
. , Hampton B.,153
. , Henry,095
. , Joel,136
. , Julia Ann,153
. , Julia,153
. , Martha E.,149
. , Martin,127
. , Moses,136
. , Phebe,100
. , Reuben,153
. , Robert Pink,153
TISCH, Adam,004
TODD, Gasper,078,103,133
TOMMERSON(Sp) John,004
TOMPKINS, W.W.,113
TRANSAN, John,007
TRANSAU, Abraham Sr.,094
. , Eva,094
. , Lydia,124
. , Magdelena,114
. , Maria,118
. , Mary Eliz.,094
. , Mary Magdaline,094
. , Feter,130
. , Philip,094
. , Philipina,094
. , Sarah,125
. , Solomon,094,125
TRANSAW(TRANSOU), Magdelene,006
. , Phillip,006
TRANSAW, Abraham,006,094
. , Catherina,006
. , Elizabeth,006
. , John,006
. , Mary,006
. , Phillip,006
. , Rosina,006

TRANSOU, Anny,067
. , Emily,013
. , Emily,061
. , Florina,061
. , Hariot,061
. , Peter,061
. , Petries,011
. , Philip,118
. , Phillip,007,011,023
. , Solomon,066
TRANSOW, Magdeline,065
TRANSU, Anna,061
. , Ben,069
. , Beningna,061
. , Eln,069
. , Maria C.,061
. , Maria Catharine,060
. , Peter,061 ,069
. , Philip Parmenio,061
TRENT, James,149
. , Wm.,149
TUCKER, Benjamin C.,143
. , Edmund,134
. , Frances,136
. , Gabriel W.,143
. , Joel,143
. , Letty,100
. , Robert A.,143
. , Sarah,111 ,134
. , Silas,136
TUGGLE, Jerry,147
TURNER, Solomon,016,017
TUTTLE, Barbara,053,115
. , Catharine,108
. , Elijah,115 ,146
. , Elizabeth,153
. , Elley,136
. , Henry,115 ,153
. , James,115
. , John,016,053,115,136,153
. , Michael,115
. , Peter,115 ,141
. , Phebe,153
. , Susannah,141
. , Thomas,108 ,115
. , William,103,115
TUTTLES, Catharine,142
TWOMY(TOOMY), Patrick,026
UPP, Jacob,017
. , Nicholas,017
. , Peter,017
VAN FLECK, Christina,135
VAN SCHEINTZ, L.D.,097
VAN VLECK, Chas.A.,135
. , Christina Susan,135
. , Jacob(Rev) 026 ,046
. , Jacob,017
. , Wm.H.,135
. , Wm.Henry(Rev),097
VANCE, John,112
. , Jon,112
. , Lucreacy,112
. , William,112
VANE, John,044
VANHOY, Abraham,016
. , Abram,082
. , Clayton,016,138
. , Edward,016
. , Iseac,082
. , James,016
. , Jemima,016 ,017
. , John M.,082
. , Iohn Sr.,016
. , John,008,016,017
. , Martin W.,138
. , Mary,138
. , Nancy,016
. , Rachel,016
. , Ruth,138
. , Susannah,016
. , Thomas,016
. , William,016
VANNER, Joseph,002
VARNUM(VERNON) Jonathan,034
. , Rebecker,034
VARNUM, Ebenezer,034
VAUGHN, Ann(Mrs),033
. , Anny,148
. , Elijah,087
. , J.B.,145,154
. , Jane,148
. , Jerome B.,148
. , Jesse,087
. , John,087,089,126
. , Joseph,089 ,126
. , Mahala,148
. , Pleasant,087
. , Polly,087
. , Reuben,087
. , W.B.,154
. , Zebulan,067
. , Zebulum,087
VAUTER(VAWTER), John,005
. , Russel,034
VAUTER, John,034
VAWTER, Alpha Monroe,090
. , Bradford,090,123
. , Chadwick,123
. , Elizabeth,127
. , George T.,123
. , Harriet J.,126
. , James M.,127
. , John M.,090
. , John,005,019,076,127
. , Joseph E.,060
. , Josiah,123
. , Julia Madison,090
. , Matilda,123
. , Paulina,123
. , Polly S.,090
. , R.T.,076
. , Russel,076
. , Sophronia,123

VAWTER, Sparks,123
. , Susanna,123
. , William,123
VAWTOR, John,005
VENABLE, Jo.,065
. , John,049
. , Polly,049
VERNON, Jonathan,009,034
. , Nancy,109
. , Polly,153
. , Richard,109
VEST, Charles,017 ,048,065
. , Chas.,017
. , Elizabeth,084,093,108
. , George,085,093
. , Isham,002,016,017,048
. , J.P.,132
. , Jno.,085
. , John,048 ,084,093,108,119
. , Lewis,114
. , Lucy,048
. , Obediah,137
. , Rachel,137
. , Samuel,019,048
. , William,002 ,019,048,093
VICKERS, Tabitha,108
VIERLING, Anne Eliz.,021
. , Benj.,001
. , Benj.Saml.,001
. , Benjamin,047
. , Caroline,125
. , D.Samuel Benj.,056
. , E.,135
. , E.A.,122
. , Eliza,125
. , Elizabeth,125
. , Ernest,126
. , Ernestine,125
. , Henrietta Frederica,013
. , Maria Rosina,021
. , Martha E.,126
. , Saml.Benj.,021
. , Samuel Benj.,010 ,125
. , Theophilus,126
. , Traugott Theo.,072
. , William,125
VINES, John,016,017
VOGLER, Charlotte,113
. , Christoph,011 ,081
. , Christopher,081
. , E.A.,139
. , Elizabeth,113
. , Gottlieb,081
. , Hanah,110
. , John,054,059,061,081,110,111
. , ,124,113
. , Mary,027
. , Michael,011,027
. , Nathaniel,081
. , Palina,081
. , Philip,090
. , Phillip,113
. , Plaulind,081
. , Regina,081
. , Timothy,081,113
VOLK, Sarah,063
VON SCHWEINETZ, Amalia L.,097
. , Lewis D.,097
VON SCHWEINITZ, Frederic Chrst.,026
. , Hans C.A.,046
. , Johanna Eliz.,026
. , L.David,097
VOSS, Sally,074
. , Thomas,044
. , William,100

WADE, Jeremiah,017
WADKINS, Henry,128
WAGAMAN, Polly,110
WAGEMANN, Polly,131
WAGGONER, Adam,090
. , Ann,033
. , Betsy,031,090
. , Delphia,109
. , ELijah L.,090
. , Elizabeth,033,073
. , Gabriel,017 ,031,033,073
. , Jesse Minter,031
. , Joel B.,090
. , John,090
. , Joseph,031,033,042,043,109
. , ,137
. , Joshiah,090
. , Lewis,017,033,109
. , Margaret,090
. , Mary,031 ,033,073,090
. , Nancy,073,090
. , Philip,090
. , Samuel,008,017,031,033,034
. , Sarah,031,033
. , Seth,090
. , Spencer,090
. , Susan,090
. , Susanna,033
. , Thomas,031,033
. , William,031 ,033
. , Wm.,016 ,089
. , Wm.Sr.,016
WALDRAVEN, John Henry,105
. , Maria S.,146
. , Mary,105
WALKER, Abner,017
. , Ann,052,124
. , David,008
. , Elizabeth,101
. , Geo.,142
. , James,124
. , Jane,052
. , John,016,025
. , Margaret,052
. , Margarit,052
. , Martha,138

MCKOIN, Rachel,002
MCMILLION, Theophilis,017
         , Wm.,091
MCMIN(?), Jehu,048
MCMURRY, John,009
       , R.,009
       , Robert,009,010
MCPHERSON, Joseph,008
MEADOWS, (Major),153
MECUM, Elizabeth,087
      , James,054
      , John,052
      , Nancy,054
      , Ruth,054
      , Samuel,054
MEDEARIS, Stephen,030
MEDERIS, Betsy,030
MEDIERESS, Thomas,011
MEINUNG, Alex.,134
       , Christian Fredr.,088
       , Elizabeth,083
       , F.C.,047 ,067,095,101,103,
         117,126,134
       , Frederic C.,082,099,107
       , Frederic,026
       , Frederick C.,120
       , Fredr.Christian,047
       , Fredric C.,063
       , Fredric,068
       , Fredrick C.,045
       , Lewis,003 ,078
       , Lisetta,120
       , Louisa,078
MELTON, John,003
MENDENGHALL, Jonathan,054
           , Joseph,007
MENDENHALL, Elizabeth,069
          , Geo.C.,134
          , Jonathan,007
          , Joseph,007 ,032,055,069
MENDINGHALL, Joseph,054
MENDINGHAM, Jonathan,043
MEREDITH, Elisha,139
        , James,099
        , John,039
        , Jonathan,139
        , Sarah,139
        , Wm.,029
MERRETT, William,032
MERRIL, William,016
MERRIT, Florence,030
       , Frankey,055
       , Wm.,030
MERRITT, Mary,065
MERRIWEATHER, Wm.D.,113
METCALF, Charles,026
MEYER, Henry,023
      , Jacob,023
      , Phillip Jacob,023
MICKE, John,138
      , Paulina,138
MICKEY, Beningna,036
       , John Lewis,036
       , John,010,018,036
       , Juliana,036
       , Lewis,018 ,098,104,112
       , Magdelene,018
       , Mary Elizabeth,036
       , Salomon,036
MICKIE, James,113
MIENUNG, Frederick,047
MIKSCH, Caroline,126
       , John,126
       , Stasia,125
MILL, Richard,058
MILLER(MUELLER), John,076
MILLER(MULLER), Jacob,014
MILLER, Ann,052
       , Anna Katherine,032
       , Anny,066
       , Catharine,058
       , Caty,076
       , Charity,058
       , Charles,058
       , Christina,121
       , Daniel,058 ,123
       , David,058
       , Eliza,134
       , Elizabeth,032 ,058,122,129
       , Emily S.,122
       , Francis,134
       , Frederic,004
       , Frederick,014 ,032,038,059
       , Fredr.,005
       , Fredric,034,050
       , George F.,133
       , George,032 ,052,122
       , Godfrey,058
       , H.,141
       , Harmon,058
       , Henry,017 ,058
       , Hermannus,058
       , J.,017
       , Jacob Jr.,029
       , Jacob Sr.,006
       , Jacob,014 ,032,038,052,059,
         074,076,077,088,134
       , John B.,089,100,117,121,122,
         129
       , John Benj.,082
       , John,014,017,029,032,052,058
         ,059,077,088,113,134
       , Jonathan,076,123
       , Joseph Jr.,021
       , Joseph,002 ,014,021,032,051,
         059,069,121
       , Margaret,058,134
       , Margaritha,073
       , Mary,058
       , Michael,017,113,134
       , Nelly,021
       , Philip,077
       , Phillip,032,076

MILLER, Regina Eliz.,029
       , Salome,058
       , Sarah,058 ,059,122
       , Synthia,052
       , Titus,122
       , Valentine,113
MILLS, Jacob,063
      , John,072
      , Margaret,063
      , Richard,039 ,091
      , Thomas,007
MILLWOOD, James,005
        , Nanny,005
MISENA, Jacob,048
       , Polly,048
MITCHEL, Anne,075
        , David,075
MITCHELL, A.,126
         , Adam M.,143
         , Adam,015 ,091,143
         , Charles A.,143
         , James H.,143
         , James,143
         , Jesse M.,143
         , John G.H.,154
         , John,128
         , Mercy,143
         , Robert,056
         , W.A.,126 ,128,143
         , Wm.A.,077,103,121,127,145
         , Wm.M.,143
MOANEE, Christina,010
MOCK, George,130
MOIR, James C.,147
     , R.F.,154
MONROE, Henry C.,060
       , Robert F.,147,148
MONTGOMERY, D.G.,149
          , Hugh,046
MOO, John L.,130
    , Margaret,130
MOODY, Alexander,053,078,150
      , Andrew,150
      , Anna,078
      , Betsy,127
      , Elizabeth J.,150
      , Elizabeth,154
      , Emma Elizabeth,150
      , Mary Emaline,150
      , Mildred,150
      , Nall,017
      , Nathaniel,078,127,149,150,153
        ,154
      , Polly,078
      , Sally,078
      , Sarah Ann,150
      , Thomas,016 ,078
MOON, John,016
MOORE (Dr),120
      , Aaron,016,030
      , Alexander Jr.,016
      , Alexander,030,032,124
      , Ann D.,117
      , Anne D.,092
      , Betsy,094,095
      , David,040
      , Edward,025 ,026,080
      , Elizabeth,124,146
      , Francis,146
      , G.E.,151
      , Gabriel B.,151
      , Gabriel,026 ,057
      , Gideon A.,151
      , Gideon,057
      , Henrietta,120
      , J.,057
      , Jackson,154
      , James Jr.,030
      , James Sr.,030
      , John,030,057,081
      , Judah,094,095
      , Lettisha,026
      , Lettitha,025
      , Littsuse,036
      , Mary,146
      , Matt R.,102
      , Matt.,026
      , Matthew R.,057 ,100
      , Matthew Red,025 ,026
      , Matthew,020 ,025,057
      , Nancy B.,146
      , Patsy,030
      , Paulina,151
      , Polly,039,057,094,095
      , Rebecca,094
      , Reuben,025 ,026
      , Reubin,029 ,057,151
      , Samuel,025
      , Susanna,057
      , Susannah C.,144
      , Tucker Woodson,025 ,026
      , W.F.,143
      , William C.,057 ,150
      , William J.,151
      , William Sr.,097
      , William,013 ,026,030,032,039,
        055,057,124,146
      , Wm.,016 ,020,066
      , Wm.C.,057,144,150
      , Wm.J.,151
      , Wm.M.,144,147
MORDYKE, Martha,040
MOREFIELD, Elizabeth,119
         , Henry,119
MOREHEAD, James T.,135
MORGAN, Benjamin,103
       , Ezekiel,008
       , Lenoah,104
       , Solomon,104
       , Susan,108
MORGE, Gabriel,025
MORRIS, Becky,030
       , Elizabeth,045

MORRIS, Hammon,016 ,045
       , Hammond Sr.,045
       , Henry,076
       , Jesse,045
       , John,016,045
       , Lewis,140
       , Martha,140
       , Mary,076
       , Presley,045,054
       , Shadrack,016,045,109
       , Thomas,045
       , Travis,017 ,045
       , William,045
MOSBY, Kellurah,004
      , Nancy,004
      , Samuel,004
      , Susannah,004
      , Thomas,004
MOSER, Christian,063
      , Francis,063
      , Henry,017,063,064,129
      , Jane,129
      , John,063
      , Leonard,063
      , M.,017
      , Margaret,064
      , Mary,064
      , Michael,016 ,017,063
      , Peter,063,064,129
      , Rebecca,064
MOTSINGER, C.,034
MOTTS, (Line),004
MOURNER, Michael,050
MUCKE, Anna Susannah,128
MURKEY, John,007
MURPHEY, David,092
MURRAY, Byne,017
NADING(NETHING), Simon,074
NADING, George,074
NADINGS, George,103
NATIONS, John,081
NEAL, Asa,116 ,141
     , Conrad,116
     , George,116,141
     , John,116
     , Joseph,116
     , Mary,040
     , Nancy,116
     , Polly,116
     , Samuel,116
     , Thomas,040,091,103,116
     , William,116
NECT, Margaretha,015
     , Rudolf,018
     , Rudolph,017
     , Rudy,015
NEEDE, Michael,018
NEELEY, John,019
       , Samuel Sr.,041
NEIDE, Catherine,038
      , Daniel,038
      , Elizabeth,038
      , Jacob,038
      , John,038
      , Joseph,038
      , Mary,038
      , Nancy,038
      , Sarah,038
      , Susanna,038
NELSON, Albert Fountain,085
       , Anna Eliza,085
       , C.H.,118
       , Clara,085
       , Constant Hardin,085
       , Elexander,043
       , Elijah,066 ,114
       , George F.,119
       , I.,085
       , Isaac,017 ,043,045,085
       , Jesse,085
       , Joseph,043 ,085
       , Mary Smith,043 ,085
       , Mary,043
       , Sarah,043
       , T.H.,127
       , Wm.F.,150
NEW, John F.,030
NEWMAN, Charles,057
       , James,057
       , Margaret,057
NICHOLS, Anna,013
        , George,146
        , Lucy,104
NICHOLSON, Dosia,096
          , Thomas,096
NICKOLSON, Anderson,131
          , Anna,131
          , Nancy,131
NIDING(NADING), Mathew,037
NIDING, Christian,037
       , Eva Catharina,037
       , George,037
       , John,037
       , Joseph,037
       , Martin,037
       , Simone,037
NISSEN, A.,078
       , Christian,061 ,065,105
NISSON, C.,097
       , Salome,055
       , Schristian,055
NODING(NOEDING), Simon,074
NOLES, Milkey,054
NORMAN, Polly,137
NORTON, John,102
NUCLSON(NICHOLSON), John,008
NUL(NULL), John,061
NULL, Barbara,047
     , Catharine,127
     , Henry,061,082,127
     , Isaac,127
     , Jacob,047
     , John Jr.,127

FRAZER, Elizabeth,046
, Francis,046
, Jacob,046
, Jeremiah,046,125,136
, John,039
, Lowel,039
, Mary,125
, Robert,049
, Stephen,046
, Thomas,046
, William,046
, Wm.Sr.,008
FRAZIER, Bennet,112
, Lowel,104
, Rhoda,084
, Sarah,059 ,104
, Susanna,087
, William,019
FREEMAN, Agnes,097
, Andy J.,154
, Elizabeth,097
, Ellender,097
, Elviry Davis,154
, Hulda,097
, James,020
, John,008 ,097
, Joshua,102
, Mary,097
, William,097
FRENCH, John,024
, William,024
, Wm.,017
FRENZEL, Anna,117
, Christina,117
, Maria,117
FREY, Geo.,015
, Henry,016
, Jacob,070,083
, Michael,017
FRIES, Francis,134
, Johanna E.,146
, Johanna Eliz.,065
, Wilh.,065
, William,082
, Wm.,063
FROST, Elizabeth B.,115
, Elizabeth,102,115
, James B.,102,115
, James,102,115
, Louisa,102
FRUANUFF, John Frederic(Rev),026
FRY, Abraham,051
, Adam,051
, Benjamin,075
, Betsy,116
, Catharine,075
, Catherina,051
, Christian,051
, D.Zadon,075
, Delith,075
, Dorothea,053
, Elijah,075
, Eliza,121
, Gabriel,075
, George,015
, Henry,015 ,017,018,051,053
, Jacob,051 ,121
, Jane,075
, Jesse,051
, John,015 ,017,051,053,075,121,
        129
, Joseph,015,051
, Lewis M.,140
, Lewis,116
, Lydia,121
, Mary,051 ,121
, Masey,115
, Massey,140,146
, Michael Jr.,051
, Michael Sr.,053
, Michael,015,017,018,051
, Milly,116
, Nancy,075
, Patsy,116
, Peter,015 ,017,018,051
, Polly,075
, Sarah,051
, Thomas,075
, Valentine Jr.,051
, Valentine,015 ,017,051,055
FUELL, Benj.,063
FULK, Christian,070
, Henry,070,105
, John Jr.,065
, Mary,105
, Peter,065
FULKISON, Nancy,039
FULKS, Adam,105
, Daniel,105
FULLER, Charles,133
FULP, Archibald,079
, Betsy,076
, Elizabeth,040
, G.,063
, Geo.Sr.,073
, Geo.V.,134
, George Sr.,070,101
, George V.,101
, George,052,076
, James M.,132
, Michael J.,120
, Michael,039 ,077
, Michel,039
, Mickel,039
, Peter,040,118
, Sally,077
, Thomas,079
, William,063
FULTEN, Samuel,143
FULTON, Allen,139
, Elisha,139
, Elizabeth,139
, Fewel,139

FULTON, Francis,139,144
, Jane,144
, Joel,139
, Martha,145
, Mary,099
, Polly,099
, Samuel Sr.,141
, Samuel,139
, Wilson,142 ,144
GAINES, Ambrose,026
, Francis T.,045
, George W.,045
, Henry P.,045,050
, James L.,045
, James S.,034
, James,026
, Louisa,045
, Mary,026
, Phillip,045
, Richard,045
, Susannah,045
, Thomas,045
, Wm.D.,045
GAINS, James L.,045
GAMBLE, Barney,090
, Hannah,090
, William,085
GAMBOL, Polly,083
GAMBOLD, Anna Maria,083,114,138
, Frederic,105
, John Christian,078
, John Fredr.,083
, John,015 ,020,083,105
, Joseph,083
, Maria Rosina,083
, Sophia Eliz.,083
GAMMEL, David,027
, Mary,027
GAMMELL, Andrew,008,009
, Betsy,008
, James,008 ,009,010
, John,008 ,010
, Joseph,008
, Lucretia,008 ,009,010
, Peggy,008
, Samuel,008
, Wm.,008,009
GARDENER, Mary,051
GARDNER, Abigail,134
, Sylvanus,009
, William,134
GARRETT, Caleb D.S.,031
, Ira,113
GARRISON, Patty,079
GARTH, Elizabeth,113
, Frances,113
, Jesse W.,113
, Thomas,113
, William ,113
, Willis D.,113
, Willis,113
, Wm.,113
GATESBY(?), Tyre,064
GATEWOOD, Dudley,102
, Elizabeth,102
, George,102
, John,102
, Mordicea,102
, Polly Carter,057
, Richard,102
, Tempy,102
, William,102
GEIGER(KIGER), Adam,058
, Jacob,058
, John,058
GEIGER, Adam,033,046,082
, Christina,063
, John,046
, Lewis,082
, Martha,084
, Peter,063
GENDER, Elizabeth,059
GENTRY, Eliza,089
, Harriet,089
, I.E.,092
, Ira,089
, James,089
, Joel,089
, John,089
, Nancy,089
, Rebecca,089
, Richard,089
, Thomas,089
, William,089
GEORGE, Andrew,018
, Betsy,110
, Isaac,016
, James,043
, Levi,133
, Martha J.,142
, Mary,110,111
, Presley Jr.,154
, Presley,073,142
, Reuben,016
, Samuel,017
GERBER, Catharine,095
, Salome,095
, Susana,095
GERNTON(?), Wm.,009
GIBBINS, Christina,114
GIBBONS, Catharine,138
, Catherine,116
, Christina,116
, John C.,116
, Mary,116
, Meryann,116
, Salome,116
, William,116
GIBSON, Isaac E.,150
, Isaac G.,140
, Isaac S.,135,136,142

GIBSON, J.,115
, J.S.,140
, J.W.,132
, Jeremiah,001,020,037,062,085
        ,098,128,140
, John W.,141
, Olivia G.,140
, Robert W.,132
, Robert,017
, Sarah,115 ,140,150
, Saray,140
, W.N.,088
, William,120
, Wm. Green,120
, Wm.,016,017
GID--, Margaretha,056
GIDEONS, Margarethe,056
GIEGER(KIGER), Adam,064
GILBLASS & GILCHREST, (?),092
GILES, John,012
GILL, William,013
GILLY, Lewis,087
GILMER, Jno.A.,135
, John A.,144
GINDER, John,084
, Julianna,084
GLADFETTER, Christina,134
, George,134
GLEN, James,004
, Jeremiah,002 ,005
, Thompson,002 ,004
GLENN, John Jr.,006
, John,006
, Thompson,007,038
, Tyre,149
GLIDEWELL, Elizabeth,154
, John L.,154
GLOVERS, Alejah,068
GOEPFORT, Geo.,010
GOGGSHALL, Peter,008
, Reubin D.,140
GOLDEN, Isaac,118 ,126,127,130,150
GOLDING, Jacky,051 ,053
, John,102
, Nancy,053
, Polly,141
, R.D.,113 ,114
, Reuben D.,109 ,141,142
, Reubin D.,137
GOODE, Charles,017
, Geo.,016
, Henry,096
, Richard,012 ,013,017
, Thomas,096
, William,062 ,096
GOPFORT, George,015
GORDON, Frances,124
, John,124
, Mary,115
, Stacy,124
, William,080
GORODN, Wm.,017
GOSLEN, Caroline,122
GOSLIN, Caroline,138
, Catherine,027
, Elizabeth,027
, John,027
, Wm.,138
GOSS, Charles,135
GRABBS, Anna Maria,083
GRABS, Christian Henry,075
, Christian,066
, John Godtfreed,075
, John,146
, William(Wilhelm),075
GRAFF, John Michael,046
, Justina,070 ,071
, Justine,083
GRAHAM, Ele,030
, Levi,008
, Thomas,026
GRANGER, Bartlett,077
, Elizabeth,077
GRANT, John,004
GRANVILLE, Earl,046
, John Earl,026
GRAUS, John,032
GRAVES, Peter,081
GRAY, Linda,060
GREAR, Wm.,016
GREEN(KROEHN), Anna,013
, Conrad,078
GREEN, Anna,013,059,096,117
, Catharine,059,096
, Christina,096
, Conrad,011 ,059
, Eliza,059
, Elizabeth,027,055,059,096
, Frederic,058
, Frederick,059,096
, Hannah,096
, Henny,031
, Jacob,056,059
, James T.,145
, John Phillip,059
, Justina,058
, Phillip,058
, Philip,096
, Phillip Sr.,059
, Phillip,027
, Salome,096
, Sarah,058
, Susanna,078
, Susannah,105
, William,031
, Phillip,055
GREENE, Phillip,055
GREENWOOD, John,020
, Mary,060
, Tabitha,057
, Wm.,057
GREGORY, Elizabeth,105
, Nancy,092

CROUS(E), John,003
CROUSE, John Sr.,019
  , Margaret,047
CROW, Thos.,008
CRUM, Godfrey,058
CRUMPLY, Irvin Asley,140
  , James M.,140
  , Nancy E.,140
CUMMINGS, Angelina,141
  , George,057
CUMMINS, Geo.Jr.,008
  , Geo.Sr.,008
  , George,052
  , Silva,030
CUNNINGHAM, Darcas,002
  , James,154
  , John J.,154
  , Martha P.,154
  , William W.,154
CUNNNGHAM, Jeremiah,057
CUNOW, John Gebhard,026,047
  , John Gebhart(Rev),046
  , John Hebbard,047
CURD, Abigal,038
CURRY, Malcom,049
  , Rebecca,049
  , Sarah,049
DAILEY, Nancy,131
DALTON, A.B.,092,117
  , Absalom B.,152
  , Benj.Kelly,032
  , Bethenia,152
  , Charles,062,072
  , Christina,152
  , David N.,152
  , David Sr.,062 ,091
  , David,011 ,016,072,075,091
  , Franklin Webb,062
  , George,036
  , Isaac,016 ,025,038,045,054,
         055,062,072,073,076,085,
         152
  , John A.B.,152
  , John,020
  , Jonathan,062,072
  , Juble L.,131
  , Madison,072
  , Margaret P.,131
  , Samuel,017
  , Susannah,072
  , Thomas H.P.,152
DANIEL, Elizabeth,022
DARDIN, John,026
DARNEL, Roll,151
DARR, E.W.,141
DAUB, John Jr.,042
  , John,044
  , M.,130
  , Margaret,068
  , Michael,125
DAULTON, Jonathan,016
DAVENPORT, Thomas,047
DAVIS, ,145
  , Abijah,010 ,011
  , Charles,016
  , Daniel,016 ,054
  , Edmund,017
  , Elizabeth,053
  , Fielder,098
  , Francis,097
  , Henry,034
  , Hezekiah,051,053
  , Isaac,053
  , James Sr.,127
  , James,002,005,028,034,038,077
         ,103,127,128,141
  , Jasper W.,151
  , Jesse,034
  , John T.W.,144,145
  , John,002,037,038
  , Joseph,037
  , Kezekiah,053
  , Margaret,127,128
  , Margery,038
  , Mary,013,024,113
  , Minerva,128
  , Nathaniel,024,025
  , Philip,137
  , Phillip,137
  , Ruchamar,005
  , Ruth,034
  , Sally,037
  , Sarah,002,037
  , Thomas,053
  , Thos. W.,113
  , Thos.W.,113
  , William Jr.,103
  , William,004 ,005,038,053,127,
         128
  , Wm.,008 ,051,077
  , Wm.Jr.,004
  , Yancy B.,146
DAWSON, Elizabeth,054 ,087,101
  , John,054
  , Nancy,087
  , Newton C.,087 ,101
  , Oney,054
  , Rebecker,054
  , Waomy,101
DAY, James,017
DEAN, Archelous,125
  , Betsy,115
DEARING, Elender,127
  , Jane,099
  , John,017
  , Rebecca,128
DEATHERAGE, Abner,036
  , Achkillas,036
  , Bird,036
  , Coleman,036
  , Geo.,016,017
  , George,004 ,036
  , James,036

DEATHERAGE, John,025,036
  , Matthew,025
  , Milly,036
  , Phillip,036
  , Polly,036
  , William,036
  , Wm.,095
DEATHRAGE, John,153
  , Matthew,153
DEAUGE, Catherine,018
  , Elizabeth,018
  , Michael,018
DEEN, Frederick,125
  , Solomon,125
  , Wm.,125
DENKE, Christian Fred.,108
  , Fredr.,109
  , Maria,108,109
DENNY, Joel,152
DENSELL, Salome,056
DENTON, Arthur,017
DIAL, Polly,089
DICKIE, Wm.,143
DILE, James,114
DILLINS, Michael,008
DILLS, Henry,011
DIXON, Benj.,016
DOBSON, Elizabeth,070
  , Fanny,114
  , Frankling,114
  , Henry B.,032,039,070
  , Henry Baker,026,041,068
  , Henry,008 ,017,068
  , Martha,068
  , Mary Ann,070
  , Pattsey,068
  , William,001,041,068
  , Wm.,008,011,070
  , Wm.P.,026
  , Wm.Polk,068
  , Wm.Sr.,068
DODSON, Agnes,051
  , Agnus,033
  , Joshua,015
  , Obadiah,060
  , Obey,033
  , Reuben,033
DOLL, George,050
  , Nicholas,050
DOLLAND, John,008
DOLLEN(DOLLAND), John,026
DOLLEN, John,026
  , Sarah,026
DOLLIN, John,041
DONNY, Lazarus,025
DOOLY, Alfred,148
DOUB, Alvira Mary Eve,107
  , Alvira,100
  , Daniel,107
  , David Westley,107
  , E. Mary,100
  , Elijah,086
  , Elizabeth,100,107
  , Gracett,074
  , H.,077
  , Henry,074,075,079,086,100
  , Jacob,100,107
  , John Boyd,107
  , John Jr.,051 ,052
  , John W.W.,100
  , John,053 ,100,107
  , Jos.,107
  , Joseph,072,079,086,100
  , M. Elizabeth,100
  , M.,075,089,105
  , Mary Eve,100
  , Mary,100
  , Michael,072 ,079,088,100,107
  , Peter,100
  , Rebecca,107
  , Susannah,107
  , Suzan,074
  , William Thos.,107
  , William,072 ,100
DOUGLASS, John,025
DOUTHERT, Elizabeth,070
DOUTHET, Anny,070
  , Benjamin,070
  , George,070
  , Isaac,070
  , Margaret,070
  , Philip,070
DOUTHIT, Benjamin,070 ,072
  , David,083 ,121
  , George,070,072
  , Isaac,070
DOWNEY, Charles,142
  , Wm.,017
DRANCH, Hanna,111
DRAUGHN, William,081
DRIEGER, George,117
DUGGINS, ,143
  , Bethany,077
  , Jane,077
  , John,077
  , Mary,077
  , Rainey,077
  , Stephen,077
  , Thomas,077
  , Usly,077
DUNCAN, Anna H.,111
  , Charles,111,155
  , James,103
  , Landon,143
  , Mary D.,143
  , Rhody,103
  , Russel,103
  , Russell,103
  , Thomas,103
  , William,103
DUNLAP, John,038
DUNN, John,044
DURHAM, A.M.,153

DURHAM, Austin,115
  , Wm.,040
DURRET, Davis,084
DURRIM, Joseph,030
DURRUM, Joseph,030
DWIGGINS, John,008
  , Patsy,115
  , Robert,044
  , Usley,115
DYER, T.B.,113

EADES, Tabina,027
  , Winston,153
EADS, Bartlet,058
  , David,058
  , Elizabeth,058
  , Isaac,058
  , James,058
  , Nancy,058
  , Polly,058
  , Robert,058
  , Sarah,058
  , Sharlet(Charlotte),058
  , William,058
  , Wm.,078
EARL, Isham,016
EARLEY, Jeremiah,026
EARLY, Asa,093
  , Mary,093
  , Polly,093
  , Samuel,093
EASON, Anna,128
  , Bethenia,141
  , Betheny,128
  , Jenny,042
  , Joseph,016 ,017
  , Sally,115
EAST, Elizabeth,041
  , Joseph,022
  , Nancy,041
  , Thomas Jr.,029,041
  , Thomas Sr.,029,041
  , Thos.,045
EASTY, Patsey,079
EATON, Camilly C.,140
  , James Morven,140
  , James,140
  , Susanna,140
  , William,120
EBERHARD, Carolina,062
  , Carolind,085
  , Juley,062
EBERT, Abraham,071
  , Ann Mary,004
  , Anna,115
  , Christina,004,039
  , Elizabeth,039
  , Eva Barbara,023
  , Geo.,017
  , George,004
  , Hannah,039 ,111
  , Hubert,122 ,124
  , John George,023
  , John Martin,023
  , John,004,039
  , Maria,039
  , Martin Jr.,005
  , Martin,005
  , Martin,004 ,023,039,058
  , Phebe,120
  , Philip,120
  , Salome,058
ECLES, John,017
EDGMON, Wm.,036
EDMON, Nancy,036
EDWARDS, Abel,029 ,041
  , Augustus T.,151
  , Daniel,129
  , Edward H.,129 ,151
  , Edward Jr.,129
  , Edward W.,151
  , Edward,030,129
  , John,129
  , Joseph,129
  , Lecetamoline,151
  , Mary C.,151
  , Nancy P.,151
  , Solomon T.,151
  , Thomas,041
  , William,129
  , Wm.,151
ELDRIDGE, Elizabeth,122
  , Pauline,122
  , Wm.,129
ELDRIGE, Levi A.,122
ELMORE, Abijah,004
  , Thomas,008 ,009
ELROD(ELROTH), Jeremiah,001
ELROD, Adam,001,020,027
  , Benjamin,100
  , Christopher,062
  , Damsey,062
  , Daniel,062
  , Jeremiah,001
  , John,062
  , Lidia,062
  , Maria,061
  , Mary,062
  , Noah,062
  , Robert,009 ,012,062
  , Sarah,062
  , Stephen,100
  , Thomas,062
ELSBERRY, Benjamin,038
  , Fredrick,038
ENDSLEY, Andrew,008,048
  , Hugh,008 ,009
  , John,008 ,026,044,048
ENGLAND, Fanny,104
ENOCK, John,043
ENSLEY, Andrew,057
  , John,057
  , Sarah,057

FOREWORD

Stokes County was formed in 1789 from Surry County.
It is in the north-central section of the state and is bounded by
Rockingham, Forsyth and Surry counties and the state of Virginia.
In 1849, Forsyth was formed by Stokes County.

Germanton was the first county seat. When Forsyth
County was created from Stokes in 1849, the county seat was moved
to present-day Danbury. The Moravian settlement at Salem,
Bethenia and Bathabra fell into Stokes County and remained until
1849, thus the numerous land transactions between those with
German names contained in the Stokes County Records.

The "Moravian Records" and tax lists have been used as
guidelines as to spelling of surnames and streams.

Abbreviations used: pds. = pounds of money,
sh. - shillings, N. S. E. W. = North, South, East and West.

X = his or her mark; otherwise it is assumed a person
could sign his or her name.

Page 1. 22 September 1792. John RIGHTS, Hatter, of Salem,
        to Mary AUST, Widow of Salem; 200 pounds hard money
to be paid yearly remainder of life to said Mary (6 pounds
with interest on 1 January eary year, payment to begin 1
January 1793). Witnesses: Peter YARRELL and Adam HAUSER.
Signed: John RIGHTS.

Page 2. 27 August 1794. Alexander STEUART, Merchant of
        Newbern, to William DOBSON; all right and claim in
black woman Venus and her 3 children, Amy, Jacob and James.
Witnesses: Francis BELL and Joseph BRITTAIN, Jurat. Signed:
Alex. STEUART.

Page 3. 30 April 1796. Joseph LADD to S. Benj. VIERLING,
        Salem, 50 pounds, Negro Woman Dorothie about 26
years old. Witnesses: John RIGHTS. Signed: Jo. LADD.

Page 3. 7 May 1799. Christian WEAVER to Abraham STEINER,
        Bethabara, 55 pounds, sorrel mare with Daniel
SHOUSE'S brand, etc. Witnesses: Christian STAUBER and Peter
(X) SCHOR (SHORE). Signed: Christian (X) WEAVER.

Page 4. 10 March 1800. Adam BOYER to Adam ELROD, Rowan
        County, $325, Negro boy Mall, 20 years old.
Witnesses: George McKNIGHT and Jeremiah ELROD (ELROTH,
ELRODE). Signed: Adam (X) BOYER.

Page 4. 25 October 1800. Robert GRINER, Power of Attorney
        to Benjamin FORSYTH, obtain grant from State for
my entry (Joseph BANNER, Entry taker), 300 acres Belews
Creek for which David FLYNT has entered Caviat against.
Witnesses: Benjamin MAJORS and Jeremiah GIBSON, Jurat.
Signed: Robert GRINER.

Page 5. 13 August 1800. Jacob BLUM, Charles Fredr. BAGGE,
        and Jacob WOLFORTH (German: WOLFAHRT, English:
WELFARE), Executors of Will of Traugott BAGGE, deceased in
consideration of release to Charles Fredr. BAGGE by Benjamin
Samuel VIERLING, 335 pounds (of 500) bequeathed to Mary
Rosina VIERLING, daughter of said Sam'l and granddaughter of
said Traugott. Witnesses: Joshua BONER, Jurat and John
GIBBONS. Signed: Chas. Fred. BAGGE, Jacob BLUM, and Jacob
WOHLFAHRT (WELFARE).

Page 5. 13 August 1800. Release from Benjamin Samuel
        VIERLING to Executors of will of Traugott BAGGE,
part money left in will to daughter of Benjamin Sam'l
VIERLING, advanced to said VIERLING. Witnesses: Gottlieb
SHOBER and Joshua BONNER, Jurat. Signed: Benj. Samuel
VIERLING.

Page 6. 9 July 1789. Will of Henry KERBEY. March Term
        1790. Wife: Susannah, plantation whereon I now
live. Son, Jesse, land on Little Yadkin, Negro Dick;

1

Granddaughter, Patsy CHILDRESS. Son, Pleasant, land I now
live on, Negroes Lucy and Diner; my 7 children, Sarah DAVIS,
Edmund KERBY, Samuel KERBEY, Sillia WILLIAMS, Darcas CUNNING-
HAM, Jesse KERBY, Pleasant KERBY. Executors: Sons, Jesse
and Pleasant. Witnesses: Matthew BROOKS, Jurat and Joseph
MILLER, Jurat by Hearsay.

Page 7. 1 February 1776. Will of Henry BANNER, Surry
         County, Planter. March Term 1790. Wife, Eleanor;
4 children: Joseph, Ephraim, Benjamin and Charity, all my
land. To Eleanor BANNER (daughter of Rachel McKOIN, alias
McGOWN), arrives at age 18 years. Two slaves, Prince and
Dinah shall choose which of my children they will belong to.
Executors: wife Eleanor, eldest son Joseph, and Traugott
BAGGE (Overseer to my true meaning). Witnesses: Jacob BONN,
Jacob MAYER, Jurat and Traugott BAGGE. Signed: Henry BANNER.

Page 9. 18 January 1790. William VEST, Senr., Surry County,
         to Isham VEST, 113 pounds, 6 shillings, 8 pense
Specie, to Isham VEST, Negro boy Amos, 17 years old. Witness:
William HUGHLETT. Signed: William (X) VEST.

Page 9. 14 March 1790. Inventory Estate of Henry BANNER,
         deceased. Joseph VANNER, Executor.

Page 10. 7 June 1790. Inventory Estate of Henry KERBY,
          deceased. Jesse and Pleasant KEARBY, Executors.

Page 11. 1 July 1789. Will of Thomas EVANS. September
          Term 1790. Wife Elizabeth, land waters Hespeth
River, little South Trace by name My Service Right, 3,840
acres. My western land to be sold to discharge my debts.
Executors: Wife Elizabeth, John ARMSTRONG and William
POINDEXTER. Witnesses: Thos. POINDEXTER, Jurat, Elizabeth
POINDEXTER, Jurat, and Valentine MARTIN. Signed: Thomas
EVANS.

Page 12. 3 June 1790. William ATWOOD to James DAVIS, 8
          pounds Virginia money, Negro woman named Sukey and
child, Theny 4 years old. Witnesses: William WALKER, Major
WILKENSON, and John DAVIS. Signed: William ATWOOD and
Sarah (X) ATWOOD.

Page 12. 18 February 1790. Giles HUDSPETH, Surry County,
          to Thompson GLEN, Stokes, 120 pounds Specie, 3
negroes, Ned 4 years old, Girl Justin 20 months, Sampson
19 months. Witnesses: Jeremiah GLEN and John (X) STEWART.
Signed: Giles (X) HUDSPETH.

Page 13. September Court 1790. Inventory Estate of Thomas
          BRIGGS, deceased, Blerlick (?) BRIGGS and John
BRIGGS, Administrators.

Page 14. 31 July 1790. Bill of Sale, Robert SMITH to
          Robert MARKLAND, 60 pounds, 14 shillings, Negro boy
Frank. Witness: Constant(ine) LADD. Signed: Robert SMITH.

Page 14. 23 November 1788. Will of Andrew FOLK (FULK),

Surry County. December Term 1790. Wife, Mary
Margaretha, furniture, stock, etc. Son, Andrew FOLK, plan-
tation I now live on. Son, John FOLK, 100 acres waters
Yadkin adjoining Henry SPOONHOUR and Adam FISCUS. My child-
ren: Adam FOLK, Ann Mary, Catharina, Christina, Magdalena,
Margaretha and Hannah FOLK have already received their
shares. Executors: John CROUS(E), Jacob SPOONHOUR (SPOEN-
HAURE, SPAINHOUR and SPAINHOWER). Witnesses: Joseph LINE-
BACK, Jurat and Francis FORDEM. Signed: Andrew (X) FOLK.

Page 16. 20 October 1790. Will of Abraham LINEBACK
          (LIONBACH). March Term 1791. Wife, Ann, planta-
tion where I now live, etc. till son Frederic comes of age
and then sold and divided equally among my children (not
named). Son Daniel. Executors: wife Ann and son Daniel.
Witnesses: Joseph BOLITJCHK (BULLITSCHEK, BOLEJACK), John
KRAUS(E), and Peter PFAFF. Signed: Abraham LINEBACK.

Page 16. 11 June 1790. Thomas McCARRELL, Granville County,
          South Carolina, to William T. LEWIS, Surry County,
163 pounds, 10 shillings, 3 Negroes, Milly 27 years, Tom and
Putney 11 months old. Witnesses: Jer. LESTER, Jurat and D.
LESTER. Signed: Thos. McCARRELL.

Page 17. March Term 1791. Inventory Estate of John MELTON,
          deceased. T.T. ARMSTRONG, D.C. and Robert
WILLIAMS, C.C.

Page 17. 6 March 1791. Inventory Estate of Abraham
          LINEBACK, deceased. Anna LINEBACK, Executrix and
Daniel LINEBACK, Executor.

Page 18. March Term 1791. Inventory Estate of John PETREY,
          deceased, by Administrator (not named).

Page 18. 9 March 1791. Inventory Estate of Major Thomas
          EVANS, deceased. John ARMSTRONG and William
POINDEXTER, Executors.

Page 19. 1 February 1790. Will of George SMITH, Blacksmith,
          of Salem. June Term 1791. My funeral according
to rites United Brethren (Moravian). Son Christian, equal
shares in personal property and my land. Daughter, Mary,
158 acres in Rowan County. Executors: Jacob BLUM, Esqr.,
John Henry HERBST and my son, Christian. Witnesses: John
RIGHT, Jurat and Lewis MEINUNG. Signed: George SMITH.

Page 20. 8 June 1791. Additional Inventory of Major Thomas
          EVANS. John ARMSTRONG and Wm. POINDEXTER,
Executors.

Page 20. 10 November 1790. Will of Sarah PEDDYCOART.
          September Term 1791. Youngest son John, Negro
Priscilla and one-half estate. My other children, Wm.
Barton, Basil, Thomas, Greenberry, Eleanor, Sarah and Lucy
other half of estate, equally divided. No Executors name.
Witnesses: Nathan PEDDYCOART, Jurat and Mary HAMILTON.
Signed: Sarah PEDDYCOART.

Page 21.   5 November 1791.   John THOMMASON, Senr. to Jesse
LESTER, Esqr., Surry County, 577 pounds, 5 Negroes
Dicy age 32, Anthony 13 years, Sarah 9 years, Delpha 6 years,
Jeffery 3 years. Witnesses: Archibald CAMPBELL and George
THOMMASON. Signed: John (X) TOMMERSON.

Page 22.   17 December 1790.   Bill of Sale.   George
DEATHERAGE to John MARTIN, 14 pounds, Negro girl
Fanny, 14 years old. Witnesses: James COFFEY and Richard
SHIPP. Signed: George DEATHERAGE.

Page 23.   20 June 1791.   Abijah ELMORE, Surry County, to
Thomas JOHNSON, 20 pounds, Negro Jacob 20 years
old who has been hired out for some years to Samuel STOTZ of
Salem. Witnesses: Richard BOWMAN and Robert (X) JOHNSON.
Signed: Abijah ELMORE.

Page 23.   28 September 1791.   Susannah MOSBY, Nancy MOSBY,
Kellurah MOSBY, daughters of the late Samuel MOSBY,
Surry County, to Thomas MOSBY, 50 shillings each, our claim
in tracts of land our father died possessed of; Yadkin River
adjoining land Phillip HOWARD, Joseph WILLIAMS, and Samuel
MOSBY. Witnesses: John SANDERS, John GRANT, and Christopher
SHOWBURGER. Signed: Susanna MOSBY, Nancy MOSBY, and
Kellurah MOSBY.

Page 24.   9 March 1792.   Bill of Sale.   John BRANSON to
James MARTIN, Junr., 350 pounds, stock and
furniture. Witness: Archibald CAMPBELL. Signed: John BRAN-
SON.

Page 25.   1 May 1789.   Will of Martin EBERT, Senr., Surry
County.   March Term 1792. My children, (not
named), 200 acres land between John WESNER and MOTTS line
to be equally divided. To Cornilues SCHNIDER (SCHNEIDER),
land for his children, both by his first wife (my daughter,
Ann Mary, deceased) and his second wife (my daughter,
Christina, now living), except daughter Christina enjoy one-
third part of 320 acres her lifetime.   Son, Martin and John
George. Sons-in-law, Adam TISCH, Cornelius SCHINEDER and
John WESNER (WEESNER). Daughter, Catherine, wife of John
WESNER. Executors: Jacob BLUM and Samuel STOTZ (a Minister).
Witnesses: Traugott BAGGE, George BIWIGHAUS (BIEBIGHAUS,
BIBIGHAUS), and John CHITTY.
CODICIL: Exception to 320 acres land not only left all
children of Cornilius SNIDER by both wives, but to all heirs
of body of my daughter, Christina, 5 May 1789. Witnesses:
Fredr. Wm. MARSHALL, George BIWIGHAUS, and John CHITTY.
Signed: Martin EBERT, Senr.

Page 28.   25 May 1792.   John LYNCH in right of my wife (not
named) of Estate of James GLEN, deceased, to
Thompson GLEN, 220 pounds, 3 Negroes Simon, Charles and
Dilse. Witnesses: William THORNTON and Frederic MILLER.
Signed: John LYNCH.

Page 29.   5 May 1791.   (Recorded September Term 1792).
William DAVIS to my son, William DAVIS, Junr. for

4

many services and good deeds done me and also part of his divident of my personal Estate, Roan mare, Bay horse and Sorrel mare. Witnesses: James DAVIS and John VAUTER (VAWTER). Signed: William (X) DAVIS.

Page 29. 5 May 1791. William DAVIS to Ruchamar DAVIS, my daughter, many good deeds done to me and part of her dividend of my personal Estate, Colt, cows, bed and furniture. Witnesses: James DAVIS and John VAWTER. Signed: William (X) DAVIS.

Page 30. 5 May 1791. William DAVIS to my son, William DAVIS, for good deeds, etc., Negro girl Doll. Witnesses: James DAVIS and John VAWTOR. Signed: William (X) DAVIS.

Page 30. 7 March 1791. William CHANDLER to Pleasant HENDERSON, Rockingham County, 41 pounds, Negro slave Ned. Witnesses: Hugh ARMSTRONG and Ja(mes) MARTIN. Signed: William CHANDLER.

Page 31. 24 June 1791. Will of James MILLWOOD, September Term 1792. Wife Nanny, plantation, 100 acres whereon I now live until my youngest child (not named) comes of age. Children mentioned but not named. Executors: Shedrick PRUIT and William SPENCER. Witness: Ja. MARTIN, Jurat. Signed: James (X) MILLWOOD.

Page 31. 5 January 1789. Will of Thomas ADAMAN, December Term 1792. Wife Mealy. Reubin MATTHEWS, my sisters oldest son, land where he now lives, Fishdam fork Thommases Creek. To Elizabeth FORRESTER, bed and money. To Nancy FORRESTER, my wife's youngest daughter, bed now called "Her'n". To William and John FORRESTER, rest of my land. Executors: William and John FORRESTER. Witnesses: Jeremiah GLEN, Jurat and Reuben (X) MATTHEWS. Signed: Thomas ADAMAN.

Page 33. September Term 1792. Inventory Estate of Martin EBERT, Senr., deceased. Bonds: Phillip ROTHROCK, Pater ROTHROCK, Bazel PETTYCORT, Peter PFAFF, John RIGHTS, Godfrey PRAZEL, Gottfried PRAEZEL, Fredr. MILLER, Peter FOLZ, Jacob PFAW (FAW), Joseph KRAUS, Miner GRIGGS, Melchor SCHNIDER, Martin EBERT, Junr., Adam FISHEL. Paid To: Cornelius SCHNIDER and John WESNER. Signed: Samuel STOTZ and Jacob BLUM, Executors.

Page 33. September Term 1792. Inventory Sale of Michael SIDES, deceased, sold 25 June 1792. Francis STAUBER, Administrator.

Page 34. December Term 1792. Inventory Estate of John PHILLIPS, deceased, by Ann PHILLIPS, Admrx.

Page 34. 9 January 1793. Inventory Personal Estate of John FARMER, deceased, divided between Phebe, the widow, Negro Peter and Peter's daughter Polly; Henry, Negro

Pell a boy; Tabitha CHILDRES, Negro Leah, a girl; John, Negro Rob, a man; Thomas, Negroes Barney and Jenny.

Page 36.   9 May 1793.   Will of William LEWIS.   June Term
            1793.   Wife, Austy, land whereon I now live, etc.
Children, Obey, James, William, Mary, John, Susannah, Anny,
Nancy, Washington, and Samuel LEWIS.   Executors: Wife Austey
and Peter HAIRSTON.   Witnesses: James LEWIS, Jehu BROWN and
William (X) BROWN.   Signed: William (X) LEWIS.

Page 37.   1793.   Will of Moses MARTIN, Blacksmith and
            Planter.   June Term 1793.   Wife Mary, 270 acres
whereon I now live until son, William come of age 21 years.
Sons, Jesse, Jonathan and Zachariah, monies from above in
case William dies before he reaches age 21.   Daughters,
Margaret and Ann.   Sons, James, Moses, John and George, 5
Shillings.   Daughter Alice Heath, 5 pounds.   Executors:
Wife, Mary MARTIN and son Jesse.   Witnesses: Joseph WINSTON,
Jurat, H. HAMPTON and John TATUM.   Signed: Moses MARTIN.

Page 39.   29 October 1798.   Robert MARTIN, Rockingham County,
            to Thomas ROGERS, 400 pounds, 3 Negroes, Solomon,
Betty and her child Lucy.   Witness: William REA, Jurat.
Signed: R. MARTIN.

Page 40.   24 August 1791.   John GLENN, Junr. to William HILL,
            City of Raleigh, North Carolina, $250, Negro boy
Edmund.   Witnesses: W.A. CRAWFORD and Sally HILL.   Signed:
John GLENN.

Page 40.   26 August 1793.   Inventory Estate of Peter BINKLEY,
            deceased, by Executors John BINKLEY and Peter
BINKLEY; appraised by Jacob MILLER, Senr. and Peter FEESER
(FEISER).

Page 41.   3 April 1793.   Will of Phillip TRANSAW (TRANSOU).
            September Term 1793.   Wife Magdalene, use of
plantation leased 29 September 1792 from Fredr. Wm. MARSHALL
in Bethania.   Son John, to rent and use above plantation.
Son Abraham, my house clock.   Children, Phillip, Mary,
Rosina, Elizabeth and Catherina, interest annually from sale
of Estate "as my other children have already received the
equilavant".   Executors: Conrod and Abraham STEINER.
Witnesses: Gottlieb SHOBER and Abraham TRANSAW.   Signed:
Phillip TRANSAW.

Page 42.   3 March 1791.   Will of Peter BINKLEY.   September
            Term 1793.   Wife Margaretha.   Sons, John, Peter,
Frederick, Joseph, Jacob and Christian BINKLEY; and John
SHEMEL, natural son of my wife Margaretha; all in State of
North Carolina, and son John Adam BINKLEY in Cumberland.
Daughters, Sarah, wife of Edward BARTLEY; Christina, wife
of Casper FISHER (FISCHER) of Cumberland; Catherine HENIG,
wife of (blank) HENIG, deceased, of Stoverstown, Virginia;
Margaretha, wife of Ulrio WOLLEWETHER of Stanton, Virginia;
Elizabeth, deceased, late wife of Georg HERBOCK of Manaskasy
of Maryland, the heirs of her body.   Son, Christian who is

simple-minded, shall live with one of his brothers.
Executors: sons, John and Peter BINKLEY. Witnesses: Abraham
STEINER, Jurat, Christian STAUBER, and Matthew ESTERLIEN.
Signed: Peter (X) BINKLEY.

Page 45.   September Term 1793. Inventory Estate of Phillip
          TRANSOU, Bethania, deceased; taken 26 April 1793
by John CONROD and Abraham STEINER, Executors. Appraised
13 May 1793 by Abraham STEINER, George HAUSER, Senr., and
Michael ROARK. Notes on Hand: Samuel PAFF and Isaac PAFF
(PFAFF), John MURKEY, Thompson GLENN, Christian HAUSER,
Gottlieb SHOBER and John TRANSAU.

Page 46.   December Term 1793. Inventory Personal Estate of
          James BLACKBURN, deceased, one Negro woman and 3
small girls, not named. Signed: Lucia BLACKBURN, Admrx.

Page 46.   31 August 1791. Will of Daniel HUFF. December
          Term 1793. Wife Ann, my house wherein I now
dwell. Son John, my home plantation. Eldest son Daniel.
Daughters, Jemima, Keziah, Mary, Elizabeth, Rebecah. Son
Jesse. Daughter Ann, a chass (chest). Executors: Son, John
HUFF and Joseph MENDENGHALL. Witnesses: Joseph MENDENHALL,
Jurat, Thomas MILLS, and Thomas MARSHALL. Signed: Daniel
(X) HUFF.

Page 47.   22 October 1793. Will of James CROOK. December
          Term 1793. Wife Elizabeth, Negroes Jacob, Phillis,
Jeam, Silla, Phill and one-fourth of my estate. Sons,
Bignal, Negro Stephen and Jenny; Jeamy, Negroes Peter and
Poll; Jeremiah, Negroes Tom and girl Mason; William, Negro
man Lamp. Daughter Mary, wife of Richard BENNETT, Negro
girl Eady. Mentions 200 acres Stewarts Creek adjoining
BOLEJACK and Wm. ALFORD. Executors: wife, Elizabeth and son
Begnal. Witnesses: Christian LASH and John SHEMEL. Signed:
James (X) CROOCK.

Page 49.   March Term 1794. Inventory goods of Sarah
          PEDDYCORT by John PEDDYCORT; appraised by John
(X) PADGET and John BLAKE 23 July 1791.

Page 50.   March Term 1794. Inventory goods of Sarah
          PEDDYCOART by John PEDDYCOAT; appraised by John
(X) PADGET and John BLAKE 23 July 1791.

Page 50.   March Term 1794. Inventory Estate of Joseph
          LAWTON, deceased. Notes on Jesse SAPP, Wm. LANE,
Levin WARD, John QUILLIN, Abijah JONES, James BURNS, Pane
STARBUCK, Abijah COFFIN, Wm. HENDERSON, John FARE, Thos.
ARNET, Zimri CHASE, Silas WORTH, James KING, John WELLS,
John ANGELL, Peter COGGSHELL, James SANDERS, Martin RING,
John COLLIN, John HOLBROOK, Constantine LADD, Drury WATSON,
Joseph STOCKTON, Obed BARNARD. Cash found in deceaseds
Cabinet. Signed: Seth COFFIN (Admr.?).

Page 52.   3 January 1791. Martin ARMSTRONG to Thomas
          Temple ARMSTRONG, for his service for one year

past and for present services in teaching his brother and
sister to read and write the English Tongue and other good
causes, Negro girl Emmy, 10 years old, daughter of Peter
and Pheby. Signed: Martin ARMSTRONG. . . . Proved March
Term 1800, oath of Wm. HUGHLETT and Joseph WILLIAMS, who
are well acquainted with handwriting of said Martin
ARMSTRONG.

Page 53.   12 October 1793.   Will of Edmon BOWMAN.   June Term
           1794.   Wife Margrit, one-fourth household furni-
ture.   Four sons, William, Richard, George and Archibald
(Geo. and Archibald when they come of age), lands on Belews
Creek.   Executors: sons, William and Richard.   Witnesses:
Michael (X) McGINNIS and John WORTMAN.   Signed: Edmond
BOWMAN.

Page 54.   June Term 1794.   Continued Inventory of Joseph
           LAWTON, deceased, by Seth COFFIN, Administrator.
List of balances due Joseph LAWTON as books now stand: From
Thomas ARNETT, Wm. ANTHONY, Joseph ARNETT, Ashley HOLT, Asa
BARROW, Edmund BOWMAN, David BROOKS, John BROOKS, John
BRANSON, Wm. BEAZLEY, Wm. BOWMAN, Zimri CHASE, John CLOSS,
Peter GOGGSHALL, Chas. CLASBY, Seth COFFIN, Thos. CROW, Geo.
CUMMINS, Senr., Geo. CUMMINS, Junr., Archibald CAMPBELL,
Andrew CAIN, Charles CASE, Henry COOK, Stephen COOK, John
COLLIN, John CLARK, Joseph CLOSS, John DWIGGINS, Wm. DAVIS,
Wm. DOBSON, Esqr., Henry DOBSON, John DOLLAND, Michael
DILLINS, Hugh ENDSLEY, Suddle ESTUS, John ENDSLY, Andrew
ENDSLY, Thomas ELMORE, Lathan FOLGER, Peter FARE, Julius
FARE, Wm. FRAZER, Senr., John FREEMAN, Michael FAIRE, Sewel
FRASER, Geo. FRASER, John HINSHAW, James HOLBROOK, John
HOLBROOK, Wm. HOWELL, Wm. HALE (Physician), John HUTCHINS,
John HESTER, Richard HARROLD, John HAM, Joseph HAM, Thos.
HAN, John GAMMELL, Wm. GAMMELL, Gabriel GRIFFIN, Levi GRAHAM,
Joshua IRONS, Benj. JONES, William JANES, Junr., Daniel
JANES, Edmund JANES (JEANS), Phillip JEANS, John JORDAN, Wm.
JEANES, Senr., James KING (ye first), Wm. KENMAN, James
KING (ye 2nd), Kerby KENDDY, Henry KING (ye 1st), Charles
LONG, Wm. LANE, Israel LONG, James LOVE, Senr., Constantine
LADD, Esqr., Peter LUDWICK, Gayer MACY, Geo. MACAY, Michael
McGINNIS, Thos. MADAIRESS, Charles MADARIS, Matthew MACAY,
Ezekiel MORGAN, Joseph MACEY, Joseph McPHERSON, John NUCLSON
(Nicholson?), Jephtha PARKER, Michael PHILLIPS, Joseph
PATTERSON, Senr., Peter PHELPS, John PATTERSON, Valentine
PHELPS, Simmons PATTISON, Joseph PATTERSON, Junr., John
PIKO, George PEARSON, Andrew RAY, John RING, Andrew ROBERSON
Esqr., Pacel STARBUCK, Senr., David SHAW, Joel SANDERS,
Jesse SAPP, Judith SWAIN, David STILLWELL, John SAPP, James
SWAIN, James SANDERS, John SWALLOW, John TALLY, John THOMP-
SON, Senr., Geo. THOMASON, John THOMASON, Junr., John VANHOY,
Joel WATSON, Charles WORTH, Leven WARD, James WHICKER, Wm.
WORTMAN, Joseph WARREN, Clayburn WATSON, John WELLS, Senr.,
David WALKER, Jarvis WILLIS, Wm. WILSON, Samuel WAGGONER,
Wm. WHICKER, Joshua GRINDER.

Page 56.   29 August 1794.   Will of James GAMMELL.   September
           Term 1794.   Wife Lucretia.   Sons, William, Andrew,
James, Joseph, Samuel.   Daughters Betsy, Peggy.   Child my

8

wife Lucretia is now pregnant with. Executors: sons, Wm.
and Andrew, wife Lucretia. Witnesses: A(ndrew) ROBINSON,
Jurat and Levin WARD. Signed: James GAMMELL.

Page 58. 12 July 1794. Inventory Estate of Joseph BINKLEY,
          deceased. Catharine BINKLEY, Martin (X) HOLDER,
Administrators. Oath of Wm. HUGHLETT.

Page 59. September Term 1794. Inventory Estate of Edmund
          BOWMAN, deceased. At public Vendue 22 July 1794,
following bought: Thomas ARNET, Margarett BOWMAN, Richard
BOWMAN, Archibald CAMPBELL, John COLLEN, Hugh ENDSLEY, John
FAIRE, Wm. GERNTON (?), Gabriel GRIFFIN, Sylvanus GARDNER,
James MEREDITH, Michael McDERMONT, Wm. WORTMAN, James
WHICKER, John WILLIAMS, (Guilford). Signed: Richard BOWMAN,
Executor.

Page 61 is missing.

Page 62. 26 September 17--. Sale of Estate of Benjamin
          PADGET, deceased, by Robert ELROD, Administrator.

Page 62. 13 May 1794. Will of William SOUTHERN. December
          Term 1794. Wife Magdalin. Daughter Judith
SOUTHERN. Son John SOUTHERN. My children, mentioned but
not named. Executor: wife Magdalin SOUTHERN. Witnesses:
Jonathan VERNON, Ford SOUTHERN, and Jonathan BARNARD, Jurat.
Signed: William SOUTHERN.

Page 63. March Term 1795. Inventory book debts of Edmund
          BOWMAN, deceased. Notes On: Hezekial STARBUCK,
Thomas ELMORE, Paul STARBUCK, Seth COFFIN, Zemri CHASE,
Thompson SMITH and William WORTMAN.

Page 64. 29 October 1794. Will of Joseph HAM. March Term
          1795. My land remain divided among my children as
formerly agreed upon among them. Wife Seth HAM. Children,
Milly HOLBROOK, Thomas HAM, John HAM, Rachel WATSON, Jacob
HAM, Ezekiel HAM and Daniel HAM. Executors: Sons, Ezekial
and Daniel. Witnesses: John (X) QUILLEN, Jurat, William (X)
BEAN, and Elizabeth (X) BURNETT, Jurat. Signed: Joseph (X)
HAM.

Page 65. 27 October 1794. Will of Robert McMURRY. March
          Term 1790. Equally divided between my wife (not
named) and son John McMURRY. Executors: Absalom BOSTICK
and Constantine LADD. Witnesses: Robert BRIGGS, Jurat, Wm.
MARTIN and Samuel STEFINE. Signed: R. McMURRY.

Page 66. 5 April 1785. Will of James HURST, late of
          Duchenfield, Kingdom Great Britain, now Salem,
Surry County, North Carolina. March Term 1795. To John
HOLLAND and Jacob WOLFART (WOLFARE) of Salem, all my cash,
chest and clothing, etc. Sister Mary HURST in Duchenfield
if she be alive; if not to children of brother, Samuel HURST.
God-Son John Fredr. HOLLAND, Salem, North Carolina. To
Single Brothers Diacony and single sisters Diacony (Mora-
vians). Executors: John HOLLAND and Jacob WOLFORT.

Witnesses: Christian LASH, Jurat and Thomas SPIESEKE.
Signed: James HURST.

Page 67. March Term 1795. Inventory Estate of Robert
          McMURRY, lotts in Germanton, etc. Signed: A.
BOSTICK and C. LADD, Executors.

Page 67. March Term 1795. Inventory Estate of John FORD
          who died 10 February 1795 at Gootlieb SPACH'S
house. Appraised by John RIGHTS and John HOLLAND. Inventory
made 21 February 1795. Signed: Jacob BLUM, Administrator.

Page 68. March Term 1795. Inventory things left in my
          possession by Benjamin SWAN, deceased. Inventory
made 28 December 1794 before Spillsby COLEMAN, Justice of
Caswell County, North Carolina. Signed: Thomas HARRISON.

Page 68. March Term 1795. Inventory of James HURST by John
          HOLLAND and Jacob WOLTFORT (WELFARE). Appraised
by Charles Fredr. STRAETER and Samuel STOTZ of Salem, 25
January 1795. Cash due HURST from John GAMMELL; to Samuel
Benj. VIERLING for Drugs; to Jeremiah SHOAF for working; to
Joseph BONNER for shaving him 6 months; to Geo. GOEPFORT for
attendance in last sickness; to John HOLLAND for digging
grave; to Jacob WOLFORT for gravestone, to John KROUSE for
coffin.

Page 69. 25 December 1794. Will of William CHANDLER.
          March Term 1795. Wife Delisha CHANDLER. Execu-
tors: Wife Delisha. Witnesses: Randolph RIDDLE, Richard
WOOD, Jurat and Mary CHANDLER, Jurat. Signed: William
CHANDLER.

Page 70. 4 September 1793. Will of Petter PENNIGAR, Farmer.
          March Term 1795. Wife Mary. Sons Matthias and
William (mentions "where Wm's. house now stands"). Three
daughters, Christiana MOANEE, Mary FLINCHUM, Catherine
FLINCHUM. Each child begotton on body of Mary PENNIGAR, my
wife. Executor: John HALBERT. Witnesses: Nathan HALBERT,
Samuel CLARK, Senr. and Samuel CLARK, Junr. Signed: Peter
PENNIGER.

Page 71. June Term 1794. Inventory of Col. John ARMSTRONG,
          deceased, by Matthew BROOKS, Administrator. Note
on John MICKEY; Certificate received of Job MARTIN assigned
by Thomas O'HARA on behalf of John BEREE (or BURCE ?), Esqr.
Paymaster General and Joseph HOWELL, Junr., Assistant
Commissioner Army Accounts.

Page 72. June 1795. Inventory Estate of James GAMMELL,
          deceased. William GAMMELL and Lucretia GAMMELL,
Executors. (3 pages of items in inventory).

Page 73. 26 July 1795. Nuncupative Will of John FARE.
          September Term 1795. In the presence of: Wife
Alice FAIRE, Andrew ROBINSON, Michael FAIR and Abijah DAVIS
and several neighbors at his bedside in his dwelling house.
Wife Alice, his plantation, Negro woman Jude for support

and rearing of his children (not named). Son John FAIRE, land after decease of wife Alice. Witnesses: Andr. ROBINSON, Michael (X) FARE and Abijah (X) DAVIS.

Page 74. September Term 1795. Inventory Estate of
Benjamin SWANN, deceased. David DALTON, Administrator.

Page 75. 4 December 1795. Inventory taken of Estate of
Henry DILLS, deceased, Sattler's (saddler) tools, two English Hymn Books, 1 German Bible, 4 German Books. Signed: Philip SNIDER (wrote in Dutch).

Page 76. 15 September 1795. Will of Jacob HINE (HEIN,
HEYN), Planter. December Term 1795. Son, Jacob William, land where I live, etc. Sons John and Frederick. Daughters, Catherine married to Moses SWAIM; Eva married to Renatur HARKE; Mary married to Alexander KOCH (COOK); Children of deceased daughter Gertraut. Executors: Jacob BLUM, Esqr. and John RIGHTS. Witnesses: Michael (X) RO-MINGER, Junr., Jurat and Michael (X) ROMINGER, Senr. Signed: John Jacob (X) HINE.

Page 76. December Term 1795. Inventory of Joseph HAM,
deceased. Ezekial HAM, Executor.

Page 76. 31 March 1794. Will of Nathan SANDERS. December
Term 1795. Wife Susanna, plantation whereon I now dwell. Eldest son Arden, North end plantation adjoining John Fendal CARR, Michael FAIR, Wm. DOBSON, Esqr. and Benjm. WATSON. Second son Merry Arthur, 150 acres South end of my plantation. Three youngest sons, Jesse, Richard and Benjamin, "until they come of age." Three sons-in-law, John LOPP, James KING and Thomas MEDIERESS (wives not named). Executors: Wife Susanna and William HOWELL. Witnesses: Archibald CAMPBELL and John Frndal CARR, (a signature in German). Signed: Nathan (X) SANDERS.

Page 78. December Term 1795. Inventory Estate of William
PITTS, deceased. Sold at Public Vendue, 10 October 1795. Signed: Isaac PITTS, Administrator.

Page 78. December Term 1795. Inventory of Michael VOGLER,
deceased. Book Debts: Gottlieb SHOBER, Samuel STYERS, Jonathan LICK, Adam FISCHEL and Conrad GREEN.

Page 79. 8 March 1796. Inventory made 23 September 1796,
Estate of Phillip TRANSOU, deceased, (a hatter), hatter tools to son Petries TRANSOU. Signed: Jacob BLUM and Christoph VOGLER, Executors.

Page 80. June Term 1796. Inventory of John FAIR, deceased,
by Alse FAIR, Executrix.

Page 81. 1 February 1796. Will of Matthew MARKLAND. June
Term 1796. Wife Aneyble. Sons Nathaniel and Joseph. My estate to be equally divided among all my children including John BLAKE, my stepson (other children

not named). Executor: son Robert MARKLAND. Witnesses:
James (X) FLETCHER, Thomas PADGET and Richard (X) LUTTRELL.
Signed: Matthew MARKLAND.

Page 82. 12 April 1796. Will of Isaac HILL. June Term
1796. Son Joshua. Daughter Mary. Rest of
estate divided equally among all my children (not named),
including Mary. Executor: Thomas PADGET. Witnesses: John
GILES, Jurat, Bazil PEDDYCORT and John BLAKE, Jurat. Signed:
Isaac (X) HILL.

Page 84. September Term 1796. Inventory of Thomas RIGGS,
deceased. Signed: Sarah (X) RIGGS and Stephen
RIGGS, Administrators.

Page 84. 20 August 1796. Will of Henry BOYER (German:
BUCHER). December Term 1796. Wife Catherine.
Children, Margaret, Adam, John, Elizabeth, Jacob, Henry,
Joseph, Isiah and Robert. Executor: Robert ELROD. Witness-
es: Henry (X) BOYER and Bryson BLACKBURN. Signed: Henry
BOYER.

Page 86. 11 November 1796. Nuncupative Will of William
JOINER (JOYNER). December Term 1796. Departed
this life 5 November 1796. Son David JOINER to take care
of my estate, my wife Mary and act as guardian to his sisters
and brother, Peggy, Sally, Atkerson and Betsy. Executors:
Joseph JOINER (no relationship given) and son David JOINER.
Witnesses: Williss (X) JOINER, Jurat, David (X) JOINER,
Martha (X) WOOLDRIDGE, and William (X) HARRIS, Jurat.
Signed: William JOINER. . . .Robert WILLIAMS witnessed
signatures of Willis and David.

Page 87. December Term 1796. Inventory Estate of Daniel
HAMM, deceased. Sold at Public Vendue 18 November
1796. Signed: Thomas HAM, Administrator.

Page 88. December Term 1796. Inventory of Nathan SANDERS,
deceased, Bible, Testament, Hymn Book, Sermon
Book, among items listed. Signed: William (X) HOWELL and
Susanna SANDERS, Executors.

Page 89. 23 September 1796. Will of William LADD.
December Term 1796. Wife Doshea (Theodoshea,
Theodotia, etc.). Son William, Negro Jacob. Child my wife
now pregnant with, Negro Dinah. My Brother, Noble LADD'S
son Moses, land bought of Peter HAIRSTON and William WILSON,
Senr. In case of death of son William and unborn child,
estate to go to Brother Noble LADD'S two eldest sons, Moses
and Noble. Executors: Brother Noble LADD and wife Theodosia.
Witnesses: Thomas HAMPTON, George BRADLEY and William
SUTHERLAND. Signed: William LADD.

Page 90. 10 December 1796. Nuncupative Will of Theodotia
LADD. December Term 1797. Henry HAMPTON and
Sarah HAMPTON made oath before Justices Richard GOODE and
Absalom BOSTICK on 2 December 1796 as witnesses to her last
Will and Testament. Her father to handle her estate for use

12

of her child 'til it comes of age and if it should die, to
be divided between her brother and sister, Thomas and Hannah
HAMPTON. Witnesses: Richard GOODE and Absalom BOSTICK.
Signed: Henry HAMPTON, Jurat and Sarah HAMPTON.

Page 90. March Term 1797. Inventory Estate of William
        JOYNER, deceased. Signed: David JOYNER and
Joseph JOYNER, Executors.

Page 91. March Term 1797. Inventory Estate of William
        BOYLES, Senr., 13 January 1797, 232 acres land,
etc.

Page 92. March Term 1797. Inventory Estate of William
        LADD, deceased, 100 acres of land, 3 negroes, etc.
Signed: Noble LADD, Executor.

Page 92. June Term 1797. Inventory Estate of Elizabeth
        WRIGHT, deceased, made 14 May 1797. Signed: S.
HAUSER, Administrator.

Page 93. June Term 1797. Inventory Estate of Mary DAVIS,
        deceased. Signed: Reuben SOUTHERN, Administrator.

Page 93. 8 March 1797. Will of Rachel TATE. June Term
        1797. Eldest son Owen TATE. Sons, Samuel and
Robert TATE. Daughters, Elizabeth and Rachel TATE. No
Executors. Witnesses: William LEACH and Elizabeth (X) TATE.
Signed: Rachel (X) TATE.

Page 95. 6 January 1789. Will of James JACKSON, Surry
        County, North Carolina. June Term 1797. Wife
Frances, 100 acres on Beaver Island adjoining John ROBERTSON,
including both plantations on Buffalow Creek adjoining James
JACKSON, Junr. and William MOORE after wife's death; 100
acres on Beaver Island with both plantations to go to Samuel
CRAWLEY; other 100 acres adjoining Wm. MARTIN'S line to
Henry CRAWLEY; 400 acres Hickory Creek adjoining John KEES-
ING and Abraham MARTIN'S line to Thomas CRAWLEY. To my two
sons and 4 daughters (not named), 1 shilling Sterling each.
Executor: Loving wife Frances. Witnesses: William RAMSEY,
William GILL, Jurat and Mary (X) FLOOD. Signed: James
JACKSON.

Page 95. 16 December 1796. Will of Johanna Elizabeth
        COLVER, Spinster, Salem. September Term 1797.
To brother and sisters, Ephraim COLVER, Anna NICHOLS, Mary
KUNCHLER, Pennsylvania money left me by my late father, 12
pounds in hand and remainder in hands of brother, Ephraim
now (or late) of New Jersey, share and share alike. To
following children, Anna Luisa STOTZ, Charlotte L. KRAMAH
(German, KRAMER), Henrietta Frederica VIERLING, Elizabeth
TRANSOU. To John Henry HERBST, tanner, Salem, remainder of
my Estate. Executors: John Henry HERBST and Anna Green
(KROEHN), Spinster. Witnesses: Gottlieb SHOBER, Jurat and
Anna Green (KROEHN). Signed: Johanna Elizabeth COLVAR.

Page 96. September Term 1797. Inventory Estate of Joseph

13

SPRAGUE, deceased, made 5 September 1797. Signed:
John MARTIN, Administrator.

Page 97. 13 June 1797. Will of Balthazar (Balthaser)
          CHRISTMANN, Bethabara. September Term 1797.
Wife Elizabeth. My children (begotton on wife Elizabeth are
under age), Benigna, Jacob and child she is now pregnant
with. Executors: Abraham STEINER and Peter FEEZER (FEISER).
Guardian of children: Abraham STEINER. Witnesses: Peter (X)
SHORE and Tency (X) FEZER (FEISER). Signed: Balthazer (X)
CHRISTMAN(N).

Page 98. September Term 1797. Inventory Estate of Rachel
          TATE, deceased. Those who bought: Samuel TATE,
Robert TATE, Elizabeth TATE, Rachel TATE, valued by Michael
SPAUENHOUR and Malekiah FRANKLIN. Signed: Owen TATE and
Elizabeth TATE, Administrators.

Page 99. September Term 1797. Additional Inventory of
          William LADD, deceased. Signed: Noble LADD,
Executor.

Page 99. September Term 1797. Inventory Estate of Thomas
          KIMBROUGH, deceased, by Fatha KIMBROUGH, Admrx.,
150 acres land, 8 Negroes, James, Nance, Geo., Peg, Dave,
Seller, Ben, and Silva. Signed: Fatha (X) KIMBROUGH, Admrx.

Page 100. December Term 1797. Inventory Estate of Balhazar
           (Balthaser) CRISSMANN, deceased, taken 24 July
1797. Signed: Abraham STEINER and Peter FISER (FEISER),
Executors.

Page 101. 15 February 1797. Will of John Marks (Marcus)
           HOINS (HOHNS, HOENS), Planter. Son Christian
Henry. Children, John Phillip, Christian Henry, Martin,
Catharina, Christina, Rosina. Son Phillip L., land in Rowan
County where he now lives. Grandchildren, John and Eliza-
beth BEROTH. Executors: Wife Anne Elizabeth and sons, John
and Christian Henry HANES. Witnesses: Henry RIPPLE, Jurat,
Jacob ROTHROCK and Robert JONES. Signed: John Marcus HANES
(wrote in Dutch). . . .7 March 1798. John and Christian
HANES, Executors, report amount of Estate of Markus HANES,
deceased, $838.50 and no other property.

Page 104. 10 October 1796. Will of Jacob MILLER (MULLER).
           March Term 1808. Eldest son, John, 250 acres he
now lives on. Son Frederick, land he now lives on. Son
Jacob, land and plantation "thereto belonging". Eldest
daughter Johanna Salome, wife of Lionhard KRAUSE in Penn.
Daughter Catherine, wife of Peter ROTHROCK. Daughter
Elizabeth, wife of Francis KETTNER. Daughter Hannah, widow
of John HAUSER. Executors: sons, Joseph, Frederick and
Jacob. Witnesses: George HAUSER and Jacob LASH. Signed:
Jacob (X) MILLER.

Page 106. 20 December 1797. Will of Hardy REDDICK. March
           Term 1798. Wife Mourning, plantation I now live
on. Son Hardy, same at decease of wife. Son John, meadow

14

tract South Spring Branch (part of). Son Abraham, meadow
tract North Spring Branch (part of). Son Thomas, CARTER
tract on Flatshoal Creek. Daughters Mourning, Sarah,
Elizabeth, Margaret, Milicent. My COLLINS tract be sold for
schooling of my children. Daughter Lovena HEATH. Daughter
Nancy CLARK. Executors: Wife Mourning REDDICK and son, John
REDDICK. Witnesses: Younger BLACKBURN, Jurat, Richard
FOUSHER, Jurat and Adam MITCHELL. Signed: Hardy (X) REDDICK.

Page 107. 13 March 1798. Will of George GOPFORT of Salem.
June Term 1798. My cousin, (blank) BAUMGARTNER,
widow; daughter of my father's brother, living now in Setiz,
Bethelhem, Pa. Executors: John GAMBOLD of Salem. Witnesses:
Thomas BUTTNER and Carl Gotlieb CLAUDER. Signed: Geo. (X)
GOPFERT.

Page 108. 3 July 1797. "Verbatim" Will of David JOHNSON.
June Term 1798. Wife Mary, as long as she lives
single and at her marriage everything be sold; ebily (Equally) divided between Matt, Nancey, Marnin, Rody, John, Eleze-
beth and Sary. No Executor. Witnesses: Matt (X) CHILDRESS
and Jane (X) CHILDRESS, Jurat. Signed: David (X) JOHNSON.

Page 109. 16 June 1798. Will of Samuel WARNOCK. September
Term 1798. All my estate reyal and personable
continue in hands of Absalom BOSTICK, Senr. for maintenance
of my son, John WARNOCK, for life; after his decease what is
remaining to be given to my daughter, Joshua DODSON'S wife;
and James WARNOCK. Witnesses: John BOSTICK, Mary BOSTICK,
Lazander Birt HOLT, and Elizabeth HOLT. Signed: Samuel
WARNOCK.

Page 110. 2 August 1798. Will of Matthew ESTERLINE.
September Term 1798. Immediately after his de-
cease, Negro Ben and other items to be sold; mentions house
in Betharbara. Wife Anne Mary, one-third of my estate. Son
Daniel. Guardian to son, Daniel, Rudolph CHRIST of Salem.
Executors: Gottlieb KROUSE and Abraham STEINER. Witnesses:
Abraham STEINER, Jurat and Christian STAUBER. Signed:
Matthew ESTERLINE.

Page 111. September Term 1798. Inventory Estate of John
RANK, deceased. Appraised 8 August 1798 by Peter
FISER (FEISER) and Henry STERR (STOHR). Signed: John RANK,
Administrator.

Page 113. 25 August 1797. Will of Valentine FRY, Rowan
County, North Carolina. December Term 1798. In
my lifetime I have sold all my lands, stock and Negroes and
given sufficient to my five sons, Michael, Valentine, Henry,
John and Peter. At my death of my personal estate to be
sold and money equally divided among my five daughters, Anna
Barbara, wife of Fredric BINKLEY; Anna Maria wife of Peter
FISER (FEISER), Margaretha wife of Rudy NECT; Rosina wife of
Adam PETREE, deceased; Christina wife of John WOLFERSBERGER
(John W. SPARGER). Executors: Fredrick BICKLE (BINKLEY),
and Michael FRY. Witnesses: John RIGHTS, Joseph FRY, and
George FRY. Signed: Valentine (X) FRY.

Page 114. 5 October 1794. Will of John VANHOY. December
           Term 1797. Wife Jemina, plantation whereon I
now live for use in raising and educating my children. Son
John, now living in Kent County, Delaware, land on Little
Neck Creek. Son-in-law, James HARRY and wife Esther (my
daughter), land in Kent County, Delaware. Son-in-law
Phinehas BOYD and wife Mary (my daughter), land in Kent
County, Delaware. My oldest son (by my last wife), Edward,
a horse. Rest of estate to be divided among James, Thomas,
William, Abraham, Nancy, Susannah, Clayton, and Rachel,
children by my last wife. Executors: Wife Jemima, Neighbor,
Archibald CAMPBELL. Witnesses: James CAMPBELL, David SHAW,
and Robert WALKER. Signed: John VANHOY, Sr.

Page 115. December Term 1798. Inventory of Joseph BITTING,
           deceased, household and other items. Signed:
Rachel (X) BITTING.

Page 116. December Term 1798. List of New Goods found at
           Petersburg, Virginia, items found in a General
Store. Signed: Rachel (X) BITTING.

Page 118. December Term 1798. Notes found in his Estate
           on: Shadrack MORRIS, Benj. BANNDER, Sr., Thomas
WINSTON, Wm. WAGGONER, Senr., Abraham MARTIN, Junr., Fredr.
SHOUSE, William CAMPBELL, Daniel DAVIS, Michael MOSER,
Phillip SUTHERLAND, James MARTIN, Thomas ARMSTRONG, Solomon
TURNER, Wm. HORTON, Ephraim BANNER, Peter PERKINS, Lewis
BLUM, Benj. FORSYTH, Gray BYNUM, Robert BRIGGS, John BANNER,
John VINES, John BOONER, John BALL, Daniel EVANS, Isham VEST,
Charles BANNER, James KING, Francis McINTIRE, and Henry FREY.
Signed: Rachel (X) BITTING.

Page 119. December Term 1798. Book Amounts on Hand:
           Charles BANNER, Robert MAJORS, Henry SAMUEL, Col.
James MARTIN, Hastin FLYNT, John MORRIS, Robert HILL, Younger
BLACKBURN, Reuben GEORGE, Phillip SUTHERLAND, Lucy BLACKBURN,
Geo. GOODE, James BOATRIGHT, Aaron MOORE, Ferdinand BOSTICK,
Alexander MOORE, Junr., John EVANS, William CARRAWAY, Charles
McANNALLY, Martha BANNER, Joshua HORNER, Jonathan DAULTON,
John HALL, Isaac GEORGE, John COOLEY, Jesse STIFF(?), David
DALTON, John HUTCHINGS, Elisha CHILDRESS, Philip WILSON,
John BOSTICK, John WALKER, Nicolas PERKINS, Thomas GRUBBS,
Paris LEWIS(?), Benj. DIXON, Thomas MOODY, Charles DAVIS,
Joseph EASON, Robert BRIGGS, Wm. GREAR, Wm. MOORE, Isham
EARL, Hammon MORRIS, Richard PRATT, Isaac DALTON, Esq., Col.
Peter PERKINS, William MERRIL, Jesse KNIGHTIN, Jesse STANDLY,
Christian CONROD, Edward COOLEY, Maj. WILKERSON, Benj.
RUTLEDGE, Richard GOODE, Jr., John DAVIS, Thomas HAMM, Abi-
jah OLIVER, Elijah RUTLEDGE, Charles CALTON, Geo. DEATHERAGE,
John SCALES, Anthony BITTING, James ANGELL, Joseph BINKLEY,
James COFFEE, Robert BLACKBURN, John APPLETON, Wm. WAGGONER,
Tandy MATTHEWS, Noble LADD, Joseph LADD, Samuel HAMPTON,
Daniel EVANS, Joshua BANNER, Wm. WALKER, John MOON, Abraham
PERKINS, Caleb HILL, Augustine SAMUELS, Francis McINTIRE,
John VINES, Wm. GIBSON, Benj. BANNER, Junr., Charles BEAZLEY,
Shadrack MORRIS, Wm. FLYNT, John TUTTLE, Absalom BOSTICK,
Junr., Micajah COFFIN, Israel BLACKBURN, Wm. RUTLEDGE, Junr.,

Wm. WILSON, Nathaniel SCALES, Christian SMITH, John HALBROOK,
Gray BYNUM, Byne MURRAY, Piann COOLEY, Wm. FRENCH, Wm. HILL,
Arthur DENTON, Jacob BINKLEY, Henry SHOUSE, Martin FLYNT,
Charles GOODE, Samuel GEORGE, Travis MORRIS, Chas. VEST,
Jeremiah WADE, James MARTIN, Fredrick AUST, Harrison HALL,
Geo. EBERT, Johnson RUTLEDGE, Fatha KIMBRO(UGH), Jonathan
BRANHAM, Theophilis McMILLION, Joshua YOUNG, Jacob HAM, John
BOLES, Mary BITTING, Henry DOBSON, Jacob PETREE, Laurance
ANGEL, Christian LINEBACK, Wm. CAMPBELL, Wm. LINVILLE, John
RING, Gottlieb WOLF, John CHESOLM, John DEARING, James
SUTHERLIN, Robert GRINDER, Nall MOODY, Michael MOSER, Jacob
SASSOM, Henry MOSER, Edward WHITWORTH, Wm. PENNIGAR, David
FLYNT, Theophilus LACY, Howell HARGROVE, Ephraim BANNER,
Richard BENNETT, Robert GIBSON, Benj. CHILDRESS, Wm. BEAVERS,
Geo. MARTIN, Edmund DAVIS, Wm. DOWNEY, John CAMPBELL, Benj.
MAJORS, Wm. CROOK, Elizabeth BLACKBURN, Thomas COOPER,
Joseph COX, Jacob UPP, John KIZER, Samuel DALTON, Samuel
WAGGONER, Benj. FORSYTH, Elizabeth FLYNT, Wm. FARRA (?),
Ezekiel HAM, Thomas CARR, Edward SAMUELS, Abraham MARTIN,
Junr., Nicholas UPP, John BANNER, Thomas OWENS, Thomas HEATH,
David POINDEXTER, George LANS (?), Henry BANNER, Wm. FOLLIS,
John LADD, Col. Joseph WINSTON, Benj. BANNER, Senr., Francis
STAUBER (?), Isaac NELSON, John WOODS, Lewis WAGGONER.
Signed: Rachel (X) BITTING.

Page 121.   November Term 1798.   Sale of Estate of Joseph
            BITTING, deceased, 9 November 1798.   Purchasers:
Robert ADAMS, Wm. CROOK, Christian LASH, Joshua COX, Richard
BENNETT, Isham VEST, Joseph EASON, Geo. HAUSER, James
MATTHEWS, Anthony BITTING, Rachel BITTING, Constantine LADD,
John KIZER, Wm. DOWNEY, Richard GOODE, Thomas CHILDRESS,
Ephraim BANNER, John HOLLBROOK, John COOLEY, Boaz SOUTHERN,
Joseph LADD, S. FERGURSON, Charles VEST, Noble LADD, Geo.
DEATHERAGE, J. MILLER, Joshua COX, Abraham PERKINS, Wm.
GIBSON, Lewis BLUM, Wm. ADAMS, John Fedol CARR, Richard
PRATT, Jack FERGUSON, Wm. CAMPBELL, Edmund JEAN, A. CAMPBELL,
R. BRIGGS, M. MOSER, Nall MOODY, Joseph BANNER, Joshua BANNER,
Martin FLYNT, John VINES, William JEAN, Wm. DOWNEY, John
BOLES, Andrew BOWMAN, Polly BITTING, John BITTING, Michael
FRY, Gabriel WAGGONER.   Signed: Isaac NELSON for Rachel
BITTING, Administrator.

Page 122.   March Term 1799.   Inventory Estate of John VANHOY,
            deceased.   Taken 25 February 1799 (sundry
household furniture, etc, 2½ pages) "due from James DAY, due
from Solomon TURNER."   Signed: Jemima VANHOY, Executrix.

Page 124.   March Term 1799.   Inventory Estate of Valentine
            FRY, deceased.   One large Bible, etc.   Notes or
bonds found in possession of said Valentine FRY: Stephen
CADLER, John FRY (7), Christian CONROD, David INGRAM, Andrew
BLACK, Peter UPP, Peter FIZER, Rosina PETREE, Peter PFAFF,
Thomas COOPER, Rudolph NECT, John BINKLE, Frederic BINKLE
(3), Christian LASH, Fetty BINKLE, Michael FREY (2), Henry
FRY (2), Peter FRY (3), Wm. GORDON, John WOLFERSBERGER,
Joseph LINEBACK, Tobias BEEBLE, Henry MILLER, John MILLER,
Phillip CRA--S, Jonas LEATHERMAN, Michael MILLER, Zack
JERVIS, John ECLES, Hardy JONES, Mark BOWLER, Samuel PECK.

Names found or charged on Book: Rudolf NECT, Arthur SMITH, Richard HOLLIS, Adam PETREE, Andrew BLACK, Duncan CAMPBELL, Peter STAUBER, David INGRAM, Adam BOYER, Abraham TANSAY, Wm. JACKSON, Henry HAUSER, John WOLFERSBERGER, Henry FRY, Peter FRY, Jacob BONN, Andrew GEORGE and Luckly GRIFFIN. Signed: Michael (X) FRY and Frederic (X) BINKLEY, Executors.

Page 126.   8 October 1798.   Will of Britain CLAYTON.   March
            Term 1799.   Wife Lucy, plantation whereon I now
live, etc.   Negroes, Seal, Hanner and Milly.   Children,
Warren Casper, Polly, Charles, Caty, Rebecah.   My children
by my first wife: Son George, Negro Aggy; Son Britain, Negro
Dick; daughter Nancy, Negro Frank; daughter Betsy, Negro
Lucy; son John, Negro Adam and Absalom; daughter Elizabeth.
Expect wife Lucy is with child, it is to have equal share
with other children of wife Lucy.   Executors: George HAUSER,
Esqr. and John CLAYTON.   Witnesses: Samuel STRUB, Jurat and
William BECK.   Signed: Britain CLAYTON.

Page 128.   2 July 1790.   Will of Michael DEAUGE.   June Term
            1799.   Wife Catherine.   Son Michael.   Daughter
Elizabeth.   Executors: Michael and Henry SPOONEHOUR.   Wit-
nesses: Henry FORTNEY and Abraham STULTZ, Jurat.   Signed:
Michael DEAUGE.

Page 129.   23 January 1799.   Will of Ann Mary ESTERLINE,
            Bethabara.   June Term 1799.   My burial to be in
forenoon of day, in afternoon of same day congregation of
Bethabara (of which I am a member) and my relations have a
Lovefeast as is common in Congregations of United Brethren,
etc.   My only living child and son, Daniel ESTERLINE who has
body and mental disabilities, I leave my Estate.   Appoint
Gottlieb SPACH, guardian of Daniel and at decease said
Daniel, remainder of my Estate to said SPACH.   Witnesses:
Abraham STEINER, Jurat, Richard BENNETT, and Christian
STAUBER.   Signed: Anna Maria ESTERLINE.

Page 130.   25 March 1799.   Will of Mary AUST, widow.   June
            Term 1799.   To Francis STAUBER, his unpaid note
and her house clock.   To Ann Gertraut, eldest daughter of
Francis STAUBER, 368 acres.   To Magdelene MICKEY, wife of
John MICKEY, a bond on Geo. HAUSER.   To Lewis MICKEY.   To
Mary HAUSER, daughter of George HAUSER, Esqr.   To Constan-
tine LADD of Germanton, a silver spoon.   Executor: Abraham
STEINER of Bethabara.   Witnesses: Michael HAUSER, Jurat and
Henry SHORE, Senr.   Signed: Mary AUST.

Page 132.   June Term 1799.   Return of Sale of Property of
            Samuel WOMOCK, deceased, made 12 March 1799.
Signed: Absalom BOSTICK, Executor.

Page 133 is missing.

Page 134.   September Term 1799.   Inventory goods and chattles
            of John LINDSAY, Senr., deceased.   Signed: John
LINDSAY, Administrator.

Page 134.   September Term 1799.   Inventory Estate of David

JAMES, deceased, made September 1799. Signed:
John VAWTER, Administrator.

Page 134. 21 June 1799. Will of Andrew PATTISON.
September Term 1799. To James Hazelwood PATTISON.
To my son, David PATTISON. To Francis BOWERS' three child-
ren: Andrew BOWERS, Elizabeth Wilkerson BOWERS and Robert
Saunford BOWERS. Executor: my daughter Mary BOWERS. Wit-
nesses: Andrew RAY and William FRAZIER, Jurat. Signed:
Andrew PATTISON.

Page 135. 8 June 1799. Will of John NEELEY. September
Term 1799. Mentions three black children, Caty
6 years, Polly 3 years and Richard 6 months, to be free when
they become of age and Mary, their mother (who was freed
before birth of said children) to live with them if she
chooses. My sisters sons, John and Abe PORTERFIELD of
Broad River, South Carolina to take charge of aforesaid
children. Executors: John CROUSE, Senr. and William VEST,
Senr. Witnesses: Samuel VEST, Michael CARVER, and John
CHITTY, Jurat. Signed: John NEELEY.

Page 137. 9 August 1799. Will of Frederick HELSABECK
(HILSEBECK), Yeoman. September Term 1799. Wife
Catherine. Children, Henry, Mary, Magdalena, Catherine,
Elizabeth, Susanna. Executors: Daniel SHOUSE and Henry
HELSABECK. Witnesses: Mary (X) CHILDRESS, Henry HELSABECK,
Jurat, Daniel SHOUSE, Jurat, Jacob (X) HELSABECK, Jurat,
(signature in German). Signed: Frederick (X) HELSABECK.

Page 138. 26 February 179eyte. Articles of Agreement
between Jacob PETREE, Senr. and Jacob PETREE,
Junr. concerning 160½ acres on Neatmans Creek, including
part of said PETREYS improvement. Witnesses: Gray BYNUM
and Thomas (X) SUTHERLAND. Signed: Jacob (X) PETRY, Junr.
(Signature in German).

Page 139. 5 October 1799. Nuncupative Will of John WOODS.
Recorded December Term 1799. Wife Nelly WOOD,
entire estate. John WOODS died 8th October 1799. Witness:
Lewis BLUM.

Page 140. 13 November 1798. Christian BINKLEY chooses "my
brother, John SHEAMEL to live with" according to
will of my father, John A(dam) WOLF, security. Witnesses:
John A(dam) WOLFF, Jurat and Patsy BONER (BOONER). Signed:
Christian (X) BRINKLEY.

Page 140. December Term 1799. Inventory Estate of Michael
CARVER, deceased. Signed: George CARVER, Admr.

Page 141. (No date). Inventory Goods and Chattles of John
NEELEY, deceased. Sold at Publick Vendue 5
October 1799. Signed: William VEST, Execr.

Page 142. 26 November 1799. Inventory of William JONES,
deceased. Seven slaves, etc. Signed: Martha
JONES, Admrx.

Page 143.   16 October 1799.   Will of Peter YARRELL, Salem,
          Skindresser. March Term 1800. Buried in the
way of the Brethren of the Society in Burrying Ground at
Salem. Wife Mary, bring up my children who are all under
age. Three children, Thomas, Anna, and Mary. Executors:
Wife Mary; Friends: Abraham STEINER, Bathabara, and Frede-
rick KUSHKIE (KUSCHKE), Salem. Witnesses: John RIGHTS,
Jurat, Rudolph CHRIST, and John GAMBOLD (GAMBOLD is German).
Signed: Peter YARRELL.

Page 144. March Term 1800. Supplemental Inventory of
          Joseph SPRAGUE, deceased. Accounts: Mary JOHNSON,
Wm. MOORE, James FREEMAN, Robert HARRIS, John DALTON - by
Matthew MOORE. Signed: John MARTIN, Administrator.

Page 144. 29 October 1799. Phillip SYTZ (SEITZ) to Jacob
          ROTHROCK, $200, Negro girl, Silvy 9 years last
April. Witnesses: Henry RIPPLE, Jurat and Adam ELROD.
Signed: Phillip SIDES.

Page 145. 15 December 1799. Will of Edward EVANS. March
          Term 1800. Wife Martha. Children Margaret, Mary,
Sarah, Rebecca, John, Hampton, Elizabeth and Rosanna.
Brother John EVANS, mentions sueing Gray BYNUM if said
BYNUM won't give right in land. Executors: John EVANS, Senr.
and Charles BANNER. Witnesses: Jeremiah GIBSON and Daniel
EVANS, Jurat. Signed: Edward EVANS.

Page 146. March Term 1800. Inventory Estate of Matthew
          ESTERLINE, deceased, taken by Gottlieb SPACH,
Administrator and appraised by Peter FEISER and John SHEMEL.
Signed: Gottlieb SPACH, Administrator.

Page 147. 18 June 1800. June Term 1800. Inventory Estate
          of John WOOD, deceased, sold by Administrator.
Signed: Lewis BLUM, Administrator.

Page 147. June Term 1800. Inventory Estate of Edward
          EVANS, deceased. Negro girl Milla, etc. Signed:
Charles BANNER and John EVANS, Executors.

Page 148. June Term 1800. Inventory Estate of Jesse
          McANALLY, deceased. (Two pages of various
articles.) Signed: Elizabeth McANALLY and Charles BANNER,
Executors.

Page 149. 2 March 1800. Will of William WEBB. June Term
          1800. Beloved wife Martha. Dear children, when
they become of age (not named). Executors: Wife Martha,
Joseph CLOUD. Witnesses: Thomas CARDWELL, Charles BEAZLEY,
Jurat, John HART ?, John GREENWOOD, and Thos. FRASLER.
Signed: William WEBB.

Page 150. 25 August 1799. Will of Traugott BAGGE, Merchant,
          Salem. June Term 1800. To Samuel STOTZ, Warden
Brethrens Congregation, all stock, etc. in my Merchant Store
in Salem and Bathabara. To Nephew Johann Lorenz BAGGE in
Germany. To Niece Caritas HERTEL, widow of Rev. Mr. HERTEL,

in Germany and her children. To Granddaughter Maria Rosina
VIERLING, money advanced to her father Samuel Benj. VIERLING
when and after he married my deceased daughter, Anne Elizabeth. To Gibhard CRENOW of Bethlehem, Trust fund for
education of above mentioned Maria Rosina VIERLING at school
in Bethlehem, Pennsylvania. To son Charles Frederic BAGGE,
my personal estate, house and lott in Salem. Mentions
2,000 acres in Wachovia deeded by Fredr. MARSHALL for James
HUTTON 1770; 2,000 in 1774; 1,937 brought from John RIGHTS
1795. Should he marry again and leave widow, Charles to
pay her $2,000. To Hannah SPACK, Spinster, for nursing my
dear late wife, Rachel in her last sickness. Executors:
Jacob BLUM, Jacob WOOLFORT (WELFARE) and Charles Frederick
BAGGE, all of Salem. Witnesses: John RIGHTS, Jurat, Peter
YARRELL and Godfreed SCHULTZ. Signed: Traugott BAGGE.

Page 155. September Term 1800. Inventory Estate of William
          WEBB, deceased, 1,135 acres land; five Negros,
Tom, Doss, Rose, Dick and Nelly; other articles.
Signed: Martha WEBB, Joseph CLOUD and Thomas CARDWELL,
Executors.

Page 156. September Term 1800. Inventory Estate of Chris-
          tian HUMMEL, deceased, taken 1 September 1800.
(2½ pages sundry articles). Signed: John RIGHTS, Gottlieb
SPACH, and Joseph BONER, Executors.

Page 157. 2 August 1800. Will of Christian HUMMELL.
          September Term 1800. Wife Mary Christina. Four
daughters Anna Maria, Anna Christina, Catherina and Susannah
Elizabeth. Executors: Gottlieb SPACH and Joseph BONNER
(BONER). Witnesses: Abraham HAUSER, Jurat and John RIGHTS.
Signed: Christian HUMMELL.

Page 158. 3 July 1799. Will of Christoph SMITH (SCHMIDT).
          September Term 1800. Wife Anna (late wife of
Abraham LINEBACK). Children John, Peter, Christian, Margaret,
Nelly wife of Joseph MILLER, Junr., and Catherine. Execu-
tors: Son Peter and son-in-law Joseph MILLER, Junr. Wit-
nesses: John CHITTY and Joseph MILLER, Jurat. Signed:
Christopher (X) SMITH.

Page 160. 26 December 1799. Will of James LOVE, Senr.
          September Term 1800. To Edmund JEAN, William
JEAN, Seth COFFIN, James CAMPBELL, all of Stokes; and Geo.
McKINNY, Junr., Reuben McDANIEL, and Travase JONES of
Guilford County. Son-in-law, Charles CLAYTON and his wife
Nancy (my daughter), one-third of estate. Son James LOVE,
one third of estate. Children of my son John LOVE by
daughter-in-law Ruth LOVE, one third of estate. Executor:
son James LOVE. Witnesses: Robert WILKERSON and A(rchibald)
CAMPBELL, Jurat. Signed: James (X) LOVE.

Page 161. December Term 1800. Inventory Estate of Christoph
          SMITH (SCHMIDT), deceased, made 10 September 1800
by Peter SMITH and Joseph MILLER, Junr., Executors. 120
acres land, etc. Also four rights of bequeasts as heirs of
Abraham LINEBACK, deceased. Also separate list bequeasts to

21

Anna SMITH his wife with notes, etc.in her possession as Execrx. of Abraham LINEBACK, deceased.

Page 162. 9 September 1800. Inventory Estate of James LOVE, Senr., deceased. Executor: James (X) LOVE. Junr.

Page 163. December Term 1800. Inventory Estate of Benjamin CANNON, deceased, given by his wife, Henningham CANNON, Admrx. Four Negroes, Nan, Charles, Eliza and Frank. Also, Joseph EAST bequeathed Mary CANNON and her heirs when youngest child comes of age if Mary CANNON still wife of deceased, Benj. CANNON, etc. etc. Signed: Henningham (X) CANNON, Admrx.

Page 164. 5 August 1800. Will of Lewis LINEBACK. December Term 1800. Wife Barbara. Two youngest children (not named here). Son-in-law Rohn RANCK, to provide for my wife. Daughter Gertraut, when she comes of age. Son Christian, plantation whereon he lives. Son Joseph, where he has lived for sometime. Eldest son John. Executors: Jacob LASH, son-in-law and Gottlieb RANKE (both of Bethania). My Executors to deed 5 acres of land to Henry KAPP. The names of six of my children are: John, Peter, Susanna (wife of Jacob LASH), Elizabeth, Gertraut, and Mary. Witnesses: Christian STAUBER and Peter (X) SHORE. Signed: Lewis LINEBACK.

Page 167. 19 September 1800. Will of John HINSHAW. December Term 1800. Wife Ann, my dwelling house, etc. Five children: John, Jesse, Benjamin, Seth and Susannah (John and Jesse, two eldest). Mentions little piece of land wife owned when married and her children to be paid their rights: David, John, Ann, Joseph and Mary PHILLIPS. Executor: Wife Ann, son Jesse, Brother-in-law, Micajah WEESNER. Witnesses: Henry WILLETS, Jurat, Samuel SCHOOLY (COOLEY), and Micajah WEESNER. Signed: John HINSHAW.

Page 168. 17 December 1796. Will of Abraham HESSLER. December Term 1800. Wife Mary Salome. Brother John William HESSLER, Hope, Sussix County, New Jersey. Sister Ann Benigna BAGGE, Bethlehem, Pennsylvania, widow of Nicholas Lawrence BAGGE of Lebanon, Pennsylvania, deceased. To Society United Brethren in North Carolina to be paid into hands of Fredr. Wm. MARSHALL. Executors: Christian Lewis BENZIEN, Salem, Hans Christian SCHWINIZ (SCHWEINITZ), Esqr., and John SHROPP (SCHROPP), Gentleman (last two of Bethlehem, Pennsylvania. Witnesses: Abraham STEINER, Jurat, Gottlieb KRAUSE and Peter (X) SHORE. Signed: Abraham HESSLER.

Page 170. 13 September 1800. Will of Almand GUINN. December Term 1800. Wife Mary, Negros Lucy and Frank, Sarah, Loosey and Nancy. Heirs, Daughter Martha, deceased: Negroes Aggy and her children, Bob, Frank, Rose and Cate. Daughter, Elizabeth DANIEL: land lying between Alex RUSSELL and Robt. ACTON. Son-in-law, Peter BURTON. Daughter, Cresan CRITTENDON, one-half my land in Halifax

County, Virginia where she now lives and Negro Miko, at her
death to her daughter, Mary CRITTENDON. Daughter Mary FARE,
Negro Hanner and other articles. Daughter Rebekah BURTON,
land I now live on and Negro Amy. Son Thornton Preston
GUINN, balance of estate including plantation on Dan River
and half land in Halifax County, Virginia; also two tracts
on Dan River I bought from William LADD; also Negroes George,
Patty, Adam, Jack, Charity, Aggy and Tab. Executors:
Thornton Preston GUIN and Peter BURTON. Witnesses: Manoah
BOSTICK, Jurat and John WILSON, Jurat. Signed: Almand (X)
GUINN.

Page 171.   5 March 1801. Inventory of Estate of John
        WILSON, deceased. Signed: John WILSON, Admr.

Page 172.   March Term 1801. Inventory Estate of Jeptha
        PARKER, deceased, taken 24 December 1800.
Signed: Clayborn WATSON, Administrator.

Page 173.   21 June 1794. Will of Jacob MEYER of Salem.
        March Term 1801. Son Phillip Jacob MEYER, I lend
my large German Bible for my grandchild, Henry MEYER. Son
Samuel MAYER, silver watch. Daughter Dorothea MAYER, my
Harpsicord. Wife Dorothea, remainder of my Estate. Grandchild John KRAUSE. Executors: Wife Dorothea MAYER, Samuel
STOTTS (STOTZ), and Rudolph CHRIST. Witnesses: Jacob BLUM
and Phillip TRANSOU. Signed: Jacob MEYER.

Page 174.   30 January 1797. Will of Eva Barbara EBERT,
        widow of Martin EBERT, deceased. March Term
1801. My body be buried at Friedburg Meeting house Grounds.
Five children: John Martin, John George, Rosina, wife of
Adam TESH; Christina, wife of Cornelius SCHNIDER; and
Catherine, wife of John WESNER. Executors: Son John Martin
and Cornelius SCHNIDER. Witnesses: Peter SEANER (SANER),
signed in German, Jurat and Peter FOLTZ. Signed: Eva
Barbara (X) EBERT.

Page 175.   3 April 1794. Will of William CARSON. March
        Term 1801. Wife Martha, one-third of estate.
Son Samuel, balance of estate. Executor: Son Samuel.
Witnesses: William SMITH and Micajah COFFEY, Jurat. Signed:
William CARSON.

Page 177.   March Term 1801. Inventory Estate of Almand
        GUINN, deceased, two pages of articles. Signed:
Peter BURTON, Executor.

Page 178.   28 February 1800. Will of George HAUSER, Senr.
        March Term 1800. Wife Barbara. Son Lorenz, my
dwelling house and lott in case he can be admitted as inhabi-
tant of this Town; in case he is not, then any other of my
Sons who may be admitted, etc. My 12 children: Henry, George,
Sarah or her heirs, Anna, Catherine, Gertraut or her heirs,
Elizabeth, Fredric, Hanna, Johny, Peter and Lorenz. Mentions
owning ¼ Grist Mill at Bethania; also 2 tracts of land on
Townfork and 500 acres in Western Waters in Mississippi;
also house and lotts in Germanton. Executors: Brother,

Peter HAUSER, Son-in-law Christian LASH and Son George
HAUSER. Witnesses: Jacob LASH and Joseph HAUSER, Jurat.
Signed: George HAUSER.

Page 180. March Term 1801. Inventory Estate of John
          HINSHAW, deceased, made 3 December 1800; 208
acres land; notes on Evans and John COSNER; Gabriel WILLETS,
etc. (4 pages). Signed: Ann HINSHAW, Micajah WEESNER, and
Jesse HINSHAW, Executors.

VOL. II

Page 1. 2 October 1799. Will of Joesph BOLETSHECK (BOLE-
        JACK) (German: BULLITSCHEK), Jiller. June Term
1801. Wife Charlotte. Six Children: Joseph, John, Samuel,
Matthew, Ann Mary, and Elizabeth. Mentions Mill and small
track land one mile from Germanton; also his land on Muddy
Creek where sons, John and Samuel now live; also that Ann
Mary is not yet Married. Executors: Wife Charlotte and son
Joseph. Witness: George BIWEGHAUSS (BIBIGHAUS). Signed:
Joseph BOLICHECK.

Page 3. 21 March 1801. Will of William FRANCH. June Term
        1801. Sons: Joseph, William, Samuel, and John, 5
shillings each. Daughter Elizabeth ABINGTON, all my property
except Negro Dilsy. Daughter, Trnrlsj HSTFMRT and her
children, Negro Dilsy. Executor: Son John FRENCH. Witnesses: Joel WATSON, Jurat, John HOLBROOK, Jurat and Betsy
WHITWORTH. Signed: William FRENCH.

Page 3. 16 September 1796. Will of James HAMPTON. June
        Term 1801. Eldest son, Thomas, Negro man Sutton
and woman Comfort, etc. Youngest son Samuel, 280 acres
whereon I now live on Townfork (excepting ½ acre for burying
ground). Youngest daughter Martha EVANS, Negro Sango and
200 acres adjoining Thomas FLYNT. Eldest daughter Margrett
HALBERT, land. Executors: Thomas and Samuel HAMPTON, Sons.
Witnesses: John BONER, Martin FLYNT, Jurat and Hastin FLYNT,
Jurat. Signed: James HAMPTON.

Page 5. 8 July 1801. Will of John SEILER. September Term
        1801. Wife Anna Elizabeth, present dwelling house.
My 8 children (not named). Executors: Samuel STRUB and Wife
Anna Elizabeth. Witnesses: Christian LASH, Jurat and
Frances STAUBER. Signed: John SEILER.

Page 7. 16 August 1801. Nuncupative Will of John CLAYTON.
        September Term 1801. In his own dwelling house
sayeth. . . To oldest son John CLAYTON, open Pond tract at
Cross Roads, bought of Wm. MARSHALL (after John arrives at
lawful age). Wife Charity. Son-in-law Nathaniel DAVIS who
married my eldest daughter Mary, land where they live. Two

youngest sons, Stephen and William, equal land with eldest.
Nine children: Mary, Elizabeth, Eleanor, John, Stephen,
Charity, William, Ruth, Nancy (as they obtain lawful age).
Executors: Wife Charity and Son-in-laws, Martin FLYNT and
Nathaniel DAVIS. Witness: Charles BANNER. Signed: John
CLAYTON.

Page 8. 25 October 1801. Will of Constantine LADD. Decem-
        ber Term 1801. Wife Mary, 250 acres adjoining Gray
BYNUM and Jacob PETREE; Negroes Will, Delse and Byner.
Sons, Milton and Newton. Three youngest children, Milton,
Newton and Mary Reynolds until they arrive lawful age.
Eldest Daughter, Judith BONER (BONNER) and her husband, John.
To daughter, Judith's children, Negro woman Hester. Brother
Joseph LADD. Executor: Brother Joseph LADD, son-in-law Benj.
FORSYTH and Isaac DALTON. Witnesses: C. BANNER, John EVANS,
Joseph BANNER and John HALL. Signed: Constantine LADD.

Page 9. 10 October 1801. Will of Matthew MOORE. December
        Term 1801. Wife Lettitha, land purchased of John
WALKER on Dan River and Double Creek including whereon I now
live; also slaves Reah, Fanny, Grace, Siphon, Sarah, Ledla,
little Sarah, Squire, Easter, little Nan, Nan wife of Squire,
Aggy, Phillis, Suckey Squire, Junr. . . .Son, Samuel MOORE:
300 acres Fishers River, Surry County, I bought of James
SHEPHERD; also Negro Bartlett. . . .Son Reuben: 390 acres
and 25 acres Snow Creek where he now lives I bought of
Thomas REID adjoining land bought of Thomas SMITH; also
Negro Moses. . . .Son Edward: 260 acres and Grist Mill
Russells Creek, Patrick County, Virginia. Also 400 acres
waters Russel Creek bought of John DOUGLASS whereon Harris
WILSON formerly lived; also tract in Pittsylvania County,
Virginia on Lawless fork bought of James WILSON; also Negro,
Joe. . . .Son Gabriel: 75 acres Arrarat River, Buel Run
Creek, including where Mary LANKFORD formerly lived, bought
of Ben WHEELER; also 100 acres on Pilot Creek adjoining lands
of Wm. HILL and Lazarus DONNY in Surry County, bought of
Wm. WALL; also 200 acres little Yadkin adjoining Elijah ROAK
and 60 acres Surry County bought of George HOLCOMB; also land
on Piney River in Amherst County, Virginia; also 300 acres
Dan River bought of Thos. ISBELL; also 320 acres Brown Moun-
tain, Stokes County, bought of Archiblad MARTIN; also Negro
Peter; Gabriel is to continue schooling. . . .Son Tucker
Woodson MOORE, land bought of John WALKER adjoining land
given to son Matthew RED on Dan River; 50 acres cultivated
by Asa OGLESBY on Dan River; 150 acres including plantation
where John ROBINSON lived bought of Matthew DEATHERAGE; 150
acres including my Old Mill on Dan River adjoining John
DEATHERAGE; 100 acres on Dan River adjoining tract bought of
John WALKER; 400 acres adjoining PERKINS and TAYLOR and John
DEATHERAGE surveys including Dusty RUTHERFORDS improvement;
200 acres adjoining Edmund TILLEY, both sides road leading
to Thomas LANKFORDS; also Negro boy Ben; Tucker Woodson to
continue schooling. . . .Son Matthew Red MOORE: part of 525
acres bought of John WALKER both sides Dan River including
Mansion House and plantation I now live on; 100 acres bought
of Wm. HORTON; 50 acres adjoining former tract; 150 acres
bought of Gamabrel BAILEY; 40 acres where James FINLEY

formerly lived; 200 acres on Finleys branch; also Negro boy
Isaac, to be his when he reaches 21 years of age; Mathew Red
to continue schooling. . . .Daughter Ann, wife of John
HUGHES, Negro Fanny. . . .Daughter Mary, wife of Ambrose
GAINES, Negroes Hannah, Patt and Arthur. . . .Daughter
Elizabeth, wife of John CLEMENTS, Negros, Lucy and Nell.
To my 7 sons and 3 daughters: bond on James SHEPPARD, land
on Grassy Creek in Surry County; bond on Edwin HICKMAN,
deceased, of State of Tennessee, for 1,000 acres in Western
Country; bond on Capt. James GAINES for 2,000 acres lying
in Western County; on obligation of Col. James MARTIN for
1,300 or 1,400 acres lying in Western Country; bond assigned
by Archibald MARTIN on John DARDIN of State of Georgia; bond
on Thomas ISBELL for 640 acres on Harpeth Creek in Tennessee.
Grandson, Matthew M. HUGHES, money for his schooling. . . .
Wills his Iron Works called Providence, be sold to pay debts
and to educate sons, Gabriel, Tucker Woodson and Matthew
Red and his grandson Matthew M. HUGHES. . . .Mentions 2,500
acres land Iron Works is on; also small tracts adjoining this
land bought of Jeremiah EARLEY, Phillip WILSON, David
SIMMINS and John FINLEY; Polecat branch of Buck Island
Creek. Executors: Wife Lettisha MOORE and Sons, Reuben,
Edward, William and Gabriel. Witness: Joseph CLOUD, Jurat.
Signed: Matt. MOORE.

Page 14. 25 September 1800. Will of John DOLLEN (DOLLAND).
        March Term 1802. Wife mentioned but not named.
Son-in-law Willey WRIGHT, 100 acres western end land on
Belews Creek adjoining Gabriel JONES, Benj. JONES, John
WELLS and myself, for which I've never received grant for.
Daughter Sarah DOLLEN, 100 acres eastern end of above land.
Son John, when he comes of age. My other children, not
named. Executors: Neighbors Henry Baker DOBSON and John
ENDSLEY. Witnesses: Archibald CAMPBELL, Jurat and Thomas
GRAHAM, Wm. P. DOBSON. Signed: John (X) DOLLEN.

Page 15. 16 December 1801. Will of Frederick William
        MARSHALL, Salem. March Term 1802. Mentions
United Brethren (Moravians): James HUTTON, Wm. CHURTON,
Charles METCALF, John Earl GRANVILLE concerning land, etc.
To granddaughter Johanna Elizabeth Von SCHWEINITZ, wife of
Rev. John Frederic FRUANUFF of Philadelphia. To grandson
Fredric Christian Von SCHWEINITZ of Salem. Executors:
Christian Lewis BENZIEN, Rev. Jacob Van VLECK of Bethlehem,
Pa. and Rev. John Gebhard CUNOW of Bethlehem, Pa. Witnesses:
Jacob BLUM, Gottlieb SHOBER, Jurat, Frederic MEINUNG, Jurat
and Conrod KREUSER. Signed: Frederic Wm. MARSHALL.

Page 19. 23 September 1794. Will of John MAJORS, Senr.,
        Shop Joiner. June Term 1802. Wife Rebecca, one-
third of estate. Son Benjm. Pollard MAJORS, 220 acres
plantation I now live on and to take special care of his
mother. Sons, Robert, Alexander and Benjamin Pollard MAJORS
my joiner and carpenter tools; mentions "all and everyone of
my dear children." Executors: Son, Benj. Pollard MAJORS.
Witnesses: Charles ANGEL and Patrick TWOMY (TOOMY), Jurat.
Signed: John MAJORS.

Page 20.   6 June 1799.   Will of George Peter HAUSER,
           Bethania.   June Term 1802.   Wife Elizabeth, all of
estate except 1,000 acres by bond from Geo. HAUSER, Esq.   I
am entitled to receive deed for in Western Country called
Cumberland and now in Territory of Indians.   Six children:
Joseph, Henry, Daniel, Johanna Gertraut, George Peter, and
Benjamin, the above mentioned 1,000 ares.   Executors: wife
Elizabeth and Sons Joseph and Peter.   Witnesses: Henry SHORE,
Jurat and Michael HAUSER, Jurat.   Signed: Geo. Peter HAUSER.

Page 21.   22 April 1802.   Will of Frederick KUINZEL (KUNZEL),
           Farmer.   June Term 1802.   Be buried on burial
ground at Friedburg.   Wife Salome, house wherein I now live,
etc.   Daughter Elizabeth (wife of Phillip GREEN), 1/3 of
estate.   Children of deceased daughter Mary (formerly wife
of Michael VOGLER, deceased), 1/3 of estate.   Two step-sons
George and Jacob LAGENOUR (LAGENAUER).   Appoints George
LAGENOUR guardian for children of Mary VOGLER, deceased.
Executors: John LANIUS and wife, Salome.   Witnesses:
Signature in German and Jacob WOHLFAHRT (WELFARE), Jurat.
Signed: Frederick KUINZEL.

Page 22.   15 February 1802.   Will of Elizabeth GOSLIN,
           widow.   June Term 1802.   Leaves friend, John
PEDDYCOART, Senr., Negro Samuel in trust for my friend, Nancy
SLATER wife of Henry SLATER at Nancy's decease, Samuel to go
to Anny PEDDYCOART wife of said John.   To Henry SLATER, who
has maintained me and my daughter since 1783 and daughter,
Elizabeth until her decease 2 December 1790.   To Grandchildren, Children of my deceased daughter, Mary YOUNG.   To
daughter, Catherine, wife of Daniel SMITH.   To Grandson (not
named), son of my deceased daughter, Tabina EADES.   To son,
John.   Executors: Horatio HAMILTON and Adam ELROD.   Witnesses: Samuel KRAMSCH, Susanna KRAMSCH, and Wm. Barton PEDDY-
COART, Jurat.   Signed: Elisaz. GOSLIN.

Page 24.   6 April 1802.   Will of Hugh McKILLIP.   June Term
           1802.   Wife, Agness, 1/3 of estate, 100 acres in
Guilford County and 200 acres in Stokes County.   Daughter
Hanna.   Heirs of daughter, Elizabeth (late wife of Michael
FARE).   Heirs of daughter, Mary (late wife of David GAMMEL).
Executors: Wife Agness, Sons, Andrew and John McKILLIP.
Witnesses: James HALBROOK, Jurat, Thomas WHICKER, and John
LINVILL.   Signed: Hugh McKILLIP.

Page 25.   25 March 1802.   Will of John George AUST, farmer.
           June Term 1802.   Oldest son, Leonard AUST, planta-
tion I now live on.   Youngest son, Frederick AUST, land in
Wilson County, Tennessee I bought of Col. Martin ARMSTRONG.
Executors: Sons, Leonard and Frederick.   Witness: William
BECK.   Signed: Jn. George (X) AUST. . . .
CODICIL: To grandchildren, Maria Margaretha AUST and Fredr.
           Wm. AUST, children of my eldest son, Leonard AUST,
bedding and clothes left me by my deceased wife, Maria
Margaretha AUST.   Witness: Wm. BECK, Jurat.   Signed: Jn.
George (X) AUST.

Page 26.   4 September 1801.   Will of Robert HAZLET, September

27

Term 1802. Wife Jean, my plantation to raise young children. Son Moses, to live on plantation with his mother if agreeable. Daughter Martha. Daughter Elizabeth, when she comes of age. Executors: James DAVIS and Wife, Jean HAZLETT. Witnesses: John DUNLAP, Senr., Jurat and James DAVIS, Jurat. Signed: Robert HAZELET.

Page 27. 30 August 1802. Will of John CONRAD, Bethania.
September Term 1802. Wife Catherine, one-room in my now dwelling and privlege of the kitchen, Negro Mary. Son Jacob, my house and lot in Bethania, 200 acres. Also to keep firewood for my wife during her life. Son John, land on Yadkin bought of Wm. WOODFORK; also Negro Milly. Son Abraham, land on Muddy Creek, formerly property of Windel KRAUS. Son Isaac. To Elizabeth ROMINGER, an orphan who has lived with my family several years. Mentions my business in keeping store together by wife and sons until Jacob comes of age 21 years. Also Executors to execute deed to heirs of "my brother Jacob, but he have lifetime privlege (privilege) to land". Also mentions new waggon at Mr. WUFRESS' Shop. Executors: Sons, John and Jacob and Wife Catherine. Witnesses: Christian LASH and Michael HAUSER, Jurat. Signed: John CONRAD.

Page 30. 18 October 1802. Will of Robert HESTER. December Term 1802. Wife Elizabeth, land where I now live. To Francis Hester. Son James. Son Henry, where I now live at death of wife. Daughter Ann HESTER. Son Stephen HESTER. Daughter Elizabeth HESTER. Sons, John, Robert, William White and Thomas Goodrick HESTER. Daughter Polly HESTER. (Note: it would appear children named as to age.) Executors: Wife Elizabeth and son Henry HESTER. Witnesses: John H. PRYOR, Jurat, Willm. W. HESTER and Elizabeth PRYOR. Signed: Robert (X) HESTER.

Page 30. 1802. Will of Jacob BLUM. December Term 1802. Wife Elizabeth. Children: Jacob, Christian, Anny, and Lewis, equal shares of estate. Executors: Christian LAST and Conrod KREUSER. Witnesses: Gottlieb SHOBER and Joshua BONER. Signed: Jacob BLUM.

Page 31. 2 September 1802. Will of Gottlob KRAUSE.
December Term 1802. Wife Christina, land and improvements formerly property of Andr. BRISING (Andreas BRUESLING) for purpose of raising "my children." Also Negroes Tim and Fan (Negro Bill to be sold). Sons: Johnny, Joseph, Samuel, Thomas and Benjamin. Executors: Joseph HAUSER and Christian LASH. Witnesses: John BUTNER (BÜTTNER) and Harman BUTNER, Jurat. Signed: Gottlob KRAUSS.

Page 32. 1 June 1802. Will of Robert SMITH, Senr., Planter. December Term 1802. Sons, John, George, Robert and Thomas, 2 shillings each. Daughters Elizabeth Harris and Ann Wilkerson, 2 shillings each. Sons, William and Bennett, 2 shillings each. To Thomas SMITH, son of Robert SMITH, Junr., Negroes Lucy, Judah, young Lucy, Tom, Friday; also stock, household furniture, etc. Thomas to take care of myself and my wife our lifetime. Executors: Wife Mary

SMITH and Grandson Thomas SMITH. Witnesses: Thomas EAST, Senr., Jurat, Abel (X) EDWARDS, and Thomas EAST, Junr. Signed: Robert SMITH.

Page 34. 14 February 1803. Will of Michael WEAVER. March Term 1803. All my Estate to go to Lenard KEEN. Executors: Daniel SHOUSE and Lenard KEEN. Witnesses: John STANDLEY, Susanah (X) STANDLEY, Markel (X) WEAVER, Henry SHOUSE and Daniel SHOUSE. Signed: Michael (X) WEAVER.

Page 34. 27 December 1802. "Verbal" Will of Samuel HAMPTON. March Term 1802. "Taken down in writing 9 days after his death." Widow Bethenia HAMPTON, keep plantation and Negroes and all property that his children be raised and schooled (children not named). Mentions Wm. REYNOLDS, John BOSTICK, and William BLACKBURN. Witnesses: Thomas (X) FLYNT, Jurat and Augustine (X) SAMUEL, Jurat. Signed: Margret HALBERT, Jurat and Susanna BLACKBURN.

Page 35. 8 December 1792. Will of Jacob MILLER, Jr. March Term 1803. His copper Still and Rifle gun be sold to pay debts, 100 acres land adjoining Abraham LASH, Michael HAUSER and John CONRAD also sold. Mentions land deeded him by his Father (not named) 21 December 1791. Wife Regina Elizabeth, Personal Estate. Son John, to have sufficient education, when he reaches age 21 to have land in North Carolina, Tennessee and Pennsylvania. Sisters Johanna Salome KRAUSE, Bethlehem, Pennsylvania; Christina SCHULTZ, wife of John SHULTZ, Stokes County. Executors: Wife Regina Elizabeth, Abraham LASH, and Henry HAUSER. Witnesses: Peter (X) CLINE, Jurat, (Signature in German), and Adam STRUB (signature in German, Jurat). Signed: Jacob (X) MILLER.

Page 36. 15 May 1803. "Verbal" Will of William TAYLOR made in presence of Shadrack SERGEANT, Reubin MOORE and John HUTCHINGS, being four days before his death. Youngest son Isaac, plantation where William lives on condition he keep and maintain his Mother. Daughter Sally Abington, 5 pounds Virginia money. Son William, 5 pounds Virginia money. Sworn to before James MARTIN 23 May 1803; proven June Term 1803.

Page 37. 20 June 1798. Will of Absalom BOSTICK. June Term 1803. Son John, Negro Milly; bond on Elisha PERKINS. Son Absalom, 250 acres he lives on; 52 acres adjoining said land bought of Mark HARDIN; 150 acres adjoining on West; 309 acres, part bought of Charles McANALLY; also six Negroes Lucy, Charlotte, Creecy, Isaac, Jane and Hannah. Son Ferdinand, 796 acres bought of Wm. MEREDITH, head Beaver Island Creek; also three Negroes James, Sib and Stephen. Son Manoah, 866 acres Dan River whereon I now live, adjoining Larrence ANGELL, Thos. CASE, the Bent, including land where son John now lives (in the whole 1,050 acres); also seven Negroes David, Jincy, Bartie, Bibbe, Francis, York, and Williamson. Daughter Bethenia, Negroes Sarah, Dolph, and Selah. Daughter Susana, Negroes Nancy, Solomon, Daniel (Flo's son). Daughter Anne, Negroes, Beck,

Rhoda, Mero (Hager's son). Daughter Christina, Negroes, Hagar, Murer and Dick to remain with my wife until Christina is 18 years old. Bond I have on Wm. T. LEWIS for 2,000 acres divided, 500 acres to Son John; 500 acres to son Absalom; 250 acres each to four daughters named above. Lend my wife seven Negroes (not named) and at her death divided among sons John, Absalom, Ferdinand; Daughters Bethenia HAMPTON, Susanna BLACKBURN, Ann GUINN, and Christina BOSTICK. Executor: Son Manoah BOSTICK. Witnesses: Thos. (X) SPRAGGINS, Laurence ANGEL, and Joseph DURRIM. Signed: Absalom BOSTICK. CODICIL: Negroes lent to my wife for life by name, Harry, Dinah, Cloe, Bynor, Nancy, Hannah, and Sam. Witnesses: Thomas (X) SPRAGGINS, Laurence ANGEL and Joseph (X) DURRUM.

Page 38. 14 July 1803. Will of Fredrick FERNSLER (FARNSLER). September Term 1803. Sister Elizabeth LINEBACK, all of estate. Executor: Christian LINEBACK. Witnesses: Gottlieb SHOBER, Jurat and John Fredr. KUSCHKE. Signed: Fredrick FERNSLER.

Page 38. 8 July 1803. Will of John TATUM. September Term 1803. Wife Molly, my land, etc, Negro Silvy. Son Edward. To Aaron BARRER and Ele GRAHAM. Son John, land. Son Thomas, plantation where he lives. Daughter Mary, Negro girl Selah. Daughter Lucy, Negro boy Ben. Sons, Seth and William, all land whereon I now live. No Executors. Witnesses: John F. NEW, Jurat, Matthew BONTHALL, and Daniel BONTHALL. Signed: John TATUM.

Page 39. 1 July 1803. Will of John KERR, Farmer. September Term 1803. Wife Sarah, 1/3 of estate. Children mentioned but not named. Execurors: Wife Sarah KERR and Daniel SCOTT. Witnesses: John MARTIN and Edward (X) EDWARDS, Jurat. Signed: John KERR.

Page 40. 27 March 1803. Will of Alexander MOORE. September Term 1803. Son John, 100 acres Townfork, blacksmith tools. Sons Aaron and Alexander, 150 acres Townford adjoining John MOORE; also 200 acres adjoining where I now live. Daughter Florence MERRIT. Son William, 200 acre Plantation and dwelling where I now live. Daughters Sarah BOLES, Mary FERGUSON and Nancy MARTIN have already received their portions. Grandson James MOORE, son of James MOORE, Sr. Granddaughter, Patsy MOORE. Executors: Son John MOORE and Boaz SOUTHERN. Witnesses: Henry SHORES, Jurat, Wm. MERRIT, Jurat, and Gottlieb CRAMER. Signed: Alexander MOORE.

Page 41. 31 October 1803. Will of William JEAN, Senr. December Term 1803. Wife Huldah, chattels, etc.; Negroes Penny and girl Mary. Son Joseph, woman Penny and girl Mary at decease of wife. Daughter Becky MORRIS, 5 shillings. Daughter Betty BOBBIT, 5 shillings. Other 7 children: Phillip, John Joseph, William, Patty PEGRAM, Silva CUMMINS and Nancy WILLIAMSON. Executors: William and Joseph JEAN (sons). Witnesses: Boaz SOUTHERN, Jurat, Stephen MEDEARIS, Jurat, and Betsy (X) MEDERIS. Signed: William (X) JEAN, Senr.

Page 42. 29 January 1803. Will of John HUNTER, Senr.
          December Term 1803. Wife Rachel, to live in <u>Knew</u>
house as long as she remains widow. Sons Thomas, David,
John, and Benedictus, 5 shillings each. Son William, plantation I now live on of 300 acres; he is to maintain me and
my wife. To Rachel PHILLIPS and Elizabeth TATE, 5 shillings
each. To Mary and Sarah HUNTER, furniture and cow each.
Executors: William HUNTER and wife Rachel HUNTER. Witnesses:
Henry SHORES, Jurat and Elizabeth (X) SHORES, Jurat.
Signed: John (X) HUNTER.

Page 43. 1 October 1795. Will of William SMITH. No
          Probate Date. To William JOYCE, provided he don't
marry into James YOUNG'S family. Granddaughters Margret
PARR, Sarah JOYCE and Mary JOYCE. Daughter Molly JOYCE,
Negro Fillis. To Elizabeth JOYCE, Shubuckles and Shubuttons.
Executor: Samuel CLARK. Witnesses: Alexander JOYCE and
Samuel CLARK. Signed: William SMITH.

Page 44. 28 December 1803. Will of Thomas BALLARD. March
          Term 1804. Wife Elizabeth, Home Plantation, life-
time. Son Thomas, Home Plantation at decease of wife.
Executors: Son Byrum BALLARD and Wife Elizabeth BALLARD.
Witnesses: Caleb D.S. GARRETT, Joseph BOND, and Samuel BOND.
Signed: Thomas BALLARD.

Page 44. 18 October 1803. Will of William HOWELL. March
          Term 1804. Son-in-law John THOMASON, 5 shillings.
Son-in-law George THOMASON, 5 shillings. Son Phillip HOWELL.
Daughter Rebeckah HOWELL, colt formerly Daniel BARHAM'S.
Son John HOWELL. Daughter Polly HOWELL, money. Mentions
"Beloved wife" several times, but does not name her.
Executors: Beloved wife and Son-in-law John THOMASON.
Witnesses: Daniel BARHAM, Jurat and Nicholas (X) HENDRICKS.
Signed: William HOWELL.

Page 46. 19 September 1803. Will of William WAGGONER, Senr.
          March Term 1804. Wife Sarah, all of estate. Son
William, land where he lives. Grandson Thomas, son of Wm.,
50 acres adjoining his father. Son Thomas, 62½ acres adjoining grandson Thomas. Son Jesse Minter, 62½ acres adjoining
son Thomas. Son Samuel, 75 acres adjoining Jesse Minter.
Grandson, William GREEN, son of daughter, Henny, deceased,
money. Daughters Betsy and Mary, money arising from sale of
Negro Phebe. Son Joseph, same as Betsy and Mary. Executors:
Gabriel WAGGONER (friend) and Samuel WAGGONER (son). Witnesses: Tarrance BURNS, Thomas HAM, Jurat and Samuel HAM, Jurat.
Signed: William WAGGONER.

Page 47. 10 September 1803. Will of Henry PETREE. June
          Term 1804. Wife Margaretha, estate during her
widowhood. 8 Children: John, Catherine, Soloman, Henry,
Mary Barbara, Ann Margareth, Elizabeth, and Ann Eva, all to
share equally. Executors: Wife Margaretha, Friend John
ZIMMERMAN, and Peter FOIZER. Witnesses: John RIGHTS, Senr.
and John RIGHTS, Jurn., Jurat. Signed: Henry PETREE.

Page 48. 27 January 1803. Will of Matthew HILL, Senr.

31

June Term 1804. Wife Lucy, ½ of my stock, etc.
Son Matthew, ½ my stock, etc. at decease of wife. Grandson
John HILL. Son Samuel HILL. Other children not named.
No Executors. Witnesses: Joseph CLOUD, Jurat and James
BOHANNON. Signed: Matthew (X) HILL.

Page 49. 29 April 1804. Nuncupative Will of William
        HAWKINS. June Term 1804. In presence of Hugh
MARTIN and wife, Elizabeth MARTIN. Wife Nancy, what little
property I have and take care of children until they come
of age. Children: Benjamin, Nelly, Betsy, William, Lazarus,
James, Gail and Nancy. Executor: Wife Nancy HAWKINS.
Sworn before James MARTIN 11 May 1804.

Page 50. 24 August 1803. Will of William RUTLEDGE. June
        Term 1804. Wife Matilda, all estate her natural
life. Eldest son Johnson, slaves, Frank, Hannah and young
Roger. Son William, 8 shillings. Son Peter, Negro Lewis.
The heirs of my son, Benjamin, Negro Charles. Son Benjamin,
8 shillings. Daughter Sarah, 20 pounds to be paid by sons
Benj. and Elijah. Son Elijah, 5 slaves Sam, Holly, Anthony,
Hannah and Ben; also my lands and everything belonging to
Plantation whereon I now live. Executor: Son Elijah
RUTLEDGE. Witnesses: Alexander MOORE, Jurat, William
MERRETT, Jurat, and William MOORE. Signed: William (X)
RUTLEDGE.

Page 51. 16 September 1800. Will of Daniel STOCKTON. June
        Term 1804. Wife Mary, 1/3 of estate. Eldest son
Joseph, money. Second son Clayton, money. Third son John,
money. Youngest son Doughty, 100 acres South end my
Dwelling Plantation. Three daughters, Mary LUNDY, Content
WORTMAN and Elizabeth LUNDY. Granddaughter Mary LUNDY.
Executors: Wife Mary and Joseph MENDENHALL. Signed: Daniel
STOCKTON. . . .Not witnessed, but proven by oaths of Archi-
bald CAMPBELL, Henry B. DOBSON and Moses PAYDON who believes
handwriting is that of Daniel STOCKTON.

Page 52. 13 April 1804. Will of Joseph MILLER. June Term
        1804. Wife Anna Katherine. Eldest son Jacob,
money. Son Joseph, land adjoining Benj. Kelly DALTON. Son
George, land adjoining John MILLER, CROOK and Jacob MILLER.
Son Frederick, land between Joseph and George. Daughter
Elizabeth, money. Executors: Sons, Jacob and Joseph.
Witnesses: Jacob MILLER, Jurat, Geo. SHAMEL, and Phillip
MILLER. Signed: Jacob MILLER.

Page 54. 18 September 1803. Will of Jacob PETREE, Farmer.
        September Term 1804. Two sons, Henry and Jacob,
my Plantation both sides Neatman Creek. Balance of estate
to be divided as follows: Daughter Eva Barbara (married to
Adam WOOLF, Esq.). Children: John Henry, Jacob, Adam, John,
Mary Catharina, Mary Dorothy, Elizabeth, Margaratha and
Johanna. Two of my sons, Adam and John are already dead,
their share to be divided among their children: Adams
Children: Sarah, Barbara, Elizabeth, Mary Catherine and
Francis. John's Children: Susanna, Jacob, William, Mary,
John, Henry, and George. Executors: John GRAUS and Sons,

Henry and Jacob PETRI. Witnesses: John RIGHTS, John (X) BECKER, and Johnson (X) RUTLEDGE, Jurat. Signed: Jacob PETRY.

Page 55. 25 October 1800. Will of Richard BEASLEY, Planter. September Term 1804. Wife Martha, Estate during lifetime. Son Jeremiah, Home Plantation to share with his mother. Children: William, Peggy COOPER, Benjamin, Robert, Richard, Molly FAYLOR (or TAYLOR), Patty HARRISON, James, Sally NUNN, Thomas, Sukea COOMER, 5 shillings each. Executors: Friends and neighbors, namely, James COOK and Tyro RIDDLE. Witnesses: Isaac PENNINGTON, Joseph PENNINGTON, Jurat and Caleb SUMNER. Signed: Richard (X) BEASLEY.

Page 56. 26 June 1804. Will of Anthony BITTING. September Term 1804. Daughter Mary, Negro woman, Ann and child, Permelia and 1/3 lott on Main Street in Germanton. Daughter Elizabeth, Negro Leddy and Jane and 1/3 of above property. Daughter Martha and son-in-law, Joshua BANNER, Negro Sterling, ½ value of Negro Florah, and 1/3 above property in Germanton. Son John, Negro Auston, 2 lotts in Germanton including Mansion house I formerly lived in. Youngest son Anthony, 198 acres including my Mansion House I now live in by deed of Gift 25th instant when he arrives of lawful age. Son Lewis and grandson Joseph BITTING, son of Joseph BITTING, deceased, they have received their share and I will that they receive no more. Executors: Joseph BANNER, Senr., Joshua BANNER (son-in-law), and Mary and Elizabeth BITTING (daughters). Witnesses: Charles BANNER, Jurat, Casper STOLTZ, Jurat and Adam GEIGER. Signed: Anthony BITTING.

Page 58. 27 August 1804. Will of William BEASLEY. December Term 1804. His wife should keep children together and raise them (no names). Witnesses: Tyre RIDDLE and William (X) BURRIS. Signed: William (X) BEASLEY.

Page 58. No date. Nuncupative Will of Reuben DODSON, deceased, the 10th instant, declared in presence of Obey DODSON and Mrs. Ann VAUGHN on his death bed. Wife, Agnus DODSON, to have home plantation, etc. To Obey DODSON, Plantation where he now lives. Other estate to be equally divided among his children not named. Proved December Term 1804 by oath of Obey DODSON, Jurat and Ann VAUGHN, Jurat, before James MARTIN, J.P.

Page 59. 26 August 1804. Will of Hastin FLYNT. December Term 1804. Wife Mary, estate "for raising these children", not named. Executors: Mary FLYNT, David FLYNT, and Martha FLINT. Witnesses: Richard FLYNT, Tarrance BURNS, and Henry SAMUEL, Jurat. Signed: Haston FLYNT.

Page 60. 23 January 1805. Will of Samuel WAGGONER. March Term 1805. Wife Mary, all estate and all property that will fall to us from Mr. Adam TATE, deceased. Grandson Lewis WAGGONER, 50 acres Southeast fork of Oldfield Creek. Sons, William, Joseph, Gabriel, Thomas, 5 shillings each. Daughters: Elizabeth, Susanna, Mary, Sarah and Ann, 5 shill-

ings each. Executors: Peter HAIRSTON and Wife Mary.
Witnesses: Charles PERKINS, Jurat, Bethenia (X) PERKINS,
Jurat, and Thomas (X) MARSHALL, Jurat. Signed: Samuel
WAGGONER.

Page 61. 2 June 1803. Will of Henry DAVIS. March Term
         1805. Wife Ruth, all estate including 50 acres
whereon I now live bought of Wm. Fredr. MARSHALL. Daughter
Mary (Wife of Jacob HARRY). Son Jesse, 200 acres bought of
Wm. Fredr. MARSHALL and Surveyors instruments. Son James,
where he now dwells, 230 acres bought of John HINE. Granddaughter, Sarah BOLING, 150 acres in Rowan County at Peter
BOTENGHAMMERS corner in Stokes County line and Fredric
MILLERS corner. Daughter Ruth (wife of Eleazer SMITH), 150
acres conveyed to John RIGG in MOTSINGERS line. Granddaughter Sarah BOTINGHAMER to have equal share with my own children. Executors: Sons, James and Jesse DAVIS. Witnesses:
John WYRUK (?) and Marget WYRUK (?). Signed: Henry DAVIS.

Page 62. 18 October 1803. Will of Jonathan VARNUM (VERNON).
          June Term 1805. Wife Rebecker, money John TERRY
owes me. Daughter Hanner TAYLOR, $1.00 as she was portioned
off at marriage. Son Ebenezer, land in Virginia he lives on.
Son Jonathan, $1.00. Daughter Irene CHILDERS, $1.00. Daughter Racher (Rachel) WARD, $1.00. Executor: Russel VAUTER
(VAWTER). Witnesses: John VAUTER, Jurat, John WRIGHT, and
John TERRY. Signed: Jonathan VERNON.

Page 63. 2 February 1805. Will of Thomas HUNTER, Planter.
          September Term 1805. Wife Elizabeth, home Planta-
tion during widowhood. Eldest son John, young bay mare.
Sons: John, Thomas, Solomon and William, 200 acres to be
divided when William becomes 21 years of age. Daughters
Rachel and Molly. Executor: Wife Elizabeth and Brother
David HUNTER. Witnesses: Michael SPOONHOUR and William
HUNTER. Signed: Thomas HUNTER.

Page 64. 1 December 1805. Will of John NUNNS. March Term
          1806. Wife Mary, all property and increase She
brought here, use of Negro Adam. To Henry FLOYD, land South
big Dan River; Negro girl Nance. To James NUNNS, land fork
Dan River. Son Thomas NUNNS, balance of land; Negroes Ben,
Geo., and Janny. Executors: Brother Wm. NUNNS and James S.
GAINES. Witnesses: Wm. WHITE and Caleb FLOYDE, Jurat.
Signed: John NUNNS.

Page 65. 29 November 1805. Will of James Dudley ROBERTS.
          March Term 1806. Wife Polly, plantation I now
live on. Son Alfred when he comes of age. Daughter Sabory.
Mentions "my two children". Executors: Wife Polly and
Brother, Naaman ROBERTS. Witnesses: John C. COX and Naaman
ROBERTS, Jurat. Signed: James ROBERTS.

Page 66. 9 January 1804. Will of Jacob HAUSER. March Term
          1806. Wife Lenora, home Plantation; Negroes Gill
and Charity; to raise my children. Children: Jacob, Hanah,
David, Adam, William, Christian, John, Joseph and children
of Catherine by Jacob SHOAR (SHORE). Daughter Hanah to have

equivilant I've given daughters, Catherine and Magdalena.
Executors: Wife Lenora and Sons, Jacob and Adam. Witnesses:
Bryson BLACKBURN and John CHITTY, Jurat. Signed: Jacob
HAUSER.

Page 67. 6 February 1806. Will of Peter FOLS (FOLZ). June
          Term 1806. Son Peter, money. Children: Andrew,
Jacob, John, Frederick, Henry, Elizabeth, Eva, and the 5
children of my daughter, Rosina, deceased, equal share of
money arising from sale of my house in Salisbury Town in
Rowan County. To Elizabeth and Mary ROTHROCK, daughters of
Valentine ROTHROCK, household furniture. Executor: Henry
RIPPLE. Witnesses: Jacob (X) SHOTT, Jurat, Henry RIPPLE,
and Jacob ROTHROCK. Signed: Peter FOLS (FOLZ).

Page 68. 24 February 1806. Will of Jack FORGUSON. June
          Term 1806. My estate to Robert MARTIN for use of
my wife, Annaky and my children who are slaves belonging to
Abraham MARTIN, Senr. Executor: Robert MARTIN. Witnesses:
Robert SIMMS, Jurat, A. MARTIN, and William MARTIN. Signed:
Jack (X) FORGUSON.

Page 69. 21 March 1806. Will of John HINE. June Term 1806.
          Wife Juliana Catharine, property during widowhood,
at her decease to be divided among my nine children: John,
Mary, Catharina, Phillip, Christina, Juliana, Henry, Peter,
Susannah. Daughter Elizabeth, to have only $1.00, but her
son, John to have a half share. Executors: Fredric BECKER
and wife Juliana Catherine. Witnesses: John RIGHTS and
Henry SHOUSE, Jurat. Signed: John HINE.

Page 70. 22 October 1802. Will of James MATTHEWS. June
          Term 1806. Son Tandy, Home tract Townfork 248
acres; also 600 acres bought of Chas. BEASLEY adjoining
above; also 100 acres Blues Creek (late property of John
THOMPSON); also 900+ acres in hands of John GRIFFITH in
Virginia; also Negro Dicy and his wife Anaky, Stephen 4 years
old and man Frank. . . .To Joseph HOLLENSWORTH in trust for
his Son, James, 600 acres bought of Charles BEAZLEY including
Mansion House "Stone Chimneys"; also Negro Silla. . . .To
Tandy HOLLINSWORTH (infant son of Mary and Joseph), Negro
Rachel. . . .To Mary HOLLINSWORTH, Negro Rachel's increase.
To son Tandy, 900 acres known as The Walnut Cove in lower
Powells Valley in trust for Betsey's children. . . .To
Joseph HOLLINSWORTH, 600 acres, balance of tract bought of
James BEASLEY and Negroes Doll and Jenny (in trust for my
Son William's children). . . .To son Tandy, 200 acres Panther
Crook (in trust for James MATTHEWS, son of my son John and
his wife Polly MARTIN) and 230 acres in Amherst County,
Virginia on Pee Vine in trust for Nancy MATTHEWS, daughter
of my son John and his wife Polly MARTIN. . . .Son John, 500
acres Waters of little Yadkin. . . .To Obediah BRANNUM, 235½
acres known as Blackburns. . . .To Irvin BRANNUM, 300 acres
late property of James COFFEY, also to Obediah and Irvin,
Negro girl Courtney now in possession of Lurance BRANNUM.
To James MATTHEWS, son of Tandy, Negro Stephen. . . .To
Tandy JAMES, son of my daughter Betsy JAMES, Negro Adam.
To James HOLLINSWORTH, son of Mary and Joseph, 136 acres

ajoining tract bought of Zigler. . . .To John MATTHEWS, son
of James, 150 acres Peters Creek, late John FIELDS land,
also 75 acres, late HUMPHREYS land. Residue of my Estate to
be divided between Tandy MATTHEWS, Betsy JAMES and John
MATTHEWS. Executors: Son Tandy MATTHEWS and Joseph HOLLINS-
WORTH. Witnesses: Andrew ROBINSON, Jurat and Lurance (X)
BRANHAM. Signed: James MATTHEWS.

Page 71. 26 October 1806. Nuncupative Will of George
        BIBIGHOUSE (BIBIGHAUS). December Term 1806. On
his death bed said, "I have no children; everything belongs
to my wife." Not named. Signed: John RIGHTS, Senr.

Page 72. 30 September 1806. Will of Henry SHOUSE. Decem-
        ber Term 1806. "I am going on a journey to the
Western Country and not knowing if I will see home again do
make my last Will and Testament." Wife, Elizabeth, my estate
during her life and at her decease to be equally divided
among my children (not named). Executors: Elizabeth SHOUSE
and Brother-in-law John NULL. Witnesses: John BUTNER, Jurat
and Harmon BUTNER, Jurat. Signed: Henry SHOUSE.

Page 72. 2 October 1805. Will of Samuel DALTON. March
        Term 1807. Revoking all Wills made by me as con-
cerning one mare and two colts which I now bequeath to
daughter, Littusue MOORE as the above property was disposed
of in my former will in manner contrary to my wish and
desire. Witnesses: Wm. CAMPBELL and John STONE, Jurat.
Signed: Samuel (X) DALTON.

Page 73. 15 December 1801. Will of George HOFFMAN. March
        Term 1807. Wife not named, house and land I now
tend her lifetime. Three sons, Lewis, George and Henry, land
we live on. Two daughters, Caty and Barbara, household
furniture, etc. Executors: Geo. HAUSER and Jacob LASH.
Witnesses: Joseph HAUSER, Jurat and Fredr. HAUSER. Signed:
George HOFFMAN.

Page 73. 10 December 1806. Will of George DEATHERAGE.
        March Term 1807. Wife Milly, to live on land
whereon I now dwell until youngest son (not named) comes of
age. Children: Nancy wife of Wm. EDGMON; Bird; Abner; Ann,
wife of George CLOUD; Polly; Ursley, wife of Ashley JOHNSON;
John; Phillip; James; William; Coleman; George and Achkillas,
to have in proportion to what have already had. Negro girl,
Edy to remain in possession of wife til youngest son reaches
age 14. Executor: George CLOUD. Witnesses: Joseph CLOUD,
William (X) LANKFORD, Jurat, Phillip (X) DEATHERAGE, and
James LYON, Junr. Signed: George DEATHERAGE.

Page 74. 1 April 1806. Will of John MICKEY. March Term
        1807. All estate sold and divided into three
parts; two parts to my three children: son John Lewis and
Daughters Mary Elizabeth and Beningna. Wife Juliana and her
two children, John and Salomon and one not yet born, one-
third. Executors: Son John Lewis MICKEY and Christian LASH.
Witnesses: Peter PFAFF, Jurat and Joseph HOLDER, Jurat.
Signed: John MICKEY.

Page 75.   Nuncupative Will of Tristram BARNARD, Cooper.
        June Term 1807. Wife Lavinia, linen made since we
were married. Proved by oath of Seth COFFIN and Latham
FOLGER.

Page 75.   10 March 1807. Will of Robert Sharp HAMILTON.
        June Term 1807. Wife Polly, Negroes Abraham, Jude,
Isaac, Ester, Wm., boy Abraham, Hannah, Peter, also 200 acres
laid off of my 1,000 acres on Elk River in Tennessee. Two
sons, John and Hance, above property when they come of age
and 800 acres on Elk River in Tennessee; also 150 acres
Rocky Branch in Guilford County; also 100 acres Snow Creek
in Stokes County. Executors: My uncle, General John HAMIL-
TON, Andrew ROBINSON, and wife Polly HAMILTON. Witnesses:
A(ndrew) ROBINSON, Jurat, Wm. COTRILL, Jurat and Cornelius
COOK, Jurat. Signed: R.S. HAMILTON.

Page 76.   19 December 1806. Will of John HIRT, Senr. June
        Term 1807. Wife Catherine, Estate her natural
life. Granddaughter Polly HIRT, 10 pounds. Daughter-in-
law Polly HIRT, 10 shillings. Mentions "his children before
they come of lawful age". Executors: Wife Catherine, John
HIRT, Junr. and Peter BINKLEY (unless my son Abraham HIRT
moves back here; then he take the place of Peter BINKLEY).
Witnesses: John H. PRYOR, Henry HOLLOMON, and Jacob (X)
BLACK, Jurat. Signed: John HIRT.

Page 77.   26 August 1806. Will of Jacob ROTHROCK. June
        Term 1807. To be buried in burying ground at
Friedburg. My brothers and brother-in-law to have my clothing one month after my decease. Wife Elizabeth, Negro Mark
until he reaches age 12, then to be hired out for benefit of
my unborn child, also furniture she had from her parents.
Mentions father, mother, brothers and sisters (not named).
Executor: Christian HANES. Witnesses: Frederick ROTHROCK
and John ROTHROCK, Jurat. Signed: Jacob ROTHROCK.

Page 78.   6 April 1807. Will of Mathew NIDING (NADING).
        June Term 1807. Wife Eva Catharina. Six children:
George, John, Simone, Christian, Martin, and Joseph.
Executors: Wife Eva Catharina, Son George and John FOLZ.
Witnesses: Gottlieb SHOBER and Christopher REICH. Signed:
Matthew NIDING (NADING).

Page 79.   5 September 1807. Will of Sarah DAVIS. September
        Term 1807. Daughter Sally DAVIS, Negro Winny to
be valued by Jeremiah GIBSON and Jesse BRIGGS. Sally to pay
rest of my lawful heirs (not named). Son John, Negro Will.
Executors: Sons, Joseph and John. Witnesses: Jesse BRIGGS,
Jurat and Charity BRIGGS. Signed: Sarah (X) DAVIS.

Page 80.   20 April 1807. Will of Fredric HAUSER. September
        Term 1807. Wife Elizabeth, my estate and any
estate coming to me from my Father's estate. Executors:
Wife Elizabeth and Friend John Henry HAUSER. Witness:
Jacob CONROD. Signed: Fredric HAUSER.

Page 80.   1 July 1807. Will of Jacob WOHLFAHRT (WELFARE).

September Term 1807. Mentions wife and children, but not by name. Executors: Samuel STOTTS (STOTZ) and Conrod KREUSER. Witnesses: Samuel KRAMSCH and Wm. Barton PEDDYCOART. Signed: Jacob WOHLFAHRT (WELFARE).

Page 81.   25 April 1807.   Will of John COOK.   September
           Term 1807.   My Sister Mary.   My brother William.
My niece Dicy COOK.   My cousin Betsy BOLES (formerly COOK).
Executors: Caleb SUMNER and Jacob CARSON. Witnesses: John
FARGUSON, Jurat and Johanna FARGUSON, Jurat. Signed: John
COOK.

Page 82.   12 November 1802.   Will of John DAVIS.   September
           Term 1807.   Wife Margery, to raising and schooling
of children and as each comes of age except: Sons, John and
William, land called White's Place, 120 acres when they come
of age.   Executors: William DAVIS and Wife Margery DAVIS.
Witnesses: James DAVIS and John (X) DUNLAP. Signed: John
DAVIS.

Page 82.   3 May 1807.   Will of Elizabeth BROWN.   September
           Term 1807.   My estate resides in Bohemia Manor,
Maryland.   I am daughter of Michael NEEDE who died in same
place.   My brothers and sisters: Joseph (eldest), Mary,
Daniel, Catherine, John, Susanna, Nancy, Sarah, and myself
(Elizabeth) and Jacob NEIDE.   After my father died, my mother
married Jacob OZIER who at his decease bequeathed her con-
siderable estate which she willed to my sisters, Nancy,
Catherine and myself, but I never went to claim my estate.
I married in Bohemia Manor, Cecil County, Maryland, Benjamin
ELSBERRY, son of Fredrick ELSBERRY and after Benj. decease,
I married Christian BROWN and came to North Carolina.   Four
years ago Christian BROWN deserted me for another woman,
leaving me in forlorn state.   My sister Nancy's son, Jacob
MILLER, has allowed me to live with him, therefore I leave
him my estate in Maryland.   Executor: Jacob MILLER.   Wit-
nesses: Archibald CAMPBELL, Jurat and Samuel PHILLIPS,
Jurat.   Signed: Elizabeth (X) BROWN.

Page 84.   14 October 1807.   Will of Thomas GRUBBS.   December
           Term 1807.   Wife Patsy, all my property for my
small children.   Executors: Wife Patsy and Isaac DALTON.
Witnesses: Benj. BRIGGS, Micajah ALLEN, and Martin (X)
MARSHALL (from Albermarle County, Virginia).   Signed: Thomas
(X) GRUBBS.

Page 84.   24 November 1801.   Will of David STEWART (STUART).
           December Term 1807.   To Jamiah HARRISON, Hezekiah
RANKIN, Lydia POTTER and Abigal CURD, 20 shillings each.
Five sons: John, David, Reubin, Samuel and Thomas, all my
estate; also Negroes Murrah, Nan, Ned, Simon, Bob and
Lannaretter.   Wife Abigail STEWART, to be maintained.
Executors: John and Reubin STEWART.   Witnesses: Thompson
GLENN, Frederick MILLER, and Henry HOLDER, Jurat.   Signed:
David (X) STEWART.

Page 85.   8 October 1807.   Will of William Barton PODDYCOART,
           deceased, Planter.   December Term 1807.   Children:

38

Greenberry, Thomas, Horatio, Sarah and Lucy. Daughters
Milea and Elizabeth who formerly received Negroes, etc.
Executors: Brother John PEDDYCOART and son Greenberry.
Witnesses: Samuel KRAMSCH, Jurat and John (X) PADGET, Senr.
Signed: Wm. Barton PEDDYCOART.

Page 86. 2 December 1802. Will of Jacob KAPP. December
          Term 1807. Wife Louisa, house clock, furniture.
Five children: Frederick, Ann Mary, Henry, Jacob and Louisa.
Executors: Gottlieb SHOBER and Gottlieb FOCKEL. Guardian
of children during their minority: Abraham STEINER. Wit-
nesses: Henry STOR (STOEHR) and Henry BUTTNER, Jurat.
Signed: Jacob KAPP.

Page 87. 21 November 1807. Will of Peter LUDWICK (LUDWIG).
          December Term 1807. Wife Margret, everything
except land. Four Sons: Jacob, ¼ of my 400 acres adjoining
Michel FULP, John HESTER, and Henry B. DOBSON; William, ¼
of my 400 acres adjoining Reuben LONG and William WALKER;
Peter, ¼ of my 400 acres adjoining SANDERS on West; and John
¼ of my 400 acres adjoining Mickel FULP on north. Executors:
Michael FULP and Henry B. DOBSON. Witnesses: Henry DOBSON,
Jurat and Michal (X) FULP, Jurat. Signed: Peter LUDWICK.

Page 88. 7 July 1807. Will of Mary HESTER. March Term 1808.
          To my trusty and faithful son-in-law, Lowel FRAZER,
who has maintained me for 20 years without compensation, all
of my estate and appoint him my Executor. Witnesses: Charles
BARHAM and John FRAZER. Signed: Mary HESTER.

Page 89. 16 December 1807. Will of Martin EBERT. March
          Term 1808. Wife Hannah, remain on Plantation
where I live during widowhood with son, John and daughter
Elizabeth. Son Martin, pay debt I owe Cornilus SNIDER'S
Estate, also to have land he lives on. Son John, pay residue
of my debts, also have plantation I now live on. Three
daughters, Christina, Elizabeth, and Maria, 30 acres adjoining Peter FOLZ. Executors: Wife Hannah and Henry RIPPLE.
Witnesses: Charles CHITTY and John ZIMMERMAN, ("one other
whose name is written in Dutch"). Signed: Martin EBERT.

Page 89. 9 January 1808. Will of William MARTIN, Senr.
          March Term 1808. Wife Rachel, 207 acres where I
now live; also Negroes Will, Patt, Zelpha, Lucy, and little
Patt; also household furniture. Daughter Nancy FULKISON,
Negroes Phebe and Hannah. Daughter Sarah HUGHES, Negroes
Edy and Phillis. Daughter Susanna Childres MARTIN, Negroes
Dolpha and her 4 children, Charlotte, John, Jerry and Mary.
Daughter Jincy CLARK, Negroes Judity, Mary and Begger.
Daughter Polly MOORE, Negroes Milly and her 2 children,
Charles and little Will. Son William, Negroes Lewis and
Patt, daughter of old Patt; also 200 acres adjoining where
I live, bought of John MEREDITH. Son Samuel, 207 acres
where I now live after death of his mother; also Negroes
Nathan and Isaac. Executors: William MARTIN and Samuel
MARTIN and William MOORE. Witnesses: Peter SCALES, Jurat,
Richard MILLS, Jurat and Joseph SCALES, Jurat. Signed: Wm.
MARTIN, Senr.

Page 91.   14 November 1807.   Will of John ZIMMERMAN.   March Term 1808.   My body to be buried in Friedburg buring ground.   Wife Rosina, 310 acres where I now live; 118 acre plantation Reedy Creek, Rowan County; all other estate her widowhood; also Negro woman Jude.   Three sons, John, Christian and Phillip, equal share of my property after decease of wife.   Four daughters Elizabeth, Sarah, Catharina and Rosina, same as above.   Mentions when younger children become of age.   Executors: Henry SHORE, Christian HEANS (HANES), and wife Rosina.   Witnesses: John HEONA (HANES) and ("one other wrote in Dutch").   Signed: John (X) ZIMMERMAN.

Page 93.   29 April 1808.   Will of Thomas NEAL.   June Term 1808.   Wife Mary, "by her industry and good conduct hath greatly assisted me in raising one family", all my estate to be hers.   Mentions all my children, but does not name them.   Executor: Wife Mary NEAL.   Witnesses: James MARTIN and Nancy (X) CRAWLEY.   Signed: Thomas NEAL.

Page 93.   24 April 1807.   Will of Robert JOHNSON, Planter. June Term 1808.   Wife Cecila, her choice of household articles, that part of land and house I reserved for myself.   Sons, Elisha, Thomas, Archelaus, Anderson, Ashley, William, and Elijah, my dwelling house and land known to be mine.   Daughters Martha MORDYKE and Judith BROOKS.   Executors: Anderson and Wm. JOHNSON.   Witnesses: John PITTS, Samuel PITTS, and Isaac PITTS, Jurat.   Signed: Robert (X) JOHNSON.

Page 94.   26 March 1808.   Will of Thomas RAPER.   June Term 1808.   Wife Patty, land on which I live for lifetime.   Daughters Elizabeth, Wife of Peter FULP and Patty, wife of Edward COOLEY, above land at decease of wife.   To Jane FOUNTAIN, wife of Stephen FOUNTAIN, household furniture. To Hannah and Stephen HAM, daughter and son of Mordicai and Rebecka HAM, $15.00 each when they come of age.   Executors: Peter FULP and Edward COOLEY.   Witnesses: James FOUNTAIN and Stephen FOUNTAIN, Jurat.   Signed: Thomas (X) RAPER.

Page 95.   1 January 1807.   Will of James BOHANNAN.   June Term 1808.   Wife Frances, estate during natural life.   Children mentioned, but not named.   Grandson James MATTHEWS, 5 pounds.   Executors: Wife Frances BOHANNAN and son James BOHANNAN.   Witnesses: Joseph CLOUD, Jurat, David MOORE, and Wm. DURHAM.   Signed: James BOHANNAN.

Page 96.   3 June 1808.   Will of John BANKS.   September Term 1808.   Wife Agga, estate.   Children mentioned, but not named.   Executors: Wife Agga BANKS and Ferdinand BOSTICK. Witnesses: Adensten PRUIT, Francis (X) STEEL, and Samuel (X) BANKS, Jurat.   Signed: John (X) BANKS.

Page 96.   19 June 1808.   Will of Phillip LAGENAUER. September Term 1808.   His land and property and money arising be divided between Wife Mary and unborn child. Executors: Jacob LAGENAUER, Senr. and John CLAUS.   Witnesses: Charles F. BAGGE, George LAGENAUOR, Jurat and a signature in German.   Signed: Phillip (X) LAGENAUER.

Page 97.   28 March 1807.   Will of Thomas EAST, Senr.
            September Term 1808.   Children of my daughter
Caty BROWN, at her decease, Negroes, girl Patt, boy Jim
(son of Jim and Sal).   Children of my daughter Elizabeth at
her decease, Negroes Nancy and Sally (daughters of old Jim
and Sal).   Children of my daughter Nancy at her decease,
Negroes Jim and Sal and their daughters Rebecca and Jude.
Son Thomas EAST, Junr., Negroes Hannah, Enoch, also my blacksmith tools and 400 acres land where I now live.   Two grandsons, Jesse BROWN and Thomas East BROWN, 200 acres Hollow
road adjoining above tract, Abel EDWARDS corner, near meeting
house spring, Samuel NEELEY, Senrs. corner.   To my old Negro
woman Fanny, to have her house and lott and all her posses-
sions.   To my three daughters mentioned above, my Stocks of
every kind.   Grandson Thomas EDWARDS, son of Abel EDWARDS.
Executors: Son Thomas EAST and Henry Spain HOWARD (SPAIN-
HOUR?).   Witnesses: Jeremiah KING, John STONE, and Henry
(X) JURAT.   Signed: Thomas EAST, Senr. . . . .September
Term 1808 proved in open court before Jury empanniled and
sworn on a Caviat against same.   Jury ordered Will to be
recorded.

Page 99.   11 October 1808.   Will of Christoph BUTNER (BUTT-
            NER).   December Term 1808.   Wife Elizabeth, personal
estate and 1/3 of Home Plantation.   Son Thomas, two shares
of my estate.   Daughters Catharine, Sarah, Alyte (?), Mary,
Magdalena, and Ann Elizabeth, one share each.   Negro Shepherd,
to be sold in case he doesn't behave himself.   If my Mother
needs assistance in her old age, my Estate to bear equal
with my brothers in her maintenance.   Executors: My brother
John BUTNER and Wife Elizabeth.   Witnesses: David (X) ANDORS
and Bartholemus WILLIAMS.   Signed: Christoph BUTNER.

Page 99.   24 August 1808.   Will of Richard WOOLFOLK.   Decem-
            ber Term 1808.   Wife Heneretor, land and Planta-
tion whereon I now live, also Negroes Arthur, Peter, Judy,
Jamimma, Lucy, and Carter.   Daughters Polly Virginia WOOLFOLK,
Sally Dalton WOOLFECK, and Elizabeth Biggers WOOLFOLK.   Sons
Lewel WOOLFOLK and Richard Thomas WOOLFOLK.   Mentions
children coming of lawful age and being educated.   Executors:
Wife Henereter and Brison BLACKBURN.   Witnesses: John Henry
PRYER, Henry HOLDER, Jurat (written in German), and Elias
(X) HOPKINS.   Signed: Richard WOOLFOLK.

Page 101.   20 November 1806.   Will of Gabriel JONES.   Decem-
            ber Term 1808.   Wife Isabella, my still "until
she marrys another man", then Still into hands of Guardian
of my Son, William till he comes of age.   Son William, 2/3
of Plantation I live on at decease of wife.   Daughter Sarah,
100 acres deeded me by Executors of John DOLLIN, deceased.
Daughter Isabella, 100 acres adjoining above deeded me by
Hartwell BARHAM.   Daughter Martha, $100.00 when she reaches
18.   Executors: My brother Benjamin JONES and Neighbor Henry
Baker DOBSON.   Witnesses: Archibald CAMPBELL, James LOVE,
Michael (X) FAIR, and William DOBSON.   Signed: Gabriel (X)
JONES.

Page 102.   21 March 1807.   Will of Elijah ROARK.   December

Term 1808. Son Timothy ROARK, 10 shillings.
Daughter Sarah LINVILL, 10 shillings. Son John ROARK, 10
shillings. Wife Judith ROARK, balance of my estate until
my youngest child comes of age; then divided between her and
my other six children: Polly, Nancy, Elijah, Rebeckah,
William and Delilah. What I have given my children Timothy,
John, and Sarah LINVILL when they went from me, I wish them
to keep and enjoy. Executors: Wife Judith ROARK and
Timothy ROARK, Senr. Witnesses: John MARTIN, Bruce (X)
LINVILL, Henry LINVILL, Jurat and Sarah (X) CARR. Signed:
Elijah ROARK.

Page 103. 23 April 1809. Will of John PATERSON. June Term
1809. Wife Hannah, to raise my children (not
named). Executors: Wife Hannah and My father, Simmons
PATERSON. Witnesses: John HULL, Jurat and John REDDICK.
Signed: John PATERSON.

Page 103. 17 August 1809. Will of John PURYEAR. September
Term 1809. Son Richard Clausel PURYEAR, all my
part of estate my Grandfather, John PURYEAR, now in possession of my grandmother, Martha PURYEAR; all my part of estate
of my Father, late John PURYEAR; also the portion of the
estate of my wife's father, late Calusel CLAUSEL, now in
hands of Susanna CLAUSEL, which falls to my wife at decease
of Susanna; also my land in town of Vienna, Stokes County;
and land adjoining said land purchased from Naaman ROBERTS
(now of Kentucky) to be sold to pay debts. Wife, Sally S.
PURYEAR, residue of estate. Executors: George HAUSER, Esq.
of Bethania, Wife Sally, and Brother-in-law, Alexander
CLAUSEL, Mecklenburg County, Virginia. Witnesses: John
DAUB, Jr., Reubin (X) STEWART, and Zebdee BILLITER. Signed:
John PURYEAR.

Page 105. 20 September 1809. Will of Joseph PATTISON.
December Term 1809. Son John, 250 acres lower
end tract where I now live adjoining Sam'l PITTS. Son
Joseph, remainder between what I've given John and what he
bought from his brother, Jordin. Daughter Elizabeth, furniture and privilege of the Shed Room at East end of my house
as long as "she remains in an un-married state." My children Simmons, Jordan, Joseph, John, Jemima, Sarah, Anna, and
Elizabeth, residue of my estate. To Jenny BEASON'S children
Joseph, William, Elizabeth, June, Jemima and Sarah, to have
1/9th part of estate. Executors: Son Simmons PATTISON and
Benjamin BENSON. Witnesses: John PITTS, Jurat, John BROOKS,
and William PATTISON. Signed: Joseph PATTISON (PATTERSON).

Page 105. 23 February 1800. Will of Stephen FOUNTAIN.
March Term 1810. Eldest daughter Martha FOUNTAIN,
furniture, cow, etc. Youngest daughter Sally FOUNTAIN,
furniture, cow, etc. Wife Jane, land whereon I now live her
lifetime. To Stephen FOUNTAIN, son of James FOUNTAIN, above
land at decease of wife. To Fountain MARSHALL, son of
Richard MARSHALL. Four children, Martha FOUNTAIN, Polly
MARSHALL, James FOUNTAIN, and Sally FOUNTAIN, residue of
estate equally divided along with wife. Executors: Joseph
WAGGONER and James FOUNTAIN. Witnesses: James FOUNTAIN and

Joseph WAGGONER. Signed: Stephen FOUNTAIN.

Page 106. 21 December 1809. Will of Richard COX. March
           Term 1810. Wife Jane, tract of land and planta-
tion I now live on; also 95 acres adjoining above; and
Negroes Seller, Lil, Aaron and Jacob. Son Joshua, Above at
death of my wife; also my Smith tools, but not remove them
off plantation; also Negro man, Bob. All other tracts of
land to be equally divided between my seven daughters: Eldest
daughter Sally, Negro Lewis; Next daughter Polly, Negro Amy;
Daughter Caty, Negro Rebecca; Daughter Agness, Negro Mimey;
Daughter Nancy, Negro Sampson; Daughter Betsy, Negro Martin;
Daughter Sinthia, Negro Jane. Son-in-law George CAMPBELL,
money in his hands. Executors: John WHITLOCK, George
CAMPBELL, and son Joshua COX. Witnesses: James COOK, Tyre
RIDDLE, and James GEORGE. Signed: Richard COX.

Page 107. 1 February 1810. Will of Wm. H. ROBERTSON.
           March Term 1810. Wife Sally, money from sale of
Bond, Gold Watch and Stud Horse for her maintenance and to
educate My little children. Children: Mildred Douglas
ROBERTSON, John Strange ROBERTSON, Lucy Fox ROBERTSON,
William James, David Wilson, Judith Turner ROBERTSON, all
children born in wedlock to Wm. H. and Sally ROBERTSON.
Also will as these children according to their names comes
of age, they receive in proportion to what Sally Redd JESSOP,
wife of Elisha JESSOP and daughter of William H. and Sally
ROBERTSON, received when she married. Executors: Wife Sally
and Abijah PENSON. Trustees: Joseph JESSOP and Drury
BRENDURANT. Witnesses: Jacob HORTON, Thomas BOND, James (X)
RITTER, Isaac (X) JOYCE and Elijah JESSOP. Signed: Wm. H.
ROBERTSON.

Page 108. 1 January 1804. Will of Joseph NELSON. June
           Term 1810. Son Elexander NELSON, deceased, 5
shillings. Children of Elexander NELSON, deceased: Joseph,
Sarah and Mary Smith NELSON, 5 shillings each. Wife Mary
NELSON. Daughter Rachel BITTING, residue my estate equally
divided among Son Isaac NELSON, those three. No Executor.
Witnesses: Seth ALDAY, Jeremiah STEGALL, and Samuel CLARK.
Signed: Joseph (X) NELSON.

Page 109. 14 April 1810. Will of Owen WILLIAMS. June Term
           1810. Wife Sarah. Daughters Margaret and
Elizabeth. My will if my daughter (not named) marry with
John ENOCK, she shall have 50 pounds. Sons, Owen and James,
10 shillings each. Son Isaac, place formerly John PIKE'S.
Son Jesse, place where I now live after decease of my wife.
Executors: Wife Sarah and Jonathan MENDINGHAMM. Witnesses:
Micajah WEESNER and Jesse WEESNER. Signed: Owen WILLIAMS.

Page 110. 17 May 1810. Will of George SPRINKLE. June Term
           1810. Wife Elizabeth, part of plantation her
lifetime. Son George, land adjoining LONGINO. Son John,
land adjoining George's. Son Peter, land adjoining John's
corner and Michael's line. Son Michael, land adjoining
Peter. Son Thomas, saddle and 50 acres my son George and I
now own. Daughter Cloe, furniture. Daughters Polly, Amy,

43

and Cloe, division money. Executors: Wife Elizabeth and Son Peter. Witnesses: John DAUB and Henry (X) WALLER. Signed: George (X) SPRINKLE.

Page 112. 3 March 1810. Will of Andrew McKILLIP. June Term 1810. Wife Elizabeth, south half of my Plantation, raising and educating children. Son John, 100 acres Mill Creek bought of Edward LAWTON adjoining Moses BARROW, John DUNN, Clayborn WATSON and McDOWELL. Sons Andrew, Archibald, land adjoining John's. Son William, 100 acres adjoining John ENDSLEY. Son Hugh, remainder of above, also 16 acres adjoining Robert DWIGGINS. Daughters Anna, Margaret, and Jane, equal share of furniture, etc. Daughters Elizabeth and Mary, equal share furniture, etc. when they become of age. My land adjoining Michael FAIRE and John QUILLEN, 150 acres, to be sold to pay legacies to my daughters. Sons Archibald and William when they arrive at 21 years. Executors: Hugh McKILLIP (son) and John ENDSLEY (neighbor). Witnesses: Archibald CAMPBELL, Jurat, John Vane, and Thomas VOSS. Signed: Andrew McKILLIP.

Page 113. 15 May 1809. Will of Charles McANNALLY. September Term 1810. My estate be equally divided among my lawful heirs, except what any of my children is owing me be deducted out of their part, including Negroes and land I have gaiv or lent them. To Richammer HORNER, 25 pounds and mother's clothes when she marries or comes of age. All that has a right to my estate is: John McANNALLY, Sarah BANNER; orphans of Jesse McANALLY, deceased, Mary LADD, Lois EVANS, Ruth BURNS and Richarmor HORNER (according to her legacy). Executors: Joseph BANNER, John EVANS, and Samuel WELSH. Witnesses: John EVANS, Charles EVANS, and Ann (X) BARRET. Signed: Charles McANNALLY.
CODICIL: Since signing within, I have paid Honor BARRETT full sufficient for her service, and $20.00 I allowed be payed her I now desire to be applied for use of little Jesse McANNALLY; also little Negro child I gave little Mary McANNALLY, I confirm to be her property. To little Molly EVINS, daughter of John EVANS, 1st Negro child born to Negro I gave little Mary McANNALLY. To Polly LADD, daughter of Molly (Mary) LADD, I confirm Negro I gave her. Also what is charged in my book against Honor BARRET is not to be charged against her. 25 February 1810. Witness: John EVANS. Signed: Charles McANNALLY.
Codicil #2. 30 June 1810. My home plantation be divided into lots 1,2, and 3 and my daughter, the Widow LADD, have middle lot with houses, etc. for service she has "done for me". Witness: George BOOTHE. Signed: Charles McANNALLY.

Page 115. 7 May 1809. Will of Phillip SHOUSE, Yeoman. December Term 1810. Children, Daniel, Frederick, Henry, John, Susanna, Catherina, and Salome, share equally in money from sale of my property. Executor: John NULL and William BECK. Witnesses: John NULL and William BECK. Signed: Phillip (X) SHOUSE.

Page 116. 7 June 1810. Will of John RIGHTS, Senr. December

Term 1810. Wife Maria Magdalina, 1/3 of estate.
Eldest son John RIGHTS, 2/6th share for service rendered
myself and family. Four children: Matthew, Joshuah, Joanna
Elizabeth and Lulanith. Eldest daughter, Joanna Elizabeth
RIGHTS, $12.00 above her share, it being her legacy from her
Uncle Adam KOFFLER, deceased. Son Joshuah, hath carried on
my Hatter's Shop, whether he continues at my decease is left
to my Executors, in conjunction with Elders of Salem Congre-
gation. Executors: Son Matthew RIGHTS and Friend, Fredrick
C. MEINUNG. Witnesses: John Christian BLUM and Jacob BONN.
Signed: John RIGHTS.

Page 117. 20 October 1810. Will of Hammond MORRIS, Senr.
December Term 1810. Mentions all his heirs in
an indijent circumstance and cannot afford Negro George who
bequeath to Isaac DALTON who is to pay my heirs following:
Sons William, Jesse, Travis, and Thomas, various sums.
Daughter Elizabeth, money and furniture. Sons John, Hammon,
Shadrack, and Presley, various sums and Presley all my land.
Executors: Isaac DALTON, Esq. and Isaac NELSON, Esq. Wit-
nesses: David WESTMORELAND and Harbard (X) BARHAM and Talor
(X) WESTMORELAND. Signed: Hammond MORRIS.

Page 118. 19 September 1810. Will of Robert BEAZLEY. March
Term 1811. Wife Caty, estate during widowhood.
Two eldest sons, James and Isham, "when they come of age".
Mentions "my children" but does not name them. Executors:
My brother Benjamin BEASLEY and James COOK. Witnesses:
James L. GAINS and Thomas BEAZLEY. Signed: Robert BEAZLEY.

Page 119. 12 December 1810. Will of George CRISMAN
(CRISTMANN). March Term 1811. Wife Dinah, inter-
est from Bond held of John FISLER (FISCHEL) for land said
John lives on; also Bond on Horation BONER (BOONER). Negro
girl Anne to be sold. Granddaughters Mercy and Elizabeth,
daughters of my deceased daughter, Marget, 150 acres Crooked
Run Creek. Son Charles, my books that are in Print. Grand-
son George (son of Charles), 67 acres bought of Thos. EAST.
Daughters Catharine and Elizabeth, remainder of estate.
Executors: John STORIE and John FISLER. Witnesses: Thomas
SMITH and William STONE. Signed: George CRISSMAN.

Page 120. 8 January 1811. Will of Thomas GAINES. March
Term 1811. Wife Susannah, whole of my estate.
Son Phillip, shall have no part of my estate for he has al-
ready received. Son Richard, shall have no part of my estate
for it has been a long time since I have seen him and I do
not know if he is dead or alive. Granddaughter, Louisa
GAINES (daughter of above Richard), horse, bridle and $200.
My following children: James L. GAINES, Elizabeth BOHANNON,
Wm. D. GAINES, Henry P. GAINES, Fanny CARDWELL, Susannah
SMITH, George W. GAINES and Francis T. GAINES, balance of
estate shared equally except $250 to be deducted from Eliza-
beth BOHANNON, part of bargain I gave Philimon BOHANNON in
land sold him on Reedy Creek; also $200 out of Susanna
SMITH'S part. Executors: John MARTIN and Johnson CLEMMENT.
Witnesses: James LYON, Jurat and William BOYLES. Signed:
Thomas GAINES.

Page 121. 8 April 1811. Will of Andrew FESSLER. June Term
         1811. Wife Mary, all lands I have lawful title
to on day of my death. Nine Children: Caty SHOUSE, Peter,
Tener, Henry, John, George, Susannah, Pegge and Adam.
Executors: Adam GEIGER and Samuel KENAMON. Witnesses: Adam
GEIGER, Jurat and John GEIGER. Signed: Anderw (X) FESSLER.

Page 122. 24 January 1811. Will of Stephen FRAZER. Septem-
         ber Term 1811. Wife Ann, use of estate to raise
and school my children. Children: Francis, Thomas, Jacob,
Jeremiah, William, and Elizabeth. Executors: John HESTER
and Latham FOLGER. Witness: Asa BARNARD. Signed: Stephen
FRAZER.

Page 123. 17 June 1807. Will of David LINVILL. September
         Term 1811. Wife Dorothy, 100 acres whereon we
now live, also 18 acres adjoining. Sons, David and Fowel,
above divided after death of wife. Five last born children:
Charity, Barbara, David, Fowel, and Dorothy. My son Moses,
50 acres West side Belews Creek bought of Rich. LINVILL.
My son John, 37½ acres bought of Tally WHICKER. My son
George, 5 shillings. Daughter Betty Ann WHICKER, 5 shillings,
Daughter Nancy WHICKER, 5 shillings. Remaining estate
divided between wife and ten children, mentions still and
distillery vessels. Executors: Worthy wife Dorothy and
Worthy son George. Witnesses: David LINVILLE, Jurat and
Wm. CREWS and Wm. LINVILLE. Signed: David LINVILLE.

Page 124. 30 August 1807. Will of John HOLLAND. September
         Term 1811. Wife Jacobina, monies arising from
sale of estate. Son Timothy, 300 acres Tantrough Branch,
Oldfield Creek, bought of John HANKS. Son Thomas, 140 acres
Panther Creek granted me by State 22 December 1796. Son
William, 100 acres Oldfield Creek, same as above. Son
Benjamin, 190 acres Belews Creek, Nelsons line, granted me
17 April 1797. Son John, rest of estate. Executors: Wife
Jacobina and John LINEBACK. Witnesses: John Fredr. BECKER
and Samuel SCHULTZ. Signed: John HOLLAND.

Page 125. 19 November 1811. Will of Benjamin BANNER, Junr.
         December Term 1811. Three brothers, Joshua, Henry,
and Ephraim. Sister Sally BANNER. Executors: Joshua BANNER
and Henry BANNER. Witnesses: Charles BANNER, Fredr. Wm.
BALDRIDGE, and Joseph BANNER. Signed: Benjamin BANNER.

Page 126. 2 June 1804. Will of Christian Lewis BENZION,
         Clerk, Salem. December Term 1811. To Rev. Jacob
Van VLECK, Nazareth, Northampton County, Pennsylvania, lands
in Pennsylvania and New Jersey devised to me by will of Fredr.
Wm. MARSHALL, Salem, 16 December 1801; and by will of Hans
Christian Alexander Von SCHWEINITZ of Pennyslvania 27 Septem-
ber 1796. To Rev. John Gebhart CUNOW, Bethlehem, Northampton
County, Pennsylvania, lands in North Carolina and Georgia and
elsewhere in America by wills of two above to maintain
settlements Unitas Fratrum, etc., mentions land in Wilkes
County, North Carolina; Earl GRANVILLE, Henry COSART, Hugh
MONTGOMERY, Esq., and John Michael GRAFF. Wife Dorothea
Sophia Elizabeth (formerly BOTTICHER), $1,1200 she owned at

46

our marriage and sums that will come to her from late Uncle
Benj. JUNGE (JUNG) of Escqueb (?). Also wife to be guardian
to my children. Children: Wm. Lewis and Lydia Theodora,
$1800. left them or to me by their grandmother in Germany.
To Jacob Van VLECK, rest of my estate found in Pennyslvania
and New Jersey. To John Gebhard CUNOW, rest of my estate
found in North Carolina and Georgia. Executors: Jacob Van
VLECK, John Hebbard CUNOW, Rev. John SCHROPP, Bethlehem,
Pennsylvania, and Rev. Samuel STOTZ, Salem. Witnesses:
Samuel KRAMSCH, Benjamin VIERLING, Fredrick MIENUNG, and
Gottlieb Benj. REICHEL. Signed: Christian Lewis BENZIEN.
Codicil, 8 September 1807: In place of Rev. John SHROPP,
            deceased, I Hereby appoint Rev. Andrew BERNHARD,
Bethlehem, Pennsylvania one of Executors. Witnesses: F.C.
MEINUNG and Gottlieb Benj. REICHEL. Signed: Christian Lewis
BENZIEN.
Codicil #2, 15 December 1808: The Grandmother of my children
            lately departed this life; I revoke whole para-
graph in my will concerning legacy from said Grandmother and
give wife $1,800 and children, $2,000. Also add my friend
Frederick Christian MEINUNG to Executors. Witnesses: Samuel
KRAMSCH and Gottlieb Benj. REICHEL. Signed: Christian
Lewis BENZIEN.

Page 130.   29 May 1805. Will of Jacob NULL, Yeoman. Decem-
            ber Term 1811. Wife Barbara, dwelling house
where I now live, etc. Son John, 2/7th part. Son Jacob,
2/7th part. Daughter Elizabeth SHOUSE, 2/7th part. Grandson Jacob SHOUSE, son of my daughter, Cala SHOUSE, deceased,
1/7th part. Executors: Son John JULL and William BECK.
Witnesses: John RICH and Thomas (X) DAVENPORT. Signed:
Jacob (X) NULL.
Codicil, 30 May 1805: Leaves sons, John and Jacob addiditonal
            personal estate. Witnesses: Thomas (X) DAVENPORT
and Robert WILLIAMS. Signed: Jacob (X) NULL.

Page 131.   23 March 1812. Will of Samuel BOND, Farmer.
            March Term 1812. Wife Elizabeth, cleared land,
etc. Son Ornan, to settle on above 328 acres of land.
Three youngest daughters, Rachel, Elizabeth, and Ruth at
coming of age. My married Children: Joseph, Thomas, Samuel,
Dorcas and Margaret, have given them all I ever expected to.
Executors: Children, Thomas, Margaret and Rachel BOND.
Witnesses: Byrum BALLARD, Adin BALLARD, and Elizabeth BOND.
Signed: Samuel BOND.

Page 132.   10 December 1809. Will of William ALFORD. March
            Term 1812. Wife Mary, all freehold lands I
possess during her widowhood. Children: William, Joseph,
Andrew, John, Ann, Mary, Esther, and Sarah, estate equally
divided. Daughter Margaret CROUSE, 10 shillings and no more.
Executors: Wife Mary and Sons Andrew and John. Witness:
Bryson BLACKBURN. Signed: William ALFORD.

Page 133.   23 May 1803. Will of Isable LOWRAY. June Term
            1812. Son John, land whereon I live. Grand-
daughters, Anabell LOWRAY and Margaret LOWRAY, daughters of
James LOWRAY, furniture. Grandson Hugh McKILLIP, $1.00.

Daughter-in-laws Hannah LOWRAY and Jean LOWARY, 2/3 balance
of estate. Daughter Mary WALKER, 1/3 balance of my estate.
Executor: Son John LOWARY. Witnesses: John ENDSLEY, Jurat
and Andrew ENDSLEY. Signed: Isable (X) LOWRAY.
CODICIL, 11 December 1809: Bequeaths additional articles to
two daughter-in-laws and daughter above mentioned.
Witness: John ENDSLEY, Jurat. Signed: Isable (X) LOWRAY.

Page 134. 7 July 1811. Will of Andrew SCHAWITS (SCHWARZ,
SCHWARTZ). September Term 1812. Debts by my
former wife not to be paid out of my estate as she left me
without cause. Daughter Susannah, $1.00 and no more.
Former wife (not named), $1.00 and no more. To Matthew
REICH, rest of my estate for kindness to me in my last days
and illness. Executors: Samuel STOTZ and Conrad KREUSER,
Salem. Witnesses: John LINEBACK, Christopher REICH, and J.
Jacob BLUM. Signed: Andrew SCHAWITS.

Page 134. 3 August 1812. Will of Henry STOEHR, Senr.
September Term 1812. Only Son, Henry, house and
lott in Bethabara to maintain wife. My three children:
Daughter (not named-Moravian Records states she was Johanna
Elizabeth) and son-in-law, Thomas BUTTNER; Daughter (not
named-Moravian Records state she was Anna Dorothea) and son-
in-law, Christian FOCKLE; and son Henry, three cows but
Christian and Henry to furnish my wife with milk her life-
time. Wife Dorothea, household furniture, etc. Executor:
John BUTTNER. Witnesses: Henry WINDLEY and Samuel (X)
KROUSE. Signed: Henry STOEHR, Senr.

Page 135. 6 December 1810. Will of William MARTIN.
September Term 1812. Wife Elenor, Negro girl
Lousey. Four children: John, William, Lewis MARTIN, and
Mary REDDICK. Old Negro woman to choose which of my child-
ren she lives with. Son-in-law David REDDICK. Executors:
Wife Elenor, Son John MARTIN, and Charles BANNER. Witnesses:
Charles BANNER, Sarah MARTIN, and Betsy (X) BLACKBURN.
Signed: William MARTIN.

Page 137. 2 April 1809. Will of Sebe ANGEL. December Term
1812. Daughters, Jemima, Elizabeth, Nancy, Sebe,
Frances, Rebeckah and Barbara, 5 shillings each. Sons,
Lawrence, John, and Josiah, 5 shillings each. Sons Charles
and James, my property. Executors: Sons, Charles and James.
Witnesses: Ann (X) HAM, Benj. ANGEL, Jurat and Jehu MCMIN
(?). Signed: Sebe (X) ANGEL.

Page 138. 26 July 1812. Will of William VEST. December
Term 1812. Wife Lucy and my nine children:
Samuel, William, Charles, Isham, John, Mary (wife of Phillip
SUTHERLAND), Polly (wife of Jacob MISENA), Jane (wife of
Thomas BENNETT), Elizabeth (wife of John SIZEMORE), money
arising from sale of estate equally divided except less what
I have already given Samuel, Wm., Isham, John, Polly MISENA,
and Jane BENNETT. Executors: Sons John and Charles.
Witnesses: Charles VEST and Samuel KENNAMAN. Signed:
William (X) VEST, Senr.

Page 138. 19 November 1812. Will of Mary RUSSEL. December
          Term 1812. Son Hiram, horse and saddle. Daughter,
Elizabeth, bed I now lie on and it's furniture. Two little
daughters, Sally and Levina, my other bed and furniture.
Son Robert, money arising from sale of estate. Executors:
Neighbors Robert FRAZER and John THOMASON. Witnesses:
Archibald CAMPBELL and Elizabeth (X) THOMASON. Signed: Mary
(X) RUSSEL.

Page 140. 3 May 1812. Will of Samuel PITTS. March Term
          1813. Wife Elizabeth, all lands except 50 acres.
Sons Andrew, Samuel, Benj., Isaac, and Levi, above lands
equally. Son John, my homeplace after his mother's death.
Son Cadwallader, 50 acres including his farm and buildings.
Daughters Martha and Elizabeth, bed and furniture, cow when
married. Executors: Isaac PITTS and Cad. PITTS. Witnesses:
James PITTS, Andrew PITTS, and Samuel PITTS. Signed: Samuel
PITTS.

Page 140. 6 October 1812. Will of Malcom CURRY. March
          Term 1813. Daughters Sarah and Rebecca, Planta-
tion whereon I now live. Daughters Peggy, wife of E.
FERGUSON, tract of land adjoining mine or she chooseth to
give it to her children, Curry and Polly. Daughters Polly,
wife of John VENABLE and Bethsey, wife of John STONE, Bond
of 100 pounds on Anthony CROTCHETT in Western Country.
Executors: John RANDLEMAN and Christian LASH. Witnesses:
George HAUSER and Henry HAUSER. Signed: Malcom CURRY.

Page 141. 6 November 1811. Will of William SWAIM, Farmer.
          March Term 1813. Wife Nancy, all estate except
13 acres adjoining Jacob HINES. Son Jonathan, above 13
acres. Sons Silas and Michael, my lands where I now live
after death of wife. Married children already portioned off,
Elizabeth BODENHAMMER, Charity IDOL, Mary CLAMPET, Nancy
WILLYARD, Isabell RICH, Jesse SWAIM, Milly KILLION and Moses
SWAIM, 10 shillings extra. Grandsons Elijah SWAIM and
William BENNETT. Executors: Wife Nancy and son Jonathan.
Witness: Thomas LLOYD, Jurat. Signed: William SWAIM.

Page 142. 19 February 1813. Will of John SHAMEL. March
          Term 1813. Wife Hannah, property she brought
with her when I intermarried her; also my Mansion house,
Plantation where I now live of 200 acres, Still, and all
slaves except girl Franky. My eight children, Joseph, John,
Elizabeth, George, Jacob, Abram, Mary, and Peter, above
equally divided at wife's death except property she brought
with her. Sons John and Jacob, 75 acres each adjoining
Hauser Town land. Mentions what he gave daughter, Eliza
KITNER, when she married and left him; also son Peter, be
bound to some good trade, etc. Executors: Joseph HOLDER,
Senr., William BECK, and Charles BANNER. Witnesses: Charles
BANNER, Jurat, George RAY, Jurat, and Joseph (X) HOLDER,
Jurat. Signed: Jon SHMEL.

Page 144. 19 March 1813. "Word of Mouth" Will of John
          LAWSON. June Term 1813. At house of William
HOOKER where he resided for several weeks about last February,

1813. Daughter Ressia, my horse and bridle for her care of me. Witnesses: Jesse LAWSON and Patsy (X) LAWSON.

Page 145. 8 July 1811. Will of Henry SMITH, Tanner. June Term 1813. Daughter Mary YATES, 10 shillings besides what she has already had. Sons Henry and Jacob, 10 shillings each, etc. Son James, half of land I live on, etc. Wife Mary, residue of above during her lifetime. Executors: Wife Mary and a person of James's choice. Witnesses: William THORNTON, Thomas THORNTON, and Polly (X) CHILDRESS. Signed: Henry SMITH.

Page 146. 16 November 1813. Will of William BINNEGER. December Term 1813. Wife, Elizabeth, lend her my land, etc. Son William, 5 shillings as he has already had his full share. Son Lenwood, my land, house and mill after wife's death. Daughters Nancy SMITH, Sarah KIMBROUGH, Polly BINNEGAR, Betsy BINNEGAR, Susannah BRINNEGAR and Peggy BINNEGER, furniture, etc. at decease of wife and privilege of house and land during wife's life. Executor: David POINDEXTER, Jacob SMITH, and Wife Elizabeth. Witnesses: Abraham REDMON, Jurat, Michael MOURNER, Jurat and Wm. SLAUGHTER. Signed: William (X) BINNEGER.

Page 146. 26 January 1807. Will of Nicholas DOLL. December Term 1813. My children who are living (not named). Son-in-law John HUFFINES. Grandson Fredereick HUFFINES. Executors: Son George DOLL and Son-in-law Fredric MILLER. Witnesses: Henry (X) STIPI, Jurat and John H. PRYOR. Signed: Nicholas (X) DOLL.

Page 147. 9 April 1813. Will of Michael RANKE, Bethania. December Term 1813. Wife Elizabeth, rents from leasehold Estate and Mill. Son Gottlieb, to tend Leasehold Estate, Bethania, I leased from Fred. Wm. MARSHALL and pay my wife yearly out of estate; also Negro Henry. To Society (Moravians), money. Daughter Elizabeth, to have extra portion for loving attendance of her parents. Executors: Son Gottlieb and Jacob LASH. Witnesses: Christian LASH, Henry HAUSER, Jurat and John H. HAUSER. Signed: Michael RANKE.

Page 149. 14 January 1814. Will of Alexander BURGE. March Term 1814. Wife (not named), land I live on, etc. and at her decease to be equally divided among all my children (not named) except my two daughters Lucy and Susannah. Executor: Wife (not named). Witnesses: Henry P. GAINES, George CLARK, and Thomas CARDWELL, Jurat. Signed: Alexander (X) BURGE.

Page 150. 15 December 1813. Will of Jonathan PERRY. March Term 1814. Only son, Wyatt, when he comes of age, 100 acres of land. My Father (not named), have the timber. My Father and Mother (not named), to have fruit. My Wife (not named) and child, remainder. Executor: Clabourn WATSON. Witnesses: Edward BULLOCK, Eleazer PETTY, Jurat and John HILL. Signed: Jonathan (X) PERRY.

Page 150.   4 December 1813.   Will of Gray BYNUM.   March Term
          1814.   Son Hampton, $5.00 as I have done good
part by him; lands where he now lives, 300 acres Little
Sandy Creek of Townfork adjoining Wm. DAVIS, Hampton, etc.;
100 acres adjoining Jacky GOLDING, Big Sandy Creek.   Daughter
Martha BLUM, Negro woman Phillis and Old Phillis' children.
Other slaves to be sold.   Eldest son, John BYNUM, $10.00 in
addition to what he has received.   Eldest daughter Mary
GARDENER'S (deceased) children, $1.00 as she received her
legacy in her lifetime.   Daughter Sally FORTNER (deceased)
children, $10.00 as she received legacy.   Son Gray BYNUM,
$1.00 besides what have already given him.   Other children:
Benjamin BYNUM, Martha BLUM, and Nancy BOWMAN, residue of my
estate divided equally.   Executor: Son Benjamin.   Witnesses:
Chas. BANNER, Jurat, Hezekiah DAVIS, Jurat and Wm. ROZELL.
Signed: Gray (X) BYNUM.

Page 152.   21 November 1813.   Will of Zebade BILLITER.
          March Term 1814.   Wife Anna, to stay on Plantation
with all my Children under age.   Son Mark, already received
his share.   Children: Daniel, John, James, Polly, (already
given their share), Joel, Samuel and Elias.   Executors: Son
Daniel BILLETOR and Joseph MILLER.   Witnesses: John DOUB,
Junr., Jurat and John HENNINGS.   Signed: Zebadoe (X) BILLETER.

Page 153.   24 March 1811.   Will of Charles WHITLOCK.   June
          Term 1814.   Wife Esteer, be maintained by son,
John, out of estate.   Son John, 240 acres on Snow Creek
where I now live; Negro boy London, and he is to pay heirs of
my son, James; my son William, my son Thos., my son Alexander,
my son Charles, my daughter Agnes DODSON, my daughter Mary
PRUIT.   Executors: Sons, Thomas and John WHITLOCK.   Witnesses: Charles BEAZLEY, Jurat, John FARR, and Edmond BEAZLEY,
Jurat.   Signed: Charles WHITLOCK.

Page 154.   14 April 1814.   Will of Valentine FRY, Junr.
          June Term 1814.   Wife Catherina, 200 acres Planta-
tion whereon I now live, Negro Katy.   Children: John, Jacob,
Peter, Adam, Michael, (children of my deceased daughter Mary),
Christian, Henry, Catherine (wife of Lewis MARTIN), Valentine,
Abraham, Sarah (wife of Michael FRY, Junr.), and Joseph,
equal shares.   Executors: Sons, Adam and Valentine.   Witness-
es: John FRY and Solomon PETREE, Jurat.   Signed: Valentine
(X) FRY.

Page 155.   18 June 1814.   Nuncupative Will of William SHELTON,
          Senr.   September Term 1814.   William SHELTON,
Junr. and Mary WOOD maketh oath few weeks before death of
Wm. SHELTON, Senr. that they were witnesses to his last Will
and Testament.   Wife Mary SHELTON, to enjoy and possess his
estate her natural life and at her death be equally divided
amongst his children and her children which she had before
he intermarried with her.   Children not named.   Witness:
John WHITLOCK, J.P.   Signed: William SHELTON, Junr. and Mary
WOOD.

Page 155.   12 June 1814.   Will of Jacob SPAENHOUR.   September
          Term 1814.   Wife Elizabeth, all estate and one

51

half the Mill. Executor and Guardian to my children (not named): Wife Elizabeth. Witnesses: Fredric WOLFF, Jurat and (Signature in German). Signed: Jacob (X) SPANEHOUR.

Page 155. 19 May 1814. Will of Godfrey FIDLER (FIELDER). September Term 1814. Wife Katharine, household furniture. Balance of estate to be sold and equally divided between wife and children (not named) except part coming to daughter, Elizabeth remain in hands of Executors and given as needed as her husband, George FULP, is a drinking man and would spend it. Executors: Son George FIDLER and Jacob MILLER. Witnesses: Henry STOLTZ, George MILLER, and Phillip STOLTZ, Jurat. Signed: Godfrey FIDLER.

Page 156. 4 August 1814. Will of William WALKER. September Term 1814. Wife Mary, plantation whereon I now dwell; Negro Aggy. 4 Children: Son Robert; 3 daughters, Margarit, Jane and Ann, have 2/3 of estate divided equally. Daughter Margaret, 200 acres bought of George CUMMINS. Grandson Abner WALKER, son of Margaret, $20.00. Granddaughter Synthia (minor), daughter of my daughter Ann (Now John MILLER'S wife), $100.00 and Synthia be raised by my wife, her grandmother, til she comes of age. Executor: Son Robert WALKER. Witnesses: Archibald CAMPBELL, John MECUM, Owen EVANS, and David MARTIN. Signed: William WALKER.

Page 158. (Not dated). Will of George THOMASON. December Term 1814. Wife Milly, all my living to support herself and children when they come of age. Children: Edy, Mary, and John, have had their saddles; Nancy had her bed; mentions "among my children" but none others named. Executors: Wife Milly and Son John. Witnesses: Harmon McGEE, Jurat and George BOWMAN. Signed: George THOMASON.

Page 158. 21 June 1814. Will of Martin HAUSER. December Term 1814. Wife Leah, continue to live on Plantation with children and educate them. Children: Joseph Martin, Moses, Samuel, Elijah, Martin, William, Susannah Mary (married to Joseph HAUSER), Rachel and Leah. Mentions William coming of age and mentions a sawmill. Executors: Jon Joseph HAUSER, and John DOUB, Junr. Witnesses: Daniel SPANEHOUR, Jurat, Isaac CHURCH, and Thomas W. YATES. Signed: Martin HAUSER.

Page 161. 19 November 1808. Will of David BROOKS. March Term 1815. Wife Sarah, all of estate during widowhood. Son Jesse, 200 acres where I now live at death or marriage of mother. Sons John and Jesse, care of my Negro man Harry. Seven children: Elizabeth, John, Jane, Mary, Sarah, Jesse, and Martha. Executors: John and Jesse (sons). Witnesses: John PITTS and Elijah JOHNSTON. Signed: David BROOKS.

Page 162. 16 February 1815. Will of Joseph PFAFF. March Term 1815. Son Peter, colt, plantation I formerly lived on adjoining Wachovia. Two daughters, Susannah Elizabeth and Sarah. Daughter Catharina, wife of Jesse STYERS. All my children: Peter, Mary Catharina, Susannah

Elizabeth and Sarah. Executors: Joseph HOLDER and John DOUB. Witnesses: John H. HAUSER and Peter PFAFF, Jurat. Signed: Joseph PFAFF.

Page 163. 15 June 1815. Nuncupative Will of Robert HAYNES.
        June Term 1815. Statement by Alexander MOODY, during last sickness of Robt. HAYNES, his brother William HAYNES, to have his property.

Page 163. 9 February 1815. Will of Phillip HINE. June
        Term 1815. Wife Mary, property. Two daughters Anna and Maria Melinda, all my Heirship due me from my father. Brother, Peter HINE, to buy my horse. Executor: John BUTNER. Witnesses: Henry HINE and Peter HINE. Signed: Phillip (X) HINE.

Page 164. 25 March 1815. Will of Michael FRY, Senr. June
        Term 1815. Children: Barbara, wife of John TUTTLE; Mary, wife of John LAIRD; Sally, wife of Jacob PINKLEY (BINKLEY); Caty, wife of Anthony HINKLE; Elizabeth, wife of Adam BUTNER; and Henry FRY - Bond I have on John FRY to be divided equally except Elizabeth's share to go to her children and not Adam BUTNER. Mentions all my children to share in sale of rest of estate after decease of wife. Mentions Negro slaves to my wife (not named - according to Salem Records, she was Dorothea). Executors: John TUTTLE and William COX. Witnesses: Thomas T. ARMSTRONG and James PATTERSON. Signed: Michael (X) FRY.

Page 165. 21 January 1815. Will of William DAVIS. June
        Term 1815. Wife Elizabeth, to enjoy plantation and dwelling on Sandy Creek; also Negroes Bob, Harry, and Hagar and her children. Three sons, Isaac, Thomas and Hezekiah, land. Son-in-laws, Malery SMITH and Robert WINSTON. Children of daughter Sally (wife of Austin SMITH). Children of daughter Nancy (wife of Jacky GOLDING). Son Hezekiah, Negroes Dick and Mary. Daughter Sally SMITH, Negro Lewis. Daughter Nancy GOLDING, Negro Jim. Daughter Elizabeth, wife of Malery SMITH, Negro Ben. Son-in-law Joshua HORNER and Theodocia, his wife, $1.00. Mentions 273 acres on Meadows Creek to sons and sons-in-law. Executors: Isaac, Thos., and Hezekiah (sons). Witnesses: Archibald CAMPBELL, Jurat and Solomon PETREE, Jurat. Signed: William DAVIS.

Page 167. 9 February 1815. Will of Henry BURCHAM. June
        Term 1815. Wife mentioned but not named. Daughter Jemima and her son Squire. My son's (not named) daughter Nancy, who now lives with me. Mentions land, 198 acres on Toms Creek to be sold and equally divided between Isaiah FIELDS, James BURCHAM, Thomas HILL and Wm. HYATT. To Robert BLACKWELL, Daniel SMITH and Ephraim THOMPSON, 5 shillings each "and no more as their part of my estate." Executors: Shubel BURCHAM and Thomas OLIPHANT. Witnesses: John P. HALE, Isaiah GYMON, Jurat and Jacob JESSUP. Signed: Henry BURCHAM.

Page 168. 12 April 1814. Will of Joseph WINSTON. June
        Term 1815. Son Robert, 100 acres lower tract

Evans ford on Townfork, 100 acres Sandy Creek named Musken-
dine Bottom, my desk, ox cart, etc. Son Joseph, balance of
land including where I now live, also what I purchased of
Daniel DAVIS and the Mill Seat including 700 acres, also 8
Negroes Cato, Will, Doctor, Vilet and all her children; also
my Blacksmith tools, etc. Daughter Sally, my bureau. Son
Lewis, Negro Lydia and my watch. All my children (not here
named) except sons Joseph and Fountain. All my children
(not here named) except Joseph, 5,000 acres Western Lands
and 3,000 acres bought of Wm. Terrel LEWIS. Son Joseph, to
take care of my old Negroes Tom and Cloe. Son William, my
old sword because he was wounded in defense of his Country.
Son Joseph, my sword presented to me by Legislature of North
Carolina and he use it in defending his Country ONLY. Son
Samuel, diamond Kneebuckles. Son Fountain, my Gold sleeve
buttons. Executors: Neighbors Isaac DALTON and Andres
BOWMAN. Witnesses: Archiblad CAMPBELL and Hampton BYNUM.
Signed: Jos. WINSTON.

Page 169. (No date). Nuncupative Will of Nancy MECUM.
        September Term 1815. Nancy MECUM was sickened and
died about 2nd Friday in June last. Wiley and Isabella
JONES, sworn witnesses. Her brothers James and Samuel to
have a piece of her clothing and James to have 3 shillings.
Her half-sister Ruth MECUM, to have rest of her property.

Page 170. 7 March 1815. Will of John DAWSON. September
        Term 1815. Daughter Rebecker DAWSON and Milkey
NOLES, 1 shilling Starling each. Wife Elizabeth; daughter
Oney; daughter Elizabeth, rest of estated divided three ways.
Executor: Wife Elizabeth. Witnesses: Isabella JONES and J.
LOVE, Jurat. Signed: John DAWSON.

Page 170. 18 June 1815. Will of John HAISLEY. September
        Term 1815. Son Alexander HAISLEY, 54 acres where
I now live. Wife Mary, house and plantation til son arrives
at 21 years. Three daughters, Elizabeth, Grace, and Mary.
Executors: Jonathan MENDENGHALL and Wife Mary HAISLEY.
Witnesses: Joseph MENDINGHALL, Jurat and Samuel PHILLIPS.
Signed: John HAISLEY.

Page 171. 3 September 1812. Will of John Peter SHEYAR
        (SCHREYER), Salem, Yeoman. December Term 1815.
Only son Jacob. Executors: John LINEBACK, Shoemaker and John
VOGLER, Silver Smith. Witnesses: Matth. RIGHTS and Henry
R. HERBST, Jurat. Signed: Peter (X) SHREYER.

Page 172. 19 October 1815. Will of Presley MORRIS. Decem-
        ber Term 1815. Wife (not named), plantation
whereon I now live; at her death equally divided between my
children, male and female alike (not named); also my Negro
Harrot. Wife to give all my children English Education, as
children come of age. Executor: Wife (not named). Witnesses: Archibald CAMPBELL and Absalom BOSTICK. Signed: Presley
(X) MORRIS.

Page 173. 18 March 1811. Will of Abraham MARTIN, Senr.
        December Term 1815. Wife Sally, 75 acres adjoining

Ephraim BANNER and Valentine FRY including Mansion house;
also Negro Diner and her children. Sons William and Abraham,
balance of land where I now live (Wm., the south end where
he now lives). Children: William, Robert, Matthew, Abraham,
widow Mary FOLLIS, Judith LINNS, and Martha BOLEJACK. Grandchildren which my deceased daughter Sally BANNER had by
Ephraim BANNER (not named). Granddaughter Sally BANNER.
Executors: Son Wm. MARTIN and Joshua and Charles BANNER.
Witnesses: Charles BANNER, Jurat, Sally MARTIN, Jurat, and
Frankey MERRIT, Jurat. Signed: Abraham MARTIN.

Page 174. 13 February 1816. Will of Jonas LAWSON. March
          Term 1816. Five daughters: Mary CLOUD, Anna
LAWSON, Martha ALLEN, Sarah LAWSON, and Nancy WOOD, 10
shillings each. Wife Milly, all estate. My last children:
William, Jonas, Lemuel, Adam, James, and Robert. Executors:
Wife Milly and Son William. Witnesses: John WEBB and William
MOORE, Jurat. Signed: Jonas (X) LAWSON.

Page 175. 16 December 1815. Will of Henry WILLETS. March
          Term 1816. Wife Charity, use of house and planta-
tion, blacksmith tools, etc. Two sons Joseph and Henry, 200
acres of land. Granddaughter Rhoda. Son Gabriel, 10 shill-
ings. Daughter Charity, Spinning wheel, etc. Daughters:
Sarah, Ann, Achjah, Elizabeth, Mary, Jemima and Charity.
Children of deceased daughter Margaret. Executor: Wife
Charity and Friend Michael WEISNER. Witnesses: Joseph
MENDENHALL and Richard CLAMPIT. Signed: Henry WILLITS.

Page 176. 18 August 1809. Will of James COFER. March Term
          1816. Wife Partheney, my plantation whereon I
now live. Son James, land Lick Fork and road leads from
John HALBROOKS and Samuel FOWLERS. Son Jacob, land between
Jacob COFERS line and John HALBROOKS and Samuel FOWLER. My
children that is now living (not named). Granddaughter Sally
MARSHALL, her mother's one-twelvth part of my estate.
Executors: Sons James and Jacob. Witnesses: Isaac DALTON,
Jurat and John and Susannah COX. Signed: James COFER.

Page 177. (Not dated). Will of Michael TAGUE, Senr. June
          Term 1816. Wife Mary Ann, estate. Son Jacob
and daughter Feby, should they marry and leave their mother,
to have same as my others when they left me. Notes of
Michael, George and Henry not to become payable til after
their mother's death. My children: Caty, Henry, George,
Elizabeth, Michael, Jacob, and Pheby. Executors: Son Michael
and Solomon SPANEHOUR. Witnesses: Daniel SCOTT, Eh. SCOTT,
and William LONDON. Signed: Michael TAGUE.

Page 177. 1 February 1816. Will of Salome KINSEL (KUNZEL).
          June Term 1816. Daughter Elizabeth GREEN, wife
of Phillip GREENE, ½ of my wearing apparel. Three granddaughters, Caty RANK, wife of John; Salome NISSON, wife of
Schristian; and Elizabeth REID, wife of Charles (all daughters of my daughter Molly). My property, notes or money
divided 4 ways: Jacob LOGENEUR, Senr. (LAGENAUER), George
LOGENOUR, Elizabeth GREEN and children of my daughter Molly.
Also Joseph KERNER pay money he owes me. Executors: Joseph

KERNER. Witness: Jacob GREEN. Signed: Salome (X) DENSELL.

Page 178. 20 October 1815. Will of Anna Catharana ERNST,
        Salem. (No probate). To Heathern Missions of
United Brethren, to Lewis D. SCHWEINITZ. To Rebecca BAGGE,
Silver Smelling Bottle. To Charles BAGGE, Gold Sleeve
Buttons and best Silver lead pencil. To Christiana BEAUGHAUSS
(BIWIGHAUSEN), my clothes. To D. Samuel Benj. VIERLING,
my walking cane. To Juliana EVERHARD (EBERHARDT), Small
Silver Snuffbox. To Carolina EVERHARD, desk and Earrings.
To Christian EVERHARD, Gold Medal. To Susannah STOTZ,
Knitting Spool. To Sister PFOHL, large Silver Snuffbox.
To Dorothes BYHON (BYHAN), my bed Curtains. To Samuel STOTZ,
$100.00. Balance of estate to be divided among poor and
widows of Salem and "not forget Mary SAMUEL near Bethabara."
Executor: Samuel STOTZ. Witnesses: C.F. BAGGE and Christiana
BEVIGHAUS. Signed: Anna Catharana ERNST.

Page 179. Last page of Richard PHILLIPS will - see below.

Pages 180, 181, 182 is missing.

Page 183. 19 March 1807. Will of Richard PHILLIPS.
        December Term 1816. To Foster PHILLIPS, my
brother's son, 50 acres Fishing Island and money to maintain
me my lifetime and what is left put to use of his own children: Hezekiah PHILLIPS, John PHILLIPS, Jeremiah CORNELIUS,
and John CORNELIUS. Executors: Foster and Hezekiah PHILLIPS.
Witnesses: Michael SPANEHOUR, Senr. and Michael SPAENHOUR,
Junr., Jurat. Signed: Richard (X) PHILLIPS.

Page 183. 21 November 1813. Will of John KELLAM. Septem-
        ber Term 1816. Wife Ann, ½ of estate. Son
Joseph, provided he remove into this county and maintain my-
self and my wife; if he fail, be divided equally among five
sons: William, Thomas, James, George, and Joseph. Executors:
Neighbors Robert WALKER and Archibald CAMPBELL. Witnesses:
Joshua HITCHCOCK and Armstrong MARTIN, Jurat. Signed: John
KELLAM.

Page 185 is missin.

Page 186. (Part of this page torn and missing). 12 June
        1812. Margaretha GID---. September Term 1816.
To Robert MITCHELL of Surry County, 10 shillings. Mentions
all my Negroes heretofore sold to beloved friend, George
HAUSER. To George HAUSER, tract formerly lived on in Surry
County on Arrarat -------- 550 acres ------. Executor:
George HAUSER. Witnsesses: Jacob SHORE, Jurat and Adam
BUTNER, Jurat. Signed: Margarethe GIDEONS.

END BOOK II

Page 1. 4 March 1817. Nuncupative Will of Charles NEWMAN.
March Term 1817. Brother, James NEWMAN swears that
on 4 March 1817 he was at home his brother, Charles, who was
on his death bed. Charles willed wife Margaret NEWMAN all
his estate for to raise and support his children. Signed:
William MOORE, J.P.

Page 2. 8 May 1816. Will of Younger BLACKBURN. March Term
1817. Wife Martha, lifetime estate. Children:
Paul, Elijah, Meredy, Hewlett, Burrwin, Martha, Docia,
Elizabeth, Mary, Frances, and Nancy, land on Neatman Creek,
etc. Executors: Friend Wm. BLACKBURN and Burwin BLACKBURN,
son. Witnesses: J. MOORE, Green HILL, Robert HILL, and Joel
HILL, Jurat. Signed: Younger BLACKBURN.

Page 3. 27 October 1816. Will of Andrew ENSLEY. March
Term 1817. Executors to sell Negro Henry (bought
of James BACHAM); also land and pay Lavinia PERDEW $200.00
(no relationship given). Wife Sarah, remove to Tennessee and
buy 100 acres land and hold "my black people"; all children
(not named) have equal share with wife when reach 21 or marry
except son, Washington ENSLEY who is to have two shares to
further his education. Executors: brother, John ENSLEY and
George CUMMINGS, brother. Witnesses: Jeremiah CUNNINGHAM,
Reubin FOLGER, Jurat and Wm. STUDDARD. Signed: Andrew ENDSLEY.

Page 5. 19 September 1816. Will of Gottlieb STRICKLE.
March Term 1817. Wife Maria Elizabeth (formerly
SPACK), household furniture, share stock in Branch Bank,
Salisbury and State Bank of North Carolina; at her decease
Stock to my Brother Fredric STIKLE. Executors: Wife Maria
Elizabeth and Friend John RANK (RANCK). Witness: John C.
BURKHARD, Jurat. Signed: Gottlieb STRICKLE (STREHLE).

Page 7. 14 March 1817. Will of Anny HART. June Term 1817.
Daughter Tabitha GREENWOOD. Granddaughter Polly
Carter GATEWOOD. Executrix: Tabitha GREENWOOD, daughter.
Witnesses: Martha (X) WEBB, Wm. (X) GREENWOOD, and Charles
BEAZLY, Jurat. Signed: Anny (X) HART.

Page 8. 20 April 1817. Will of Reubin MOORE. June Term
1817. Executors to sell land on Snow Creek; Negro
woman Nanne and her children. Wife Susanna, Negroes Delph,
Charlotte, John, Jerry, Mary, Hyram, Patt which I possess
by my marriage to her. Sons William C. and Matthew, Negro
Charles. Daughter Elizabeth (wife of John CLAYTON), Negroes
Dycy and Adam. Sons Reubin, John, Gabriel, and Gideon MOORE.
Daughter Polly MOORE. Gabriel and Gideon to continue school
until acquire good English Education. Executors: Wm. C.
MOORE, son and Matthew R. MOORE, brother. Witnesses:
Johnson CLEMMENT, Jurat and William MOORE, Jurat. Signed:
Reubin MOORE.

Page 10. 2 May 1816. Will of Anthony KOSNER (Antron KASTNER),

Blacksmith. June Term 1817. Wife Catharine, live on plantation and be maintained by my son Frederick. Son Frederic to have all land whereon I live and maintain mother; pay his brother Henry KASTNER $10.00; sister Elizabeth $25.00 and $157.00 to each my other children: Mary KASTNER; Christina (wife of Joseph KERNER); Catharina (wife of William BEDWELL); Hannah (wife of John SNIDER); Salome (wife of Martin EBERT); Justina (wife of Philip GREEN) and Sarah (wife of Frederic GREEN). Son John KASTNER, $3.00 and 130 acres land. Executor: John KASTNER, son. Witnesses: Henry RIPPLE and Philip SNIDER. Signed: Andon KESNER (KASTNER). CODICIL, 5 January 1817: Appointed friend Henry RIPPLE, Executor in room John COSNER. Witness: Phillip SCHNEIDER. Signed: Andon KOSNER. CODICIL, 17 February 1817. Wife Catharina shall enjoy her legacy she had by will of her father, Godfrey CRUM and daughter Elizabeth have one acre my home tract I willed to son Fredric. Witnesses: Phillip SNEIDER and Henry RIPPLE. Signed: Andon KOSNER.

Page 13. 1 July 1816. Will of Isaac EADS. September Term 1817. Wife Sarah, homeplace, 101 acres adjoining Charles GRIFFIN, Richard MILL, William PADGET and others (not named). Sons: Robert, William, Bartlet, James, Isaac, David, Nancy, Sharlet (Charlotte). Daughters Elizabeth and Polly, estate death wife. Executors: Charles GRIFFIN and Joseph SCALES. Witnesses: James GRIFFIN and Henry (X) CAMPBELL. Signed: Isaac EADS.

Page 15. 3 June 1816. Will of Harmon (Hermannus) MILLER. March Term 1818. Son Harmon and his wife remain on my real estate. Grandchildren: Elizabeth, Margaret, Catharine, Mary, David, Daniel, and Sarah MILLER (children of Godfrey MILLER). Grandchildren: Mary, John, Henry, Harmon, Charles, Charity and Sarah MILLER (children of my son Harmon and their mother Salome). Executors: Henry HAUSER, Esq. and Henry KAPP. Witnesses: John GEIGER (KIGER), Jurat, Adam GEIGER (KIGER), and Jacob GEIGER (KIGER). Signed: Harmon (X) MILLER.

Page 17. 28 April 1818. Will of Michael ROMINGER. June Term 1818. Sons Martin and Benj., $10.00 as have already received. Balance estate divided as follows: Wife Anna Maria, two shares; Sons Phillip, George, Conrad, one share each; Daughters Catharine, Juliana, Mary, Eve, Fronica, Elizabeth, and Susanna, one share each. Executor: Geo. FREY of Rowan County. Witness: Henry RIPPLE, Jurat. Signed: Michael (X) ROMINGER.

Page 18. 24 July 1817. Will of Catherina HAUSER. June Term 1818. Son John HAUSER, West part land I live on adjoining Philip ROTHROCK. Daughter Christina (wife of Philip ROTHROCK), money and my Dutch Bible. Daughter Elizabeth, East part land I live on adjoining Philip ROTHROCK. Daughter Anna (wife of Valentine BICKLE (BOECKEL)), notes and interest. Executor: John HAUSER, son. Witnesses: Henry RIPPLE, Senr., Jurat, Henry RIPPLE, Jr., and Elizabeth (X) RIPPLE. Signed: Catharina (X) HAUSER.

Page 19. 5 September 1817. Will of Frederick MILLER.
          June Term 1818. Wife Sarah, my home and Mill and
land belonging to Mill; Negro Sarah. Son Jacob, remaining
part whereon I now live, 185 acres. Son Frederick, take
care Mill during lifetime wife. My five children: John,
Jacob, and Frederick MILLER; Margaret GRIFFITH and Elizabeth
CONRAD. Executors: John, Jacob and Fredr. MILLER, sons.
Witnesses: Charles ANDERSON, Joseph MILLER, and Samuel
BOLEJACK. Signed: Fredric MILLER.

Page 22. 5 September 1718. Will of Phillip GREEN, Senr.
          (KROCHN-KROHN). September Term 1718. Be buried
in burying ground United Brethern at Friedland. Wife
Elizabeth, house and land whereon I live; 1 shelf in house
and all there is on it. Children: Catharine, Anna, Frederick,
my son Jacob's daughter (Eliza GREEN), Christina (wife of
Jacob LANIUS), Hannah (wife of Philip ADER), Elizabeth
GENDER'S children (not named), Salome (wife of Daniel
HARTMAN. My eldest son, John Phillip GREEN, all land South
side Sweehen (?) fork. Executors: Conrad GREEN, brother and
Elizabeth, wife. Witnesses: Michael SWAIM and Godfry (X)
FIDLER. Signed: Philip GREEN (KROEHN).

Page 24. 7 November 1799. Will of Daniel CHRISTMANN, Salem.
          September Term 1818. Wife Johanna, lifetime claim
of estate. My 7 children: Phillippina, Christina, Anna,
Sabina, Dorotha, Daniel and Jacob, equal shares. Executors:
Johanna, wife, John LINEBACK, and Christopher REICH.
Witnesses: John RIGHTS (REUZ, REUTZ, REITZ) and John
STOCKBURGER. Signed: Daniel CHRISTMANN.

Page 25. 15 August 1818. Will of Israel ROBINSON. Septem-
          ber Term 1819. Wife Jane, "to raise and educate
my children." Three sons, Jacob, Michael and Charles. Two
daughters Mary and Elizabeth. Executors: Wife Jane and
father Jacob ROBINSON. Witnesses: John FAIR, Wm. ROBINSON,
Jurat and Milton CAMPBELL. Signed: Israel (X) ROBINSON.

Page 26. 23 May 1818. Will of Nathaniel SHOBER (SCHOBER).
          September Term 1818. Be buried in customary
manner in Salem. Wife Rebecca, house and lot in Salem.
My children: Henrietta, Regina and Johanna Maria, $5,000.00
each and "trinkets" to have something to remember their
father by; Lewis David SCHWEINITZ to act as their guardian
(same to go to child wife is ensient of at my decease.
Brother Emanuel, my flute. Sisters Johannah Sophia; Anna
Pauline, Hedwig Elizabeth, Maria Theresia, a trinket to each
for their attention to me during my long and protracted
indesposition. Executors: John Christian BLUM and Emanuel
SHOBER, brother. Witnesses: Gottlieb BYHAN and John VOGLER,
Jurat. Signed: N. SHOBER.

Page 29. 8 December 1817. Will of Alexander JOYCE. March
          Term 1819. Wife (not named), 250 acres Crooked
Creek; Negros Phillis, Price, Charles and Lucy. Son John,
124 acre part tract belonging to my brother, Issac JOYCE on
Crooked Creek. Daughter Sarah FRAZIER, 3 pounds, 10 shillings, balance due her from her Grandfather SMITH. Son Thomas.

Grandson William, (son of Thomas JOYCE), 27 acres adjoining
land I now live on and adjoining Virginia line, waters
Crooked Creek. Daughters Margaret PARR and Nancy POOR.
Granddaughter Linda GRAY by request of her mother, ½ legacy
her grandfather left her. Daughters Mary GREENWOOD and
Jincy BREADLOVE. Executors: William JOYCE, John JOYCE, sons,
and Andrew JOYCE, brother. Witnesses: Thomas CARDWELL,
Josiah TAYLOR, and John (X) POLLARD. Signed: Alexander
JOYCE.

Page 30. 7 January 1819. Will of John HESTER. March Term
        1819. Wife Martha, lifetime estate. Seven child-
ren (not named), all have received dowry except Polly WICKER,
she is to receive $15.00 to make her equal with other
children that are married. My children not married: Fathy,
Benjamin, Martha and Betsy. Executors: William HESTER and
Robert HESTER, sons. Witnesses: Lathan FOLGER, Jurat and
C. WATSON. Signed: John (X) HESTER.

Page 31. 12 March 1819. Will of Adam HOLSTON. June Term
        1819. Wife Polly. Four children: oldest daughter,
Phanny, shall live with her mother until she becomes of age;
Eliza, Joseph and Sally. Executors: Wife Polly and Henry C.
MONROE. Witnesses: John (X) FIDLER, Jurat and Catherine (X)
RITTLE. Signed: Adam (X) HOLSTON.

Page 31. 28 December 1818. Memorandum: Manner in which
        Charles BEAZLEY wishes to dispose of his estate.
June Court 1819. Daughter Nancy CHILDRESS (widdow of Elisha
CHILDRESS, deceased), $1.00 and support from my estate.
Wife Mary, lifetime estate. Son, Negroes Sal, Barbea, Hapton,
Hannah, Tapney, Betty, Rachel, Sarah and Gilley. Executors:
Wife Mary and son Edmond. Witness: Obadiah DODSON, Jurat.
Signed: Charles BEAZLEY.

Page 31. 14 March 1819. Will of William ORE (ORR). June
        Term 1819. Wife Mary, lifetime estate. Children:
James, John, Sarah, William, Isaac, Abner, Jacob, Benjamin,
Robert, Nancy and Elizabeth. Executors: Wife Mary and
William ORR. Witnesses: Thornton P. GUYNN, Jurat and
Joseph E. VAWTER. Signed: William ORE (ORR).

Page 32. 3 July 1809. Will of Samuel RICH. June Term 1819.
        Wife Rachel, 168 acres where I now live. Children:
Vashty, Phebe, John, Tamer, Samuel, Joseph, Sarah, Jacob,
Thomas, and Jane. Executrix: Rachel, wife. Witnesses:
Anthony RIGHT, Jurat and Reubin SHIELD, Jurat. Signed:
Samuel RICH.

Page 33. 5 April 1819. Will of Robert MANSELL. June Term
        1819. Wife Elizabeth, lifetime estate. Children:
Richard, Robert, James, Elizabeth CROSSWHITE, Mary JAMES,
and Frances JAMES, deceased son John. Executors: Wife
Elizabeth, Daniel WOLFF, and Jacob CONRAD. Witnesses: C.
LASH, Jurat, Henry HAUSER, and Lewis LASH. Signed: Robert
MANSELL.

Page 34. 5 March 1819. Will of Maria Catharine TRANSU

(TRANSOU). June Term 1819. Brother Peter. Sisters
Elizabeth SENSEMAN, Mary Magdlena LANDMANN (her half sister)
and Benigna TRANSU. Sister-in-law Anna TRANSU. Niece
Florina TRANSOU, Emily and Hariot TRANSOU. Friend Anna
SPACH. My little friends Leuisa REICH and Susan KUMMER.
Dear little nephews: Edwin Timolean SENSEMAN (silver table-
spoon, a present from dear departed Mother) and Philip
Parmenio TRANSU. Room companions in Sister House: Christina
HINE, Maria Elizabeth KUMMER, and Dorothea KREUSER. Execu-
tors: Peter TRANSU and John H. SENSEMAN. Witnesses: John
C. BLUM and John VOGLER. Signed: Maria C. TRANSU.

Page 35. 14 May 1801. Will of Jacob RIED. June Term 1819.
        To be buried among United Brethren. Wife Elizabeth
Barbara, lifetime estate. Mentions children (sons and
daughters) living with their mother, but does not name them.
Executors: Geo. LAGENAEUR and John LANIUS, Senr. Witnesses:
Christian NISSEN, Jurat and Jacob WEIRICH. Signed: Jacob
RIED.

Page 36. 7 March 1814. Will of (Rev.) Simon PETER, Salem.
        September Term 1819. Daughter Susanna Elizabeth,
my musical instruments and note, etc. Wife Martha, lifetime
estate; after decease of my daughter her legacy to go to my
brother David PETER of Gradenhuetten, Ohio and my sister
Anna PETER of Zeist, Kingdom of Holland. Executor: Samuel
STOTZ, warden of Brethrens. Witnesses: Gotthold Benj.
REICHEL and (Rev.) Magnus HULTHIN. Signed: Simon PETER.

Page 37. 27 July 1817. Will of John KRIEGER. September
        Term 1819. Wife Mary Elizabeth, 209 acres Barcas
(?) Creek adjoining John SPAINHOUR. Sons Solomon and
Themothias. Daughter Levina. Executor: Jacob CONRAD.
Witnesses: Daniel WOLFF and Jacob SHOUSE. Signed: John
KRIEGER.

Page 37. 17 July 1819. Will of Peter HINE. September Term
        1819. Wife Margaret, being pregnant; child to
have my share of our Plantation of 21 acres. Executors:
Henry HINE, brother and John BUTNER. Witnesses: Jacob
KUMMER and Joseph KROUSE. Signed: Peter HINE.

Page 38. 30 January 1816. Will of John BECK, Senr. Septem-
        ber Term 1819. Granddaughter Elizabeth BECK.
Wife Catherine, my house and land. Son Abraham BECK, house
and land after decease of wife. Children: William, Frederick,
Sary, Solomon, Clary, Salome, Henry, Abraham, and Elizabeth,
residue estate. Executors: Son William BECK and John NUL
(NULL). Witnesses: Traverse BARBER and Henry NULL. Signed:
John (X) BECK, Senr.

Page 39. 14 August 1816. Will of Maria ELROD. December
        Term 1819. Legacies of personal estate from
clothing to handkerchiefs. To Elizabeth BUTNER (daughter
of John BUTNER); Mary BUTNER (daughter of Thos. BUTNER; her
legacy to be paid to John BUTNER); Mary and Caty BUTNER
(daughters of Christopher BUTNER); my sisters Lidia McKNIGHT,
Margareth BONER and Sarah BUTNER; Sarah HAUSER (wofe of Benj.

HAUSER); Sarah ELROD (wife of Christopher); Sarah ELROD
(wife of John); Elizabeth EVANS (wife of Job); my three
brothers Robert, John and Christopher ELROD; Thomas, Sarah,
Mary, Lidia, and Daniel (children of Christopher ELROD);
Noah (son of Robert ELROD); Damsey (boy) and Mary (children
of John ELROD); Carolina EBERHARD; Juley EBERHARD; Dorotha
WARNER; Margreth KRIEGER; Johana HOLDER; Alsha JOHNSON; Mary
LEHNERT: Joshua BONER, Senr.; Christina BONER; Elizabeth
SENSEMAN; Isaac BONER, his wife Dortha and children, Polly
and Wm. Executors: Joshua BONER and John BUTNER. Witnesses:
John C. BLUM and J. Jacob BLUM, Jurat. Signed: Mary ELROD.

Page 41. 7 November 1819. Will of John HEATH. December
        Term 1820. Son Thomas, 100 acres adjoining my
deeded land. Wife Lovina, dwelling house. Sons William,
John, and Abraham. Daughters Nanny, Elizabeth, Patty and
Susan. Mentions "my two little sons", John and Abraham to
be taught at school. Executor: Son Thomas HEATH. Witness:
Jas. COFFEY. Signed: John (X) HEATH.

Page 42. 2 November 1814. Will of Ashley JOHNSON. March
        Term 1820. Wife Elizabeth, whole estate.
Executrix: Wife Elizabeth. Witnesses: Jonathan MANLOVE,
William HULET, and Wm. MANLOVE. Signed: Ashley JOHNSON

Page 42. 17 September 1819. Will of Abraham HAUSER. March
        Term 1820. Wife Mary Magdalene, lifetime estate.
My six children: Abraham, Jacob, Timothy, Martin, Susanna
Alarcy, and Anna Elizabeth. Mentions 126 acre plantation
where he now lives. Executors: Wife Mary and Matthew RIGHTS
of Salem. Witness: Conrad KREUSER. Signed: Abraham HAUSER.

Page 43. 15 March 1820. Will of Jacob ROBINSON. June Term
        1820. Wife Rebeccah, lifetime estate. Three
daughters Elizabeth CREWS, Rebeccah BENNETT, and Mary FARE.
Executors: Son William and son-in-law Joseph CREWS. Witness:
Drury KIRK, Jurat. Signed: Jacob ROBINSON.

Page 44. 1 May 1815. Will of David DALTON, Senr. June Term
        1820. Mentions entering into contract with present
wife in interest of Estates of each. Son David, land I
bought of Wm. WATSON adjoining where I now live. Son
Jonathan, Negros Peter, Ben and Patty. Son Charles, Negroes
Sam, Hannah and her sons Joe and Frank. Son-in-law John
Fendal CARR and my daughter Elizabeth, Negroes Charles, Joe,
Jim and Jess, children of Cate whom I gave said CARR years
ago; also Negroes Frank, Tildy, Riddle, Horace, Simon, Aaron
and Sangar. Son-in-law Absalom BOSTICK and wife Nancy, Negro
Anny in his possession for years; also Negro Tena, Delph and
Delph's little son George; also Negroes Jeffery, Nann and
her children (not named); also my faithful old Pegg. Son-in-
law Thomas CARR, Negro woman Lett, yellow Frank and her
children Sampson and Lewis. Grandchildren John FENDAL and
Nancy CARR (children of Thomas CARR), Negroes Fan and her
children Big George and Wilson. Son Isaac. Executors:
Thomas T. ARMSTRONG and Jeremiah GIBSON. Witnesses: William
GOODE, Jurat and Benj. YOUNG. Signed: David DALTON (Senr.).

Page 46. 4 September 1820. Will of (Rev.) Samuel STOLTZ
          (STOTZ), Salem. September Term 1820. My beloved
Friend Lewis (Ludwig) David SCHWIENITZ, my office as Warden
for Congregation in Salem and property I possess as said
Warden. Daughter Anna Louisa, 12 shares Bank North Carolina
Stock. Daughter Susanna Elizabeth, 9 shares Bank North
Carolina Stock. Executors: Lewis David SCHWIENITZ, Fredric
C. MEINUNG, and Jacob BLUM, all of Salem. Witnesses: Wm.
FRIES, Jurat, Fredric BOHLO (BOLOW, BOLO), and Rudolph
CHRIST. Signed: Samuel STOTZ.

Page 47. 27 October 1819. Will of Jacob CAMPLIN. September
          Term 1820. My kind friends: Wenny WESTBROOK and
Zachariah WALL, my estate. Executor: Zachariah WALL.
Witnesses: Benj. FUELL and Robert WALL, Jurat. Signed: Jacob
CAMPLIN.

Page 48. 12 March 1818. Will of Elizabeth LIDE (LEIDY),
          widow of Michael LIDE, deceased. September Term
1818. Sons John, George, Phillip, Michael and Lorentz.
Daughters Margaret (wife of Jacob MILLS ?); Anna (wife of
Christian LASH); Salome (wife of Samuel PHILLIPS); Caty
(widow of James FLYNT); son John have all household furniture,
etc. but is to pay brother and sisters; others to have $1.00
each. Executor: Son John LIDY. Witness: Joseph KERNER,
Jurat. Signed: Elizabeth LIDE.

Page 50. 4 December 1815. Will of Joseph JESSUP. September
          Term 1820. Wife Betsy, lifetime estate. Sons
Thomas, Jonathan and Caleb. Daughters Mary and Hannah
JESSUP and Priscilla JACKSON. Mentions if Geo. BEABOR buys
certain land of Peter HAIRSTIN. Executors: Thomas JESSOP and
Jacob HORTON. Witnesses: Jonathan JESSOP, Shadrack (X)
McKINNEY, and Jane (X) CHILDRESS. Signed: Joseph JESSOP.

Page 52. 20 July 1820. Will of Michael FAIR, Senr. Septem-
          ber Term 1820. Daughter Jane, Negro girl child
(not named). Sons Michael FAIR and John FAIR and wife Mary
Ann, balance estate divided among my six children. Executors:
R. Crawford FAIR, son and wife Mary Ann. Witnesses: G. FULP
and William FULP. Signed: Michael (X) FAIR.

Page 53. 4 June 1820. Will of Frederick KRIEGER. Septem-
          ber Term 1820. Wife Mary, Negro boy (not named).
Children: Sally, Mary, Susanna, Anna Philipina, Isaac,
Nathaniel, Abraham, and Emanuel. Executors: Wife Mary and
Joseph HELSABECK, Jr. Witnesses: Martin HOLDER and Jacob
CONRAD. Signed: Frederick KRIEGER.

Page 54. 10 February 1815. Will of Sarah BARTLEY. Septem-
          ber Term 1820. "Bed and furniture belong to
whichever child in whose house I die." Four daughters (not
named here). Be buried at burying ground where my first
husband Leonard MOSER is burried and give Executors $10.00
for stones for him and me. Children: Sarah VOLK, Peter
MOSER, Francis MOSER, Christian MOSER, Henry MOSER, Michael
MOSER, John MOSER, Ann Mary WOLFF, Elizabeth HESS, and
Christina GEIGER. Executors: Henry MOSER and Peter MOSER.

Witnesses: George BOOZE, Jurat and John BOOZE. Signed: Sarah (X) BARTLY.

Page 55. 3 November 1819. Will of Richard CLAMPETT. September Term 1820. Wife Elizabeth, lifetime estate. Sons: John, Ezekiah, George, and William. Daughter Dinah BEESON. Sons Mathias and Richard. Daughter Elizabeth TALLEY. Executors: Wife Elizabeth and son John. Witnesses: Thomas ARNET, John HENLEY, Jurat and Elizabeth HENLEY. Signed: Richard (X) CLAMPET.

Page 56. 18 March 1820. Will of Aaron McCARTER. December Term 1820. Wife Lydia, all my estate. Daughters Elizabeth and Jane "part plantation belonging to them I have no claim on???" To Charles CHRISTMANN, Reubein BURCHAM, Shadrack McKINNA and Tyre GATESBY (?). Son Henry, a deed to my land. Executor: Son Henry. Witnesses: Joshua COX, 3rd. and Thomas SHIPP. Signed: Aaron McCARTER.

Page 57. 4 November 1820. Will of Johanna HOLDER. March Term 1821. Spinster of Salem. Legacies of wearing apparel and kerchiefs, etc. to: Rebecca, Polly, Nancy, and Matilda LINEBACK; Henry HOLDER'S children: Henry and Mary; Jacob and Henry LINEBACK; Henry, Joseph, John, Rebecca and Mary HOLDER (children of George HOLDER, deceased); Rebecca LINEBACK (daughter of Joseph); Johanna SPACH. Executors: Joseph LINEBACK, brother-in-law who is to pay all debts and funeral expense and what is left to he and wife Elizabeth. Witness: Charles F. BAGGE. Signed: Johanna (X) HOLDER.

Page 58. 4 February 1821. Will of Peter MOSER. March Term 1821. All the apparel which my deceased wife Margaret brought with her, etc. My child Mary MOSER (when she becomes 18 years old). Daughter Rebecca MOSER, spinning wheel. Daughter Catherine SHOUSE for her nursing said daughter Mary after her mother's decease. Mentions "all my children." Executors: Henry and Peter MOSER, sons. Witnesses: Adam GIEGER (KIGER) and G. SHOBER. Signed: Peter (X) MOSER.

Page 59. 10 January 1821. Will of David CREWS. March Term 1821. Wife Sarah, all my land, etc. after decease my wife estate divided among my children (not named). Executor: Isaac STANLEY. Witnesses: Thomas ARNETT, Jurat and John (X) PATTISON. Signed: David CREWS.

Page 60. 11 May 1820. Will of Elijah WICKER. March Term 1821. Wife Barbara, all property she sees cause to take; any left to be divided between Barbara and my children (not named). Son Moses WICKER, my saddle and rifle gun. Executors: Tally WICKER and wife Barbara. Witnesses: G. LINVILL and Moses LINVILL. Signed: Elijah WICKER.

Page 61. 22 December 1820. Will of George SPRINKLE. March Term 1821. Wife (not named), lifetime estate. Sons George, Michael and Jesse. Mentions each of my girls when marry, but does not name them. Mentions when youngest

64

child come of age, but does not name same. Executors:
beloved wife (not named) and Thomas SPRINKLE. Witnesses:
Frederick WARNER and Owen TATE. Signed: George (X) SPRINKLE.

Page 62. 7 December 1820. Will of Julianna HINE (HEIN).
March Term 1821. Legacies apparel and small
items, etc. To John Peter HINE (son of my late brother
Peter); Samuel Benjm. HINE (son of my brother Henry). My
Mother Julianna Catharine HEIN. Brother Henry HEIN, my
share of my father's land in Friedland settlement. Sisters:
Christina SCHULTZ, Catherina HEIN, Mary HOLDER and Susan
REXTRA (possible early spelling surname RAKESTRAW). To Mary
HEIN (wife of my brother Henry); John HEIN (chest); Maria
Rebecca HOLDER (daughter of my sister Mary); Louisa HAUSER
(Lorenz's daughter). Executor: John HEIN of Bethabra,
friend. Witnesses: Henry HINE and John (X) SANDERS.

Page 64. 28 March 1815. Will of Maria Salome HESSLER
(translated). June Term 1821. Daughter Maria
Salome SCHAUB, household furniture. Son Christian NISSEN,
household furniture; items to his wife (not named). To
Johanna Elizabeth FRIES. No Executor named. Witnesses:
Wilh. FRIES and Carl Gottlieb CLAUDER. Signed: Maria Salome
HESSLER.

Page 65. 27 February 1813. Will of John JAMES. June Term
1821. Wife Hannah, Negro woman Ellin and her
child Edmund. Eight children: William Cary JEAMES; John
Beiley JEAMES; Thomas JEAMS, Cary JEAMES; Joseph JEAMES,
Martha LOVE, Mary MERRITT, and Sary POINDEXTER. Executors:
John G. POINDEXTER, Joseph JEAMES, and Samuel KINNEMAN.
Witnesses: Samuel KINNAMON and Charles VEST. Signed: John
JAMES.

Page 67. 22 April 1821. Will of Henry SPAINHOUR. June
Term 1821. Son Jacob, land and Still. Wife
Louise, lifetime claim; at death divided amongst all rest my
children (not named). Executors: Jacob SPAINHOUR, son and
Joseph SPAINHOUR, friend. Witnesses: Thomas SMITH, Peter
FULK, and John (X) FULK, Junr. Signed: Henry SPAINHOUR.

Page 68. 17 May 1820. Will of Jhon SHOUSE (SCHAUSS).
September Term 1821. Wife Mary, my land and
tennaments until Son David reaches age of freedom, then land
goes to David. Executor: Friend William BECK. Witnesses:
John L. HAUSER, Jurat and Robert (X) PRATT. Signed: Jhon
(X) SHOUSE.

Page 69. 25 December 1819. Will of John CONNELL. September
Term 1821. Wife Dinah, to live on land and not
sell it and at her death to descend to Daughter Anne SCOTT
and heirs of her body. To wife, Negroes Jenny and her
eldest son Isham and her daughters Chany, Haly and Juda.
Executor: Son-in-law Stephen SCOTT. Witnesses: Jo. VENABLE,
J. KERBY, Thos. SMITH, and F. KERBY. Signed: John (X)
CONNELL.

Page 70. 17 May 1821. Will of Henry HAUSER. September

Term 1821. Son Henry, upper half land I bought of
James FRANKLIN (Jacob CONRAD, merchant, made deed); also
Negro Patsy. Son Frederic, lower half above land. Son
George, land bought of Geo. HAUSER, Esq. adjoining John NULL
on which said George now lives; also Negro Dick. Daughter
Gertraut (now lawful wife of Jacob SCHEMEL). Daughter Mary,
plantation where I live. Wife Ann Mary, choice household
furniture, etc. Negro Jacob to be sold at private sale and
he be permitted to chose a master. My four children by my
first wife: Anna (wife of Valentine BOECKEL); Christina
(wife of Philip ROTHROCK); Elizabeth and John. Executors:
George and Henry HAUSER, sons and Jacob CONRAD, merchant.
Witnesses: Christian LASH, Jurat, Wm. A. LASH, and Wm.
HUNTER. Signed: Heinrick HAUSER.

Page 73. 7 April 1815. Will of Thompson SMITH. September
Term 1821. My five sons: Eleazer, Jacob, Moses,
Thompson and John, 290 acres land where I now live. Wife
Rachel, my dwelling house and she live on plantation lifetime.
My four daughters: Martha, Mary, Leah, and Rachel (with above
named sons), equal shares remaining estate. Executors: Wife
Rachel and Sons Eleazer and Moses. Witnesses: John SHIELD
and John SELL, Jurat. Signed: Thompson SMITH.

Page 74. 15 January 1822. Will of Gottlieb RANK (RANCK).
March Term 1822. Wife Mary, residue estate after
expenses. Mentions "my share Bethany Mill be sold; town lott
in Bethany (Bethania); land in Stokes and Rockingham
Counties. Executors: Wife Mary and Abraham LASH. Witnesses:
Joseph STOCKBURGER, R. HAUSER, Christian GRABS, and Solomon
TRANSOU. Signed: Gottlieb (X) RANK (RANCK).

Page 76. 10 May 1821. Will of Henry STOLTZ. March Term
1822. Wife Sarah, house and household furniture.
Son Philip, 100 acres where I live. Mentions "when my
Yonkis child comes of age." To Anny MILLER, $50.00. Men-
tions when son James comes of age. Children: Philip, Henry,
Sally, Nancy, William and James, Shire and shire alike.
Son Daniel, a bond I have on him $200.00 to be collected and
pay rest of the childring equal that as to say Lesabeth,
Caty, Susana, Markrat, and Jacob. Executors: Chasper
STOLTZ, and son Philip STOLTZ. Witnesses: John CONRAD and
Nancy (X) STOLTZ. Signed: Henry STOLTZ.

Page 77. 6 May 1822. Will of Ann KELLUM. June Term 1822.
All estate I am entitled to by will of my beloved
husband, deceased, to my sister Rachel RIGHT. Executor:
John C. LOVE. Witnesses: Coleman JENKINS and Martha MARTIN.
Signed: Ann (X) KELLUM.

Page 78. 18 December 1818. Will of Sally SISK. June Term
1822. Son Berry, all estate and act as Executor.
Witnesses: Wm. MOORE, Elijah (X) NELSON, and Ettil (X)
BOHANNON. Signed: Sally (X) SISK.

Page 79. 4 April 1822. Will of James YOUNG. June Term
1822. Wife Sarah, one-third part estate including
dwelling place where I live. Four daughters: Elizabeth

JOYCE (wife of Wm. JOYCE); Mary AINSWORTH (wife of James AINSWORTH); Martha STEPHENS (wife of Peter STEPHENS); Sarah JOYCE (wife of John JOYCE). Sons James and Jesse YOUNG. Remainder estate divided equally between sons and daughters. Executors: Jesse YOUNG and William JOYCE. Witnesses: Joseph CLOUD, Lemuel JOYCE, and William JOYCE. Signed: James YOUNG.

Page 80. 10 May 1821. Will of John MARTIN. June Term 1822. Wife Nancy, lifetime estate; four Negroes Edd, Ben, Frank, Sarah. Daughter Poley C. BYNAM, Negro Luse and $150 Hampton BYNAM owes me. Daughter Elizabeth HARRIS, Negro girl Mary. Son James, land he lives on; Negroes Yam and Peter. Son Joseph, land on Peters Creek adjoining Benj. COOMER and Ben BEAZLEY. Son John, balance land he and James live on adjoining Mallory SMITH; Negroes Anthony, Seal and her 4 children (not named). Son Samuel ½ value 640 acres in Jackson County, Tennessee; 2 Negroes Bob and Winney; household furniture. Son George, other half land in Jackson County, Tennessee; 3 Negroes Brice, Lillie and Cugger. Son Thomas, land adjoining my land I live on and Quaker Meeting House; also tract adjoining Timothy ROARK, Jacob PEARCE, Zebulan VAUGHN near Springfield Meeting House; Negroes Haston, Edy, Bet, and Ben. Son William Gilham MARTIN, balance land I live on on Double Creek and Little Yadkin adjoining Judith ROARK; Negro Harden, Frank and Sarah. Grandchildren: John Martin CLOUD, Maryann CLOUD and Jorameliza (female) CLOUD be educated at descretion of son, James MARTIN. To John Martin CLOUD, Negro boy Sanders; Maryann, girl Gin; Jorameliza, girl Bet. (This will stops at this point with etc, etc, etc...the original was checked in the State Archives in Raleigh, North Carolina. It also stops in the same manner, no Executors, witnesses or signatures).

Page 82. 17 August 1821. Will of John HARTMAN, Senr. June Term 1822. Wife Catherine, personal estate. Son Daniel, 50 acres off my present dwelling place. Two daughters Elizabeth and Catharina, remaining part dwelling place equally. Children: George, John, Jacob, Elizabeth, Daniel and Catharina, remainder estate divided equally. Executor: son George HARTMAN. Witness: F.C. MEINUNG. Signed: John (X) HARTMAN (Senr.).

Page 83. 7 May 1822. Will of Daniel CHRISTMANN. June Term 1822. My Mother, Johanna CHRISTMANN, $200.00. Brother Jacob, working tools, cross cut saw. Brother Thomas, rifle gun. Sisters: Phillipina SOMERS, Christina and Sabina CHRISTMANN; Anny TRANSOU and Dorotha CHRISTMAN, Silver, money and a desk. Brother-in-law J. CHRISTMANN, $12.00. Executor: Jacob CHRISTMANN, brother. Witness: Abraham STEINER, Junr. Signed: John Daniel CHRISTMANN.

Page 84. 7 January 1822. Will of William CHILDRESS, Senr. September Term 1822. Wife Anne, lifetime claim plantation. Son William, Negro boy Isaac. Daughter Elizabeth WILLIAMSON, Negro woman Jane and her two sons Lewis and Jacob; half my improvement where I live adjoining George BOAZE and Joel TANNER and Lucy CHILDRESS. Son Benjamin (deceased), land on which his widow now lives, 50 acres.

Grandsons: William, Joseph and Samuel (sons of my son Jesse), land; Negro boy Harry. Daughter Nancy, Negro girl Judah during Nancy's life; then to her daughter Elizabeth. Daughter Sally, Negro Beck her lifetime; then to her daughter Nancy. Daughter Susannah, Negro girl Rachel. Mentions old Negro woman Beck and old man Frank be sold; Beck allowed to choose her master among my children. Executors: John STONE and Solomon SPAINHOUR. Witnesses: David SPAINHOUR, Jurat, Elisha CHILDRESS, and George BOOSE, Jurat. Signed: William CHILDRESS.

Page 85. 21 July 1822. Will of Maria BELLING of Salem.
        September Term 1822. Father, Godfrey of Sheneck, Pennsylvania, my whole estate. No Executor named. Witnesses: John C. BLUM, Jurat and Abraham STEINER. Signed: Maria BELLING.

Page 86. 1 October 1821. Will of Henry MAAS, Senr.
        September Term 1822. Sons Henry and Horatio, 120 acres where I live and nothing more. Other personal property and Negroes (not named) be sold and equally divided among my other 7 children: Peter, William, Elizabeth JONES (wife of John JONES), Melca, Sally, Polly, and Lucy. Executor: John LINEBACK of Salem. Witnesses: C.F. BAGGE, Jurat and Chr. REICH. Signed: Henry (X) MAAS, Senr.

Page 87. 12 May 1815. Will of John Christian SMITH.
        September Term 1822. Wife Elizabeth, my present homeplace for lifetime; then sold and divided equally between my 5 children: Mary Elizabeth, Ann Sophia, Catharine Elizabeth, John Henry and Benjamin Solomon. Mentions note due Abigail and Mary CLAYTON dated 22 September 1814 for $60.00 be paid out of my estate. To William SNOW, $1.00 and no more. Executors: John HOLLAND and Fredric MEINUNG. Witnesses: Henry R. HERBST, Jurat, Samuel STOTZ, and M. RIGHTS. Signed: John Christian SMITH.

Page 88. 3 June 1813. Will of William DOBSON, Senr.
        December Term 1822. Wife Martha, 280 acre plantation I live on by name "Shepperd's Hill" her lifetime; also Negroes Peter and Dicey and Jeremiah. Son Henry Baker DOBSON, plantation death of wife, my silver headed cane. Son William Polk DOBSON, $200.00. Granddaughters Pattsey (daughter of son Henry) and Pattsey (daughter of son William). Executor: Son Henry Baker DOBSON. Witness: Archibald CAMPBELL. Signed: William DOBSON (Senr.).

Page 89. 5 July 1821. Will of John Jacob SPAINHOUR.
        December Term 1822. Son Joseph, My Still, hogsheads, Barrels, Casks and cooling tubs. Children of my son Jacob, deceased (not named), money. Son David, 250 acres where I live; blacksmith tools; household furniture, etc. Daughter Barbara and her 3 children: Charity, Leaney and William H. RITTER, 100 acres land I purchased of Henry BANISTER; Negro Jim as long as she remains a widow; at her marriage or death Negro Jim be sold to one of my children. Daughter Margaret DAUB, already received $200.00, etc. Daughter Rebecca LINEBACK, 250 acres known as Alejah GLOVERS

old place. Grandchild: Susanna (daughter of my daughter
Franky), 100 acres adjoining David SPAINHOUR and Fredr.
WOOLFS. Remainder estate sold and divided equally except my
daughter Franky BOROTH in consequence money advanced to her
daughter Susana by Susana's father (not named). Executors:
Sons Joseph and Solomon SPAINHOUR. Witnesses: William
CHILDRESS, Junr. and Elisha CHILDRESS. Signed: (In German
also) in English, John Jacob SPAINHOUR.

Page 91. 9 June 1822. Will of Mildred COX, Junr. December
      Term 1822. To all my brothers and sisters (not
named), $1.00 each. To Jane C. BOULDING, (daughter of
Thomas BOULDING), residue of my property. Executor: William
JOYCE. Witnesses: Reuben HUGHES, Sarah (X) SIMMONS, and
William JOYCE. Signed: Mildred (X) COX.

Page 92. 10 October 1818. Will of George WILLARD. December
      Term 1822. Wife Susannah, my home plantation
where I live her lifetime. Children: Elizabeth, Catharine,
George, Mary, John, Ann, Margaret, Barbara, Jude and Hannah,
$1.00 each; Susanna, feather bed, cow, etc. Four youngest
sons: Jacob, Daniel, Solomon, and Joseph, all my land
equally divided. Executors: Wife Susanna and son Daniel.
Witnesses: Jacob WILLARD and John FRASER. Signed: George
(X) WILLIARD.

Page 93. 20 February 1819. Will of Henry LANDMANN of Salem.
      March Term 1823. To all children my late wife
brought to me by marriage, towit: Peter TRANSU, Ben TRANSU,
Eln TRANSU (now wife of John H. SENSEMAN) and my daughter
Mary LANDMANN, share and share alike all estate by me owned.
Executors: Josiah BONER and John C. BLUM. Witnesses: Thomas
and C. David WOHLFAHRT (WELFARE). Signed: Henry LANDMANN.

Page 94. 27 September 1822. Will of Joseph MENDENHALL.
      March Term 1823. Wife Elizabeth, her riding mare,
etc. and support out of plantation as long as she remains
my widow. Five daughters: Pheba WILLIAMS, Sarah HAULEY,
Rebecka WESNER, Elizabeth WESNER and Mary HAULEY, $150.00
each. Son Jonathan (take due care of his mother), residue
of my estate. Executors: Wife Elizabeth and son Jonathan.
Witnesses: Nathan PIKE and John PATTERSON. Signed: Joseph
MENDENHALL.

Page 96. 3 May 1821. Will of Thomas COOK. March Term 1823.
      To Friend William BOLES, Junr., 11 Negroes:
Phillis, Cato, Sydner, Harry, Maria, Sam, Albea, Esther,
Mereman, Anthony and Lubendo; also residue of my estate.
Executor: Alexander BOLES, Senr. Witnesses: Thomas REDDICK,
Elijah REDDICK, and Sally (X) REDDICK. Signed: Thomas (X)
KOOK.

Page 97. 8 March 1813. Will of Benjamin KELLY. June Term
      1823. Son Canada, land North ferry road. Wife
Susany, land South ferry road and personal property. Son
Jacob, land South ferry road at death of wife. Three
daughters: Lydda, Heaster and Sarah, residue property.
Executor: Son Canada KELLY. Witnesses: Joseph MILLER and

Esther KELLY. Signed: Ben (X) KELLY.

Page 98. 20 January 1823. Will of Isaac DOUTHET. June
        Term 1823. Son George, plantation and lands he
now holds. Son Benjamin, home plantation. Heirs of Philip,
deceased: George and Anny, plantation where their Father
formerly resided. Sons George and Benj., my part of Mill in
partnership between myself and heirs of Joseph BLAKE,
deceased. Daughter Elizabeth DOUTHERT, $3.00 and household
furniture. To Margaret DOUTHET, 10 shillings. Executors:
George and Benjamin DOUTHIT, sons. Witnesses: Thomas PADGET,
Jr. and Jacob FREY. Signed: Isaac DOUTHIT.

Page 100. 3 March 1823. Will of Philip SNIDER. June Term
        1823. "I am hastening on to the grave." Wife
Elizabeth, land. Son David, notes on Henry and Christian
FULK, Daniel FISHE; also farm tools, etc. so they can
maintain my wife Elizabeth. Daughters: Mary Magdalane FISHEL
and Mary HOUGHMAN and Anny SNIDER and Sally SNIDER and Lesa
LINEBACK and Caty SNIDER, $4.00 each and cow each. Execu-
tor: Son David SNIDER. Witnesses: Chesly ROBERSON, Jurat
and Elizabeth (X) ROBERSON. Signed: Philip (X) SNIDER.

Page 101. 1 September 1823. Will of Mary Ann FARE. Septem-
        ber Term 1823. To John FARE, 100 acres taken off
home tract including plantation and house where he now lives
agreeable to Will of his father, Michael FARE, deceased.
Son Robert Crawford FARE, ½ my homestead tract where he is
now living when John's 100 acres is laid off. Son Barnabas
FARE, 80 acres Lick Creek adjoining John QUILLIN; ½ household
furniture. Son Wm. Dobson FARE, ½ homestead tract where I
live when he arrives age 21; ½ household furniture. Daugh-
ters: Mary (wife of William ROBENSON), $50.00; Elizabeth
FARE, money, etc. when she arrives 18 years; Mary Ann FARE,
gullied pitcher and mug when she arrives age 18 years.
My Sister Elizabeth DOBSON. Mentions her 3 children, Wm.
DOBSON, Elizabeth and Mary Ann. Executor: Son Robert
Crawford FARE. Witnesses: Thos. CAMPBELL, George FULP, Sr.,
Jeremy BARKHERSTT, and Henry B. DOBSON. Signed: Mary Ann
FARE.

Page 104. (No date). Will of Martha LOFLEN, late from
        Greenville County, Virginia, but now removed to
Stokes County, North Carolina, Snow Creek with my beloved
daughter Martha MARTIN, wife of James MARTIN, Senr. Son
Edmund LOFLIN, my riding mare that he drove me to her in a
little four wheeler waggon; also furniture I left in my
house in Virginia. To son Edmund and daughter Martha MARTIN,
my linen, stock, household furniture, etc. left at house of
my unkind son-in-law, William STURDIVANT, Greenville County,
Virginia, which they refused to give up when I came away.
Mentions rent from Old Plantation in Virginia rented to Mr.
Thomas SPENCER. Executors: Martha MARTIN, daughter and
son-in-law James MARTIN, Sr. Witness: Mary ROGERS. Signed:
Martha (X) LOFLEN.

Page 106. 14 February 1822. Will of Justina GRAFF, Salem.
        December Term 1823. Legacies of clothing, etc.

70

to: Niece, Johannah Maria COOPER; Sister Ann Johanna KUSCHKE;
Charles COOPER (son of Johannah Maria); Hannah SPACH; Mary
SMITH; Charlotte SHULTZ; Charles COOPER and Delia COOPER;
Maria BELLING; Christina, Christian and Dorothy SPAUGH;
Maria STEINER and Dorothy WARNER. Executor: Abraham EBERT,
Senr. Witness: John Jacob BLUM, Jurat. Signed: Justina GRAFF.

Page 107. 23 August 1823. Will of William CRAIG, Salem.
            December Term 1823. Mentions specified articles
in enclosed papers to Lewis (Ludwig) BENZINE (BENZIEN), all
other estate to Mr. Jacob BLUM, merchant for his fatherlike
treatment during "my long indesposition." Executors:
Matthew RIGHTS and Wm. Lewis BENZINE (BENZIEN). No witness.
Signed: William CRAIG.

Page 108. 5 August 1823. Will of John TEAGUE. December
            Term 1823. Wife Martha and children: William;
Elizabeth BODENHAMER; Ann EVANS; Phebe BEDENHAMER; Lydia
WELBORN; Abigail HARVEY; Polly CHARLES; and Esther BODEN-
HAMER, share and share alike. Grandchildren (not named),
children of my deceased daughters Rebeckah ROBERSON and Hulda
CHARLES. Granddaughter Rebecca ROBERSON who I have raised
in my family, furniture and mare at marriage or when she
reaches age 18 years. Daughter Peggy HARVEY, wife Martha's
legacy if Martha marries, etc. Executors: Son William
TEAGUE and son-in-law Paris HARVEY. Witnesses: Jonathan
MANLOVE and Moses SMITH. Signed: John TEAGUE.

Page 110. 14 May 1818. Will of Christopher REICH, Salem.
            March Term 1824. Children Philip, Jacob,
Catharine, Emanuel, Louisa, Henry and Henrietta REICH,
several hundred dollars each when reach age 16 or marry.
Sister Verona REICH, $50.00. Wife Catharine, interest from
money left 7 children until they reach age; also all copper
on hand not worked up and all tools of the Coppersmith trade;
my house and lot in Salem, household furniture. Son Phillip,
100 acres waters Little Yadkin purchased of Benj. WINSTON
1805. Executors: Jacob and Christian BLUM. Witnesses: C.F.
BAGGE and Isaac BONER. Signed: Christopher REICH.

Page 111. 28 November 1817. Will of Henry BLUM, living
            near Salem. March Term 1824. Wife Catharine,
54 acres adjoining lands Lewis SCHWEINITZ and Joseph WATERSON;
also my improvement on lease from Samuel STOLZ (STOTZ).
Daughter Christina Elizabeth, $100.00. Mentions at death of
wife, all estate to above daughter and all my children (not
named). Executor: John Jacob BLUM. Witnesses: Matthew
RIGHTS and Henry B. HERBST. Signed: Henry BLUM.

Page 113. 17 November 1823. Will of John Adam HENNING.
            March Term 1824. All perishable estate to be
sold. Wife Elizabeth to remain in house and Plantation
with children (not named) under age and until youngest son,
Gabriel, becomes of age. To Daughter Katharine's children:
Rachel and Elizabeth, $5.00 each. Executors to manage
estate of daughter Katharine for her. Children: Mary Anna
(wife of Peter KLINE); Christina Magdaline (wife of Peter
HUFFMAN); Katharine, Simon, Michael, Susanna (wife of Joseph

SAILOR); Christian; Adam; William; Gabriel; Anna and Sally
"according to age." Executors: Son Adam HENNING, Joseph and
Michael DOUB. Witnesses: William DOUB, Jacob SPAINHOWER,
Jurat and William JEAN. Signed: John A. (X) HENNING.

Page 116.   12 February 1815. Will of Christian HEINZE of
            Salem. March Term 1824. To Christian Thomas
PFOHL in Bethania for use of his children, my bed clothing
and linen. To Samuel Thomas PFOHL in Salem, my Godchild,
Watch and Silver Knee buckles. To five Children of Revnd.
Christian Thomas PFOHL: Thodore Christian, Gottlieb Benjamin,
Dorothea Elizabeth, Charlotte Frederecca, and Carolina Sophia,
hard money each. To my Godchild Traugott Theophilus VIERLING
of Salem, hard money. To Society of United Brethrens for
furtherance of Gospel, $10.00. To Susanna Elizabeth STOTZ
of Salem, $10.00. Executors: Worthy friend Samuel STOTZ and
John Jacob BLUM, merchant. Witnesses: Gottlieb REICHEL and
Magnus HULTHIN. (No signature recorded). . . .
We, Matthew RIGHTS and John C. BLUM, Esq. appointed to
translate the meaning, sense and construction of last Will
of Christian HEINZE from German to English language, certify
the foregoing the true meaning, etc. Signed: John C. BLUM
and M(atthew) RIGHTS.

Page 117.   14 May 1822. Will of John BLAKE, Senr.   June
            Term 1824. Son John, plantation on where I live;
balance of estate divided equally between Children: Nancy,
Polly, Thomas, John, and Phanah. Executors: Sons Thomas
and John BLAKE. Witnesses: Jacob HOLDER, George DOUTHIT,
and Benjamin DOUTHIT. Signed: John BLAKE, Senr.

Page 118.   23 July 1823. Will of Isaac DALTON. June Term
            1924. Wife Susannah, plantation where I live,
waters Oldfield Creek by name James' old place, 415 acres
including 73 acres around Mt. Tabor Meeting House; at her
death or marriage to go to my Brother, David. Also to
wife following slaves: Simon, Lewis, Easter and her two
children Anthony and Tine, Aggy, Pleasant, Bob, Stephen, Mary,
Dier, Patsy, Andrew, Hannah, Burwell, Phebe, Moll, Queen, Joe,
Anna, Violet, Paulina, Stephen, Henry, Sarah, Philip and Ben;
Also $4,000.00. Nephew Madison DALTON, Negro called
Blacksmith Sam, desk, gun. Mentions estate my Brother
Jonathan DALTON, deceased. Nephew Isaac DALTON, clock.
Brother David DALTON, 2 guns, rifle, silver watch; Books:
John MILLS' Treatise on Cattle, Hervey's Meditations, Life
and Travels of Lorenzo DOW, Young Sheppard's Guide, small
Prayer Book, Potter's Justice, Sherriden's Dictionary and
Methodist Magazine; also Bank Stock. Wife Susanna, Books:
Family Bible and Hymn Book, Walter SELLON'S Family Advise
Experience of Herter and Rogers(?), Watt's Hymns, Methodist
Discipline and Grounds of a Holy Life. Nephew, John F. CARR
$500.00 cash and $250.00, my navigation stock. Niece Nancy
LADD, $500.00 cash. To Francis CARTER and Absalom BOSTICK,
Jr., money in consequence death of Negro I sold to Charles
DALTON. Sister Elizabeth CARR, Bank stock, mentions her
children. Executors: Wife Susannah and brother David DALTON.
Witnesses: Willis PILKENTON, David WESTMORELAND, and
Christian HUCHLN (?). Signed: Isaac DALTON.

CODICIL: 6 May 1824. Names Absalom BOSTICK, Junr. as
        Nephew. Witnesses: Willis PILKENTON and Salathiel
STONE. Signed: Isaac DALTON.

Page 122. (No date of will). Will of Alexander BOLES, Senr.
        September Term 1824. Wife Sally, maintenance
from my estate her lifetime. Two daughters Isabella
RUTLEDGE and Judith KISER. Two sons Benjamin and Alexander,
balance of my land, Negroes (not named), stock, household
furniture, etc. (This will ends thusly-).

Page 122. 18 June 1824. Will of Lorentz SIDES (SEITZ).
        September Term 1824. Brother George, the debts
he owes me. Brother-in-law Samuel PHILLIPS, debts he owes
me. Brother Michael (deceased) Heirs, Frances SIDES and
Justina SHOAB (wife of Christopher SHOUB), $4.00 each.
Brother Phillip, $8.00. Sister Anna LASH (wife of Christian
LASH), $8.00. Sister Caty FLYIND (FLYNN(T)), $8.00. Sister
Margaritha MILLER, $8.00. Brother John, all my personal
property. Executor: brother John SIDES. Witness: s. KERNER.
Signed: Lorenz SIDES (SEITZ).

Page 123. 20 December 1822. Will of Gabriel WAGGONER.
        September Term 1824. Wife Mary, land I live on;
Negroes Phill, Vina, Harriet, Hannah, Jeremiah; also Hannah
I bought of Francis CARTER. Daughter Nancy WAGGONER, 400
acres at my wifes death. Grandchildren, Mary BLACKBURN and
Gabriel Waggoner BLACKBURN, remainder land. Daughter
Elizabeth WAGGONER, deceased, property she died possessed of
to go to above Nancy. Daughter Wineford BLACKBURN, share
with above Nancy. Executors: John HOLLAR of Salem, and Geo.
FULP, Senr. of Blews Creek. Witnesses: He. MAGEE, Senr. and
Benjamin BRIGGS. Signed: Gabriel WAGGONER.

Page 124. 10 July 1824. Will of Jeremiah BEAZLEY. Septem-
        ber Term 1824. Wife (not named), land where I
live, 259 acres Dan River. Son John, above at death of wife.
All my children (not named) except John, balance estate.
No Executor named. Witnesses: Presley (X) GEORGE, Malkejah
FRANCIS, Joseph FRANCIS, and James LYON. Signed: Jeremiah
(X) BEAZLEY.

Page 124. 25 July 1824. Will of Sarrah JONES. September
        Term 1824. Sister Elizabeth PITTS, pewter and
my side saddle. Nieces Elizabeth and Sarah JONES, pewter.
To Patsy PHILLIPS. Sister-in-law Mary JONES. Brother
Benjamin, what I was devised by my father's will. Executor:
Brother Benjamin JONES. Witnesses: Ezekial TEAGUE and
Isaac TEAGUE. Signed: Sarrah (X) JONES.

Page 125. 1 June 1824. Will of Michael ROMINGER. September
        Term 1824. Wife Christina, land and house where
I live. Mentions when all my children reach age 21; does
not name them except leaves half Trist and Saw Mills when
Son, Christian Lewis ROMINGER arrives at age 21. Names
Negroes Jam, Tom and Martha cannot be sold. Mentions 3
minor children (not named). Executors: Sons Christian
Lewis ROMINGER and Joshua ROMINGER. Witnesses: Jacob SHULTZ

and Joseph ROMINGER.   Signed: M. ROMINGER.

Page 127.   1820.   Will of Archibald REYNOLDS.   September
        Term 1824.   Mentions land in town of Vienna, one
tract as Holder land; lots as Chulz (?) land to be sold and
equally divided between 5 daughters and 3 sons: Nancy
REYNOLDS, Sally VOSS, Becky REYNOLDS, Suzan DOUB, Gracett
DOUB, David and Samuel F. REYNOLDS.   Mentions land on
Double Creek bought of Terry CROOK and land bought of Joseph
HOPKINS.   No Executors named.   Witnesses: J. STOCKBERGER,
Henry DOUB, and Elijah HOOPER.   Signed: A. REYNOLDS.

Page 128.   7 December 1749.   Will of Martin Wells MARSHALL.
        December Term 1824.   Sons William and James, 5
shillings each.   Son Richard, working tools and skin covered
trunk.   89¼ acres land to be sold and equally divided amongst
all my children by my last wife (not named) except Richard.
No Executor named.   Witnesses: H. MAGEE, Senr. and Harman
MAGEE, Junr.   Signed: Martin (X) MARSHALL.

Page 128.   7 December 1824.   Will of Joseph SUTTIN.   Decem-
        ber Term 1824.   All stock, plantation utensils,
household furniture to remain in hands of son-in-law Simon
NADING (NODING, NOEDING, NETHING).   Executor: Son-in-law,
Simon NADING.   Witnesses: Jacob MILLER and George NADING.
Signed: Joseph (X) SUTTON.

Page 129.   15 September 1820.   Will of William HEDGECOCK.
        September Term 1824.   Wife Elizabeth, all property
for support of her and children yet under age.   Children:
William, Joseph, Anderson, and Henderson, above divided
equally at death of wife.   Two daughters Milly and Mary,
featherbed and furniture each.   Sons Joshua and Isaac and
Daughter Nancy WILLARD, have already had share.   Executor:
Nathan PIKE.   Witness: Jesse WEISNER.   Signed: William (X)
HEDGECOCK.

Page 130.   1 May 1820.   Will of Jacob KRIEGER "being aged."
        December Term 1824.   Wife Susannah, property I
died possed of during lifetime.   Son John's widow, Mary
Elizabeth KRIEGER, 200 acres on Muddy Creek and Barkers
Creek as long as she is John's widow; land then to go to her
children Solomon, Timotheus (male), and Levinia KRIEGER.
My children: Frederick, John, deceased, Elizabeth SCHULZ,
Catharine CONRAD, and Susannah HELSABECK.   Executors: Henry
SCHULZ and Jacob HELSABECK.   Witnesses: Jacob SHOUSE, Senr.
and Jacob SHOUSE, Junr.   Signed: Jacob (X) KRIEGER.

Page 131.   29 November 1824.   Will of Nancy HITCHCOCK.   March
        Term 1825.   To a daughter of my Daughter Nancy, if
she has one by name of Nancy.   To Susan (daughter of my son
Thomas), linen.   To Nancy (daughter of my son Thomas),
household furniture.   Daughters Nancy and Elizabeth, my
wearing clothes.   Son Thomas, all other property.   Executor:
Son Thomas HITCHCOCK.   Witnesses: John C. LOVE and Robert
WALKER.   Signed: Nancy (X) HITCHCOCK.

Page 132.   24 August 1824.   Nuncupative Will of Ferdinand

BOSTICK. March Term 1825. His wife (not named) keep two Negro girls Jenny and Nelly to help raise the children (not named). Witnesses: David DALTON, Polly (X) COX, and William BLACKBURN. (No signature given).

Page 132. 9 March 1823. Will of William COOK. March Term 1825. Wife Ann, lifetime claim all estate. Son William, above at death of wife. "As I have given all my lawful heirs their porportional part; notwithstanding if Stokes Superior Court should decide in favor of my Brother Thomas COOK, etc..." Executor: Samuel WELSH. Witnesses: Richard (X) SMITH, Sarah (X) SMITH, and Patsey (X) BENNETT. Signed: William (X) COOK.

Page 133. 29 January 1823. Will of John PITTS. March Term 1823. Wife Elizabeth, all household furniture she brought from her fathers; also dwelling house and whole plantation I live on. My 7 children: James, Amelia RITCHFIELD, Martha PEGG, Henry, Andrew, John and Sarah PITTS, residue estate. Executors: Son John and wife Elizabeth. Witnesses: Thomas ARNETT and Andrew PITTS. Signed: John PITTS.

Page 134. 27 June 1823. Will of William (Wilhelm) GRABS, shoemaker. September Term 1823. Sons Christian Henry and John Godtfreed, my interest in lott in Bethania, stock, two Negroes (not named). Two granddaughters of Salem, Gertruat Lizetta SCHUTZ and Dorothea Matilda SCHUTZ (children of my daughter Anna Maria). Executors: Son Gottfreed and Abraham LASH. Witnesses: M.A. LASH and Jacob STOLZ. Signed: William GRABS.

Page 135. 12 February 1825. Will of John FRY. June Term 1825. Wife Polly, 105 acres land on waters Muddy Creek where I live; stock, household furniture, etc. lifetime, if marries, a child's part. My children: (those that was beget by my first wife whose maiden name was Nancy COLLINS): Benjamin, Jane, Delith, Elijah, Gabriel, Thomas, D. Zadon, and Nancy, land coming to me in the Western Country for my service in Revolutionary War. Executor: Wife Polly. Witnesses: Catharine (X) FRY, Thomas FRY, and John WHITWORTH. Signed: John (X) FRY.

Page 136. 28 June 1825. Will of Alexander BILLITER. September Term 1825. Wife Leah, remain on my plantation, etc. Children: Betsy, Jonathan, Dolly, Martha, Lorenzo, and Matthew BILLITER, share and share alike when Matthew comes of age 21. Daughers: Nancy (wife of George LONG) and Anne (wife of David MITCHEL), for their disobedance towards me--only $1.00 each. Executors: Elijah HOOPER and Henry DOUB. Witnesses: Elisha HUNTER and M. DOUB. Signed: Alexander (X) BILLITER.

Page 137. (Not dated). Will of Thomas FLYNT. December Term 1825. Step-son Martin, Negro boy Ben, etc. Step-daughter Polly, Negro girl Sally, etc. Step-son Haston FLYNT'S lawful heirs: Martha, Sally and Susanna, Negro Phill, etc. Step-son Richard, Negro boy Brill, etc. My children: Susanna, Negro Rose, etc; Abijah, Negro Ned, etc.; Sally,

Negro Mourning, etc.; Thomas, Negro Winston, etc.; Nancy, Negro Lucy, etc.; and Joseph, Negro girl Delf, etc. Wife Sally FLYNT, remain on estate. Executors: Martin, Richard, and Thomas FLYNT, Jr., sons. Witnesses: Tandy MATTHEWS and Thomas MARTIN. Signed: Thomas (X) FLYNT (Senr.). . . . Indorsement on back of Will of Thomas FLYNT: 1823, paid son Joseph $50.00; 1824, paid daughter Sally, $30.00; paid Sally HAMPTON sorrel mare and $40.00; 1825, paid Joseph FLYNT, 1 bay mare and $80.00.

Page 138. 12 June 1824. Will of Zachereah BRONSON. December Term 1825. Wife Jane, homeplace, stock, and household furniture until son, Daniel arrives at age 21 years. Two daughters Elizabeth and Jane Lyon BRONSON, 150 acres land. Son Eli, 100 acres land. Daughter Sarah (wife of Enoch HUTCHINS), 50 acres land. Daughter Hannah BRONSON, 55½ acres land. Daughter Sebby BRONSON, 55½ acres land. Daughter Mary (wife of Henry MORRIS), 55½ acres land. Daughter Mahala BRONSON, 40 acres known as Marshall tract. Sons Joab, Eli, and Daniel, my Still with all necessary utensils. Mentions James and Samuel KING paying his estate $120.00 as per Sheriffs sale of their father, Jonus KING, Senr. Executors: Son Joab BRONSON and George FULP, (son of Betsy FULP). Witnesses: D. LINVILL and Allen WHICKER. Signed: Zacheriah BRONSON.

Page 140. 26 October 1825. Will of William WRAY. December Term 1825. Youngest sons Moses and Labon, my old Mill Seat and land around it adjoining John VAWTER. Wife Mary, one third estate. My 8 children (not named). Mentions land sold Nathaniel PHENIX. Executors: Wife Mary WRAY and Joseph CARDWELL. Witnesses: Russel VAWTER, William WILSON, and R.T. VAWTER. Signed: William WRAY.

Page 141. 1 June 1824. Will of John HENSLEY. December Term 1825. Sons William and Henry, Saw and Grist Mills, Blacksmith Shop, etc. Daughter Elizabeth HENSLEY, to have room with fireplace in my dwelling house as long as she liveth unmarried. Mentions lands adjoining Isaac DALTON, Wm. HARGROVE, and Moravian land. No Executor named. Witnesses: William BECK and Christian (X) BECK. Signed: John HENSLEY.

Page 142. 16 February 1824. Will of Philip ROTHROCK. December Term 1825. Wife Eve Elizabeth, use of plantation and dwelling where I live; also Negro woman Rachel and a child (not named). My 9 children: Frederick, E. George, John, Joseph, Phillip, Martin, Christian, and Daniel, equal shares above at death wife. (Share coming to my daughter Eve (wife of Philip SIDES) be put in had of Rev. Mr. SHULTZ at Salem and given her as she needs it and calls for it herself). Executors: Sons, George and Philip ROTHROCK. Witnesses: John LONG and Jacob MILLER. Signed: Philip (X) ROTHROCK.

Page 143. 16 March 1823. Will of John MILLER (MUELLER). March Term 1826. Wife Caty, plantation lifetime. Sons Jacob, Jonathan, and Phillip. My daughter Caty WOLL (WOLLE) to have use plantation lifetime at death me and my wife. Daughter Caty's children: my grandchildren Mahaley, Lucy, Sally, Nancy, and Jonathan WOLLE. Daughters Margaret BARNHAM(N) and Elizabeth WHITSEL. Executors: Sons Jacob and Philip MILLER. Witnesses: John CONRAD and Jacob MILLER. Signed: John (X) MILLER.

Page 144.   22 November 1825.   Will of John DUGGINS.   March Term 1826.   Son Thomas, $28.00 in cash paid to Patsy SOUTHERN.   Daughters Bethany and Jane, bed and furniture, etc.   Son John, one mare.   Daughter Rainey, bed and furniture.   Son Stephen, mare.   Daughter Mary, bed and furniture.   Wife Usly, lands and dwelling lifetime; then divided equally between Thomas, John, and Stephen.   Executors: Wm. A. MITCHELL and Wm. DAVIS.   Witnesses: James DAVIS and Ezekiel (X) HARVY.   Signed: John DUGGINS.

Page 145.   17 November 1825.   Will of John LEDFORD.   March Term 1826.   Sons Bruis and Spruce, part of my land.   Daughter Phebe S., land and Negro boy Ellace, etc. Wife Grizzalah, Plantation, new wagon, Negro girl Dinah. Daughter Martha W., when she comes of age, Negro Rosy Mariah. Daughter Nancy, Negro Sarah.   Son John, my law book. Daughters Rebeckarr, Betsy, Suzzanah, and Grizzalah.   Son William.   Executor: Son John LEDFORD.   No witness.   Signed: John LEDFORD.

Page 146.   4 February 1826.   Will of Joseph RANSOM.   June Term 1826.   By oath of William STEEL who was present with Joseph RANSOM and his wife Mary RANSOM; said Joseph leaves estate to wife Mary lifetime and at Mary's death to go to Granddaughter Nancy RANSOM (daughter of Thomas); after death Joseph, William STEEL was with Mary RANSOM who stated she wanted granddaughter Nancy RANSOM to have her estate.   Signed: H. DOUB, J.P.

Page 147.   6 July 1818.   Will of Laurance (Lorenz) WOLFF. June Term 1826.   Wife Maria Barbara, lifetime estate.   Son of my deceased wife, Hester, who goes by name of Daniel WOLFF, to receive nothing.   Daughter Rebecca, when she becomes 18 years of age.   Executors: Wife Maria Barbara and John BILLITTER.   Witnesses: Lewis WOLFF and Wm. A. WOLFF. Signed: Lorentz WOLFF.

Page 148.   23 March 1826.   Will of Weatherington PRESTON. June Term 1826.   Wife Patsy, plantation where I live; Negro man Lewis and other slaves (not named), etc. her lifetime.   Son Nathaniel (and to his children at his death), 50 acres land, etc; Negro boy Ned.   Son Allen, interest in Saw Mill; Negro girl Levina.   Daughter Elizabeth (wife of Bartlett GRANGER) Negro woman Prenter and child Rhoda. Daughter Sally (wife of Michael FULP), Negro woman Lydia and child Lucy.   Daughter Patsy (wife of Aaron LINVILLE), cupboard, as have given her considerable already.   Daughter Temperance (wife of William BROWN), Negro woman Delphy. Son John, $1.00 as have already given him considerable. Executors: Wife Paty PRESTON and son Allen PRESTON.   Witnesses: D. LINVILLE and A. WHITAKER.   Signed: Weathington PRESTON.

Page 149.   30 December 1925.   Will of Conrad GREEN (KROEHN,
          KROHN).   June Term 1826.   Wife Anna Susanna, 10
acres land, etc. and at her decease to go to John Christian
GAMBOLD; also Negro girl Elsey 10 years old.   Executor:
Wife Anna Susanna.   Witnesses: A. NISSEN and Jacob RIED,
Senr.   Signed: Conrad GREEN.

Page 150.   20 April 1826.   Will of Thomas SCHULTZ (SCHULZ),
          shoemaker, Salem.   June Term 1826.   Legacies of
money to: Andrus BEESING (daughter of my friend Johanna
BOESING); Johanna Elizabeth SHULTZ (daughter of Samuel SHULTZ,
Senr.); Louisa MEINUNG (daughter of Lewis MEINUNG); Edward
ESIG when he becomes of age; Catharine ESSIG (wife of John
ESSIG); Lyea RIECH (daughter of Matthew REICH), my desk;
Dorothea SCHULTZ (daughter of Christian), my watch and chain;
Gertraut SCHULTZ and Wm. F. SCHULTZ and Antnetta Amelia
SHULTZ and to my Mother, Dorothy SHULTZ, balance of my estate.
Executor: Brother, Samuel SHULTZ.   Witness: John Henry SHULTZ.
Signed: Thomas SHULTZ.

Page 151.   9 December 1825.   Will of Henry SHORE (SCHOR).
          September Term 1826.   Son John, $600.00 to pay for
land where he now lives.   Son Jacob, $500.00 to pay for land
where he now lives; also 40 acres, part I now live on.   Son
Thomas, land and plantation where I now live.   Daughters:
Mary SPAUCH (SPACH) (wife of George SPAUGH) and Elizabeth
ROMINGER (wife of Benjamin ROMINGER), 110 acres land in
Davidson County, North Carolina that formerly belonged to
Frederick BICKLE (BOECKEL), deceased.   Mentions son, Thomas
reaching age of 21; mentions slaves (not named) to be sold.
Executors: Son Jacob SHORE and son-in-law George SPAUGH.
Witnesses: Nehemiah COOPER and Gasper TODD.   Signed: Henry
SHORE.

Page 153.   29 February 1815.   Will of Cadwalledder JONES.
          September Term 1826.   Son Benjamin, land I now
live on, etc.   Daughter Sarah, household furniture and house
I bought for her, etc.   Mentions estate divided equally among
my children but does not name them.   Executor: Benjamin
JONES, son.   Witnesses: Isaac and Ezekiel TEAGUE.   Signed:
Cadwalleder JONES.

Page 154.   17 August 1826.   Will of Alexander MOODY. Decem-
          ber Term 1826.   Mentions Germanton tract and
Townfork tract land; slaves be hired out, etc.   Wife Sally,
kitchen furniture and use house and lot where I live.
Children: Nathaniel, Polly, Alexander, Thomas, Anna, and
Sally, residue of my estate be divided equally.   Mentions
children coming of age.   Executors: Wife Sally and son
Nathaniel.   Witnesses: Jesse BANNER and Thomas T. ARMSTRONG.
Signed: Alexander MOODY, (Senr.).

Page 155.   14 October 1824.   Will of Frederick HUTCHENS.
          December Term 1826.   Wife Elizabeth, land where I
live.   Grandson Mark WHITE, property after wifes death.   No
Executors named.   Witnesses: Wm. C. COLE, Wm. EADS, and
Nancy SMITH.   Signed: Frederick (X) HUTCHENS.

Page 157.   24 March 1827.   Will of Michael SPAINHOUR
             (SPOENHAUER), farmer.   June Term 1827.   Wife
Elizabeth, household furniture, etc. and be maintained by
my son, Michael in my dwelling house on my plantation.
Daughter Elizabeth, 40 acres my land received in her husband's
lifetime, which Henry DOUB now owns.   Executors: Son Michael
SPAINHOUR and Michaell DOUB.   Witnesses: Joseph DOUB and
Frederick (X) LONG.   Signed: Michael SPAINHOUR.

Page 158.   30 April 1827.   Will of John PHILIPS.   June Term
             1827.   Wife Colley, money arising from sale of
property coming to me from Samuel CORNELIUS.   Mentions wife
staying on plantation where he lives provided she can get one
of her brothers to manage it; also mentions "children" several
times.   Daughters Agnes and Peggy, when come of age to
receive equally.   Mentions "legacy coming from my Father."
Executors: Henry DOUB and Jonathan W. SHORE.   Witnesses:
John HUNTER, Senr., John HUNTER, and John CORNELIUS.
Signed: John (X) PHILIPS.

Page 160.   31 March 1826.   Will of Paul STARBUCK.   June Term
             1827.   Wife Hephsebah, property she possessed
when I married her; also plantation I live on bought of
Adam SMITH; also other property.   Granddaughter Delfine
SMITH, furniture when she reaches age 18; and if she dies
divided between her four sisters (not named here).   Granddaughters Susannah, Evalind, Mary, and Elizabeth SMITH,
(daughters of my daughter Hephsebah SMITH, deceased), $10.00
each when reach age 18.   Granddaughter Martha STARBUCK and
grandsons James and Salathiel STARBUCK (children of my son
Shubel STARBUCK, deceased), $1.00 each when reach age.
Daughter Eunice SMITH, book debt I have against her husband,
Adam SMITH.   Children: Eunice SMITH; Seth, John, Paul, and
Tristram STARBUCK, my estate equally divided at death of
wife.   Executors: Wife Hephsebah and Asa BARNARD.   Witnesses:
Aaron COFFIN, Phebe COFFIN, and George F. COFFIN.   Signed:
Paul STARBUCK. . . .
CODICIL: 22 October 1826.   Asa BARNARD has moved his family
             out of this State; I appoint Moses COFFIN and my
nephew Seth STARBUCK of Guilford County Executors with my
wife.   Mentions grandchildren and Daughter Eunice SMITH.
Witness: Aaron COFFIN.   Signed: Paul STARBUCK.

Page 162.   22 December 1826.   Will of John THOMASON.   Septem-
             ber Term 1827.   Daughter Sarah, 10 acres east
dwelling house.   Son Pleasant, balance of my land.   Four
daughters: Patsey EASTY, Nancy HARROLDS, Judith HENDRIX, and
Nelly SNIPES, five shillings each.   Executor: Asa BENNET.
Witness: Hugh PATTERSON.   Signed: John (X) THOMASON.

Page 162.   (No date).   Will of Jane FOUNTAIN.   September Term
             1827.   Children: James, Patty GARRISON, Polly
MARSHALL, deceased, Heirs, 5 shillings each.   Son-in-law
Richard MARSHALL, 5 shillings.   Daughter Sally FOUNTAIN,
remainder of my estate.   Executors: Daughter Sally FOUNTAIN
and Thomas FULP.   Witnesses: Harman MAGEE, Archibald (X)
FULP, and Henry MARSHALL.   Signed: Jane (X) FOUNTAIN.

Page 163.   26 August 1825.   Will of Mildred COX.   September
            Term 1827.   Son Isham COX, $1.00.   Three daughters
Franky Anglin, Armin Boulding and Mary Vernon, $1.00.
Granddaughter Polly SIMMONS, bed, furniture and stock.   Son
John COX, ½ residue my estate equally with my daughter Sarah
SIMMONS.   Mentions her Negro women having her wearing clothes.
Executor: John SIMMONS.   Witnesses: Richard C. ALLY and Wm.
JOYCE, Senr.   Signed: Mildred (X) COX.

Page 164.   15 March 1775.   Will of Robert ESTES of Lunenburg
            County, Virginia.   13 April 1775.   Mentions Negroes
and my land where I live and it being same tract whereon
Court House stands, to be sold.   Sons Robert, Elisha, George,
Benjamin, Zachary and Bartlett, take care of my slaves.
Son-in-law Frederick COX, who married my daughter Milley, to
care for my estate.   Mentions Negro boy Sam.   Mentions
maintaining son George's wife and any children she has by
said Geo. if she be yet living (meaning the wife he carried
with him when he left Virginia).   Also mentions wife of sons
Benjamin and Zachary but does not name any of them.   Daughter
Milly, Slaves and her deceased Mother's wearing clothes.
Executors: Son Elisha ESTES and Thomas TABB.   Witnesses:
William GORDON, Wm. GRYMES, and Thomas TABB.   Signed: Robert
ESTES. . . .Note: John SIMMONS was appointed Administrator
of Robert ESTES Will in Stokes County, North Carolina,
September Term 1727.

Page 167.   25 July 1827.   Will of John Frederick BOEHLO
            (BELO), Salem.   September Term 1827.   Wife (not
named) (Maria, Moravian Records).   Children: Edward, Levin,
Lewis, Henrietta, Carolind, Theresea and Louisa (Levin,
Carolind and Louisa under 21), silver items.   Mentions
Executors to sell dwelling and shop and buy smaller house
for wife and children.   Executor: John C. BLUM of Salem.
Witnesses: M. RIGHTS and C.F. BAGGE (Charles Fredr.).
Signed: Frederick BOEHLO (BELO).

Page 168.   3 August (no year).   Will of John C. LOVE.
            December Term 1827.   Wife Flora, raise my
children (not named).   Executors: Son John N. LOVE, Wife
Flora LOVE, and Armstrong MARTIN.   Signed: John C. LOVE.

Page 169.   16 February 1813.   Will of Lewis HOFFMAN.   Decem-
            ber Term 1827.   Wife Ledia, plantation whereon I
live and at her death or marriage to return to my two
daughters, Catherine and Elizabeth.   Sons William and Henry
HOFFMAN.   Mentions undivided money of my brothers Henry and
George HOFFMAN.   Executors: George and Henry HOFFMAN, brothers
and Edward MOORE.   Witnesses: Anthony BITTING and Casper
STOLTZ (STOLZ).   Signed: Lewis (X) HOFFMAN.

Page 170.   24 June 1827.   Will of John SHAMEL (SCHEMEL).
            December Term 1827.   Brothers and sisters: Joseph;
Alizabeth KITNER (KETTNER); George, Jacob, Abram, Peter, and
Mary HAUSER, $1.00 each.   To John SHAMEL (son of Jacob),
$5.00.   To Ann HAUSER (daughter of Henry and Mary), $5.00.
To John Isaac HAUSER and William Henry HAUSER, balance of my
estate when Wm. Henry comes of age.   Executor: Henry HAUSER.

Witnesses: John NATIONS, Peter GRAVES, and William FRANKLIN.
Signed: John SHAMEL (SCHEMEL).

Page 172.   7 July 1827.   Will of Christopher (Christoph)
          VOGLER, Salem.   December Term 1827.   Oldest son
Gottlieb, 84 acres Muddy Creek where I reside which I
bought of Abram ZIGLER.   Son Nathaniel, house where I reside.
Son Timothy, $1,000.00 and new Smith Shop.   Son-in-law
Christian HEGE, $1,000.00 he owes me.   Daughter Palina,
$1,000.00 when she reaches age 18.   Youngest daughter Regina,
$1,000.00 to continue schooling.   Mentions he is presently
having a house built.   Wife (not named), furniture, etc.
Mentions Bank Stock.   All my children: Gottlieb, Nathaniel,
Timothy, Anna Maria (wife of Christian HEGE), Plaulind and
Regina.   Executors: John VOGLER and Christian HEGE, son-in-
law.   Witnesses: Christian G. STAUBER and David LIVENGOOD.
Signed: Christian VOGLER.

Page 175.   14 January 1828.   Will of James BOLES, Senr.
          March Term 1828.   Wife Mary, all estate.   Child-
ren: Alexander, Abel, William, Nancy, Rebecca, and Edward
BOLES, share equally at death of wife.   No Executor named.
Witnesses: John MOORE and David B. TILLEY.   Signed: James
(X) BOLES.

Page 175.   23 April 1828.   Will of William NUNS.   April Term
          1828.   Wife Sally, lifetime estate.   Four sons:
William, Squire, Major and Richard, estate at death of wife,
provided William comes home and discharges duties of a good
boy with his Mother; if not, he is to receive $1.00 with his
sisters Betsy, Martha, Sally, and Nisa who shall have but
$1.00 each.   Son James by my first wife (not named), $1.00.
Executors: Sally NUNS and John SIMMONS.   Witnesses: Edward
COLLINS and William (X) PRUIT.   Signed: William (X) NUNS.

Page 176.   7 September 1826.   Will of Nathaniel LASH, planter.
          March Term 1828.   Perishable estate, land where I
now live with mills and tract adjoining George CARTER and
Nathan CRAFT be sold.   Mentions money due me from Matthew
BROOKS; Negroes be sold except Sandy age 6 and Nancy Minerva,
age 6 and they go to Niece Rebecca LASH, who cared for my
late wife (not named).   To Elizabeth Goodman ANDERSON, an
orphan girl raised by me from an infant, money and household
furniture.   Mentions land in Surry County on Yadkin River
adjoining John CONRAD not to be sold until 1864.   To Mary
Josephine YEATS (formerly Mary Josephine BROOKS), $100.00
in addition to $300.00 worth property already given her.
To Allen, Grace and Andrew BRYANT, $2.00 each and no more.
Balance of estate to be equally divided between nearest legal
heirs except William DRAUGHN, who shall have $2.00 and no
more.   Executors: John C. BLUM and Matthew RIGHTS.   Witnesses:
Jeremiah H. McKENZIE, Philip STOLTZ, and Simon P. HAUSER.
Signed: Nathaniel LASH.

Page 178.   15 September 1827.   Will of Thomas JONES.   June
          Term 1828.   Wife Anna, land where I live.   Sons
Joshua and John, land.   Mentions if wife is delivered of a
boy child within 9 months he is to share land with above sons;

if a daughter two sons to pay her $20.00 when she reaches
age 21. Executor: Abram VANHOY. Witnesses: John M. VANHOY
and Isaac VANHOY. Signed: Thomas JONES.

Page 179. 14 January 1828. Will of Henry KRIEGER. June
Term 1828. Brothers George and Jacob's Heirs,
$1.00 each. Sisters Elizabeth ALBERTINI and Rosina STOLTZ
(STOLZ), $1.00 each. Wife Reghena (Regina) Elizabeth, lend
her my estate during life or widowhood. To John Benj. MILLER,
my wife's son, my estate after death of wife. Executors:
Henry HAUSER, sadler and John Benj. MILLER. Witnesses:
Anthony BITTING and Jacob SHORE. Signed: Henry (X) KRIEGER.

Page 180. 22 March 1828. Will of Dorothea SHULTS (SHULZ).
September Term 1828. Grandchildren Gertraut
and Dorothea SHULZ, $100.00 each; also bed linen, etc.
Sons Samuel and Henry, bed linen and balance of estate.
To Johanna Elizabeth SCHULZ, $100.00. Executors: Sons Henry
and Samuel. Witnesses: F. C. MEINUNG (Frederic C.) and
William FRIES. Signed: Dorothea (X) SHULTS (SCHULZ).

Page 182. 21 March 1828. Will of Matthew RIGHTS, Salem.
September Term 1828. Mentions house I occupy in
Salem and Plantation one mile below Salem adjoining Matthew
REICH. Sons S. Zacharias and Constantine L., division of
land. Daughter Susan Elizabeth, money, etc. Wife Elizabeth,
slaves (not named) and other estate for her maintenance.
Mentions wifes silver; six shares bank Cape Fear Stock; stock
goods and groceries in his store; younger son (not named)
reaching age 12 years. My 3 children: Susanna Elizabeth, S.
Zacharias and Constantine L. To John HAUPLER (?), Salem,
$5.00 and razor. Executors: John H. SUSAMAN and David
KUHLN. Witness: John LIENBACK. Signed: Matthew RIGHTS.

Page 184. 27 June 1828. Will of John L. HAUSER. September
Term 1828. Wife Patsy, plantation and dwelling
house; except REICH tract and all Negroes. Mentions land
bought of John REICH adjoining Henry NULL; also land bought
of John RANK. My six children: Lewis, George, Elizabeth,
Maria Louisa, Martha E. and Nancy Rebecca (wife of Absolum
STOLTS (STOLTZ), share money arising from sale of Negroes at
death of wife. Son Lewis, Negro boy Handy. Executor: William
LASH. Witnesses: Henry (X) HOLDER and Benjamin SHULTS
(SHULTZ). Signed: John L. HAUSER.

Page 186. 17 June 1828. Will of Elizabeth BITTING. September Term 1828. Sister Mary, my plantation; Negro
boy Elias; stock. Mary to give Negro woman Gin a house on
plantation as long as she lives. Sister Martha, Negro Lewis
and household furniture. Brother John, Negro boy Winston.
Brother Anthony, Negro woman Liddie and household furniture.
Nephew Anthony BANNER, 1/3 lot in Germanton adjoining lot my
father left sister Mary. Nephew Walter BITTING, lot in
Germanton. Nephew John Wilkenson BITTING, 50 acres adjoining
my brother Anthony. Niece Elizabeth BITTING, my Beauro (?).
Executors: Brothers John and Anthony BITTING. Witnesses:
Adam GEIGER and Lewis GEIGER. Signed: Elizabeth BITTING.

Page 188.   10 June 1828.   Will of Catharine REICH.   September
            Term 1828.   Son John Philip, $50.00.   Daughter
Catharane CLEWELL, $100.00 and my Forte Piano.   Daughters
Catharine, Louisa and Henretta, wearing clothes.   Son Jacob
to have refusal house and lot in Salem.   Three children:
Louisa, Edward and Henretta, their beds.   All my Children:
John Philip, Jacob, Emanuel, Edward, Catharind, Louisa, and
Henretta.   Executors: Sons John Philip and Jacob.   Witnesses:
Chas. F. BAGGE and John C. BLUM.   Signed: Catharine (X)
REICH.

Page 189.   27 August 1818.   Will of Christina BIBIGHAUS
            (BIEBIGHAUS), Salem.   September Term 1828.
Legacies of personal estate including money to following:
Elizabeth BIBIGHAUS; Charity SNIDER; Christian SPACH; Fredrica
REICHEL; Johanna SPACH; Dorothea WARNER; United Bretharn
Missions Among Heatherns; Mary FISHEL; Christine BRESING
(BROSING); Mary SMITH; Polly GAMBOL; Elizabeth MEINUNG:
Justine GRAFF: Margaretta KRIEGER; Rebecca HOLDER; Susan
PHILIPS; Dorothea KREUSER and each sister who dwells with
me (Moravian Sisters).   Executor: Conrad KREUSER.   Witnesses:
Jacob BLUM and Chas. F. BAGGE.   Signature in German.

Page 191.   22 June 1825.   Will of John GAMBOLD, Missionary
            Among Cherokee Tribe of Indians.   December Term
1828.   Little Godson: David Zeisberger SMITH, my English
Quarte Bible with copper plate printed by Matthew CAREY,
Philadelphia 1801.   Wife Anna Maria (late widow SHULTZ;
formerly GRABBS), my German books, household furniture, etc.
To friend John Renams SMITH, Missionary at Spring Place,
Cherokee Nation, use Mission of United Brethern among
Cherokees Indiana.   To daughters of my wife by her former
marriage, Gertraut Lisette SHULTZ and Dorothea Maria SHULTZ,
$100.00 each.   To four children of my brother Joseph
GAMBOLD: John Frederick, Sophia Elizabeth (now widow HERTEL),
Anna Renigna (wife of Philip SYFRIED ?), and Maria Rosina
GAMBOLD, $75.00 each.   Executors: Wife Anna Maria, John R.
SMITH, and Theodore SHULTZ.   Witnesses: Elijah HICKS and John
ROSS.   Signed: John GAMBOLD.

Page 193.   22 September 1828.   Will of George HAYNES (HANES).
            December Term 1828.   Wife Nancy HANES, plantation
where now live, 41½ acres, etc.   Also what her father gave
her when married.   Eldest son Edwin, plantation at decease
of wife.   Mentions when children become of age but names
only Edwin.   Executors: Brothers Thomas and Charles Lewis
HANES.   Witnesses: Jacob FREY and David DOUTHIT.   Signed:
George (X) HANES.

Page 194.   (No date).   Nuncupative Will of Jane HARPER.
            Probated December Term 1828.   Daughters to have
bed and clothing and Thomas to have a colt he calls his and
three other boys have $10.00 each; other property equally
divided.   By request of late deceased Jane HARPER on the
day of her death 3 August 1828.   Signed: Geo. F. WILSON.

Page 195.   2 October 1828.   Nuncupative Will of John RIDINGS.
            December Term 1828.   Wife Nancy, keep house and

land (except portion alloted to eldest daughter Matilda, as soon as she becomes married) and each remaining children have portions as they reach ages 18 and 21. His female slave to be returned to Davis DURRET of whom she was purchased. Signed: Geo. F. WILSON.

Page 196. 11 September 1828. Will of Henry HUFFMAN. December Term 1828. His part land be sold and divided equally between brother William and Catharine and Elizabeth HUFFMAN. Executor: Brother William HUFFMAN. Witnesses: William A. WOLFF and John SPEAS. Signed: Henry HUFFMAN.

Page 196. 25 October 1828. Will of Peter FIDLER (FIEDLER). March Term 1929. Son John, home plantation of 115 acres where I now live and balance of property to be equally divided among my five children: Gottfried, Peter, Catharine (wife of John FISHEL), Elizabeth (Wife of Abraham SHAMEL) and Julianna (wife of John GINDER ?). Executors: Son John FIDLER and son-in-law Abraham SHAMEL. Witnesses: Samuel Thomas PFOHL and Ann Elizabeth PFOHL. Signed: John Peter FIDLER (FIEDLER).

Page 197. 19 October 1828. Will of John MASTEN, Senr. March Term 1829. Wife Elizabeth, dwelling house and gardens and furniture for lifetime. Daughters Mary CHIPMAN and Matilda CREWS, above at death of wife. Son William, land and farm tools. Mentions tracts land adjoining Thomas CREWS and Lucy BODENHEIMER. Daughter Rhoda FRAZIER. Son Mathias, to share in property at death of wife. Executor: Son William. Witnesses: Darias MASTIN and Joseph CREWS. Signed: John MASTEN, Senr.

Page 198. 2 March 1829. Will of Frederick KASKY (KASKE). June Term 1829. To Louisa WARNER (wife of Benj. WARNER), for her care during my sickness. To Elizabeth SPACH, Martha GEIGER, Mary FOLTZ, and Rebecca FETTER, money. To brother John KASKY (KASKE) residing in Pennsylvania near town Nazreth, residue estate. No Executor named. Witnesses: Henry R. HERBST and John C. BLUM. Signed: Frederick (X) KASKY (KASKE).

Page 199. 22 April 1829. Will of Matthew REICH. June Term 1829. Be buried in custom of United Brethren Church. Wife (not named) and children who are still living with her at my decease. Son Solomon, already received horse. Two other sons (not named) receive $30.00 each. Mentions children "I had by my former and by my present wife." (No other children named). Executor: Daniel C. WELFARE and Wm. Lewis BENZINE (BENZIEN). Witnesses: George FOLTZ and John LINEBACK. Signed: Matthew REICH.

Page 201. 4 January 1825. Will of George RAY. June Term 1829. Wife Mary, estate divided between her and my children and grandchild. Children: Elizabeth (wife of John VEST); Rebecca (wife of William BARR); Anna (wife of John BARR) and Ruth who is now single. Grandchild Eleanor (daughter of William BARR). Executors: Sons-in-law John VEST,

and John BARR and daughter Ruth. Witnesses: Chas. BANNER,
Jno. VEST, and George VEST. Signed: George RAY.

Page 202. 4 July 1820. Will of Isaac NELSON. June Term
         1829. Daughter Anna Eliza, Negroes Nance, Jim,
Edmund, Fan and Poll; also furniture. Daughter Mary Smith
NELSON, Negroes Seal, Phillis, Lueaza and Robt.; also
furniture. Son Joseph, Negroes Mariah, Moses and Rachel.
Son Albert Fountain NELSON, Negroes Jack, Alexander and
Eveline. Son Constant Hardin NELSON, Negroes Stephen, Peter
and Mourning. Mentions the children to have good education;
also when children come of age. Executors: Jeremiah GIBSON
and Isaac DALTON. No witnesses: Signed: I. NELSON. . . .
Proven by oaths of Thomas FLYNT, Tandy MATTHEWS, Chas. L.
BANNER and John HILL, handwriting that of said Isaac NELSON,
deceased.

Page 204. 26 August 1828. Will of Elizabeth NUNNS. Septem-
         ber Term 1829. Two sons John and James, land
where I now live. Daughter Clara NELSON, 50 acres land. No
Executor named. Witnesses: Joshua COX and Tyre RIDDLE.
Signed: Elizabeth (X) NUNNS.

Page 204. 10 October 1829. Will of Verlinda BOSWELL.
         December Term 1829. Brother-in-law Thomas
SULLIVAN, Senr., personal property and 125 acres where I now
live on, Oldfield Creek, if he support and maintain my sister
Sally BOSWELL. Executor: Thomas SULLIVAN, Senr. Witnesses:
William GAMBLE and Philip REED. Signed: Verlinda (X) BOSWELL.

Page 205. 20 October 1826. Will of Jacob CRIM. December
         Term 1829. Wife Mary, property I now possess,
furniture stock, etc. lifetime; at her death to be equally
divided among Female Sect. To Lewis CRIM, pay $40.00 to
William CRIM for his part tract land where I reside; also
James CRIM and Lewis CRIM to manage my estate after my de-
cease. No executors named other than above. Witnesses:
Jesse NELSON, James CRIM, and Lewis CRIM. Signed: Jacob
CRIM.

Page 206. 13 June 1828. Will of Elizabeth RANK. December
         Term 1829. Legacies of clothing, etc. to follow-
ing: To Dorothea Warner (money due from Revd. Theodore SHULZ
(SCHULZ)); Mary SHELTON and Catherine SHAFFNER (SCHAFFNER),
my sisters; Nieces Lavenia HAUSER and Lydia HUNTER; Mary
SMITH of Salem; Barbara LINEBACK; Catharine RANK; Mary RANK
(sister-in-law); Sis SHORE (my nephews wife); Betsy SHORE
(Sis SHORES daughter); Pauline SHORE; Polly (sister Mary's
daughter); Elizabeth BIEWIGHAUS; Magdeline TRANSOW; Mary
STEINER; Carolind EBERHARD; Malinda STOCKBERGER; Catherine
HINE (born FEISER); Mary WHITE; Sally WATERSON; Polly PHILIPS;
(3 Moravian Sisters employed in kitchen); Elizabeth REIDE,
Elizabeth FOCKEL, and Rebecca SHUTT (SCHOTT?). Executors:
John Jacob BLUM, merchant of Salem. Witnesses: John C. BLUM
and Chas. F. BAGGE. Signed: Elizabeth (X) RANK.

Page 207. 5 October 1829. Will of Frederick LONG.
         December Term 1829. Wife Mary Elizabeth, live in

my house and plantation during lifetime and my children live
with her until they come of age. Mentions his Still and
other property be sold. Mentions barrel of whiskey and barrel
of brandy be kept for use and support of family. Son Jesse,
to have some land when he comes of age. Youngest son Solomon,
land. Son Jacob, pay 1/5 part what he raises on land. All
my children: Jacob, Thomas, William, Jesse, Sarah, and
Solomon. Executors: Joseph DOUB and son Thomas LONG. Witnesses: Henry DOUB, Andrew THOMASON, and Elijah DOUB. Signed:
Frederick (X) LONG.

Page 210. 18 March 1830. Will of Zepeniah HARPER. June
          Term 1830. Son Edgar and his heirs, viz: Alfred,
William Asberry, Josiah Burgis, Milton and Edgar HARPER and
their heirs, my home plantation of 166½ acres. To Jane
HARPER (widow Eliphas HARPER, deceased), land where she lives
provided she give up a note given by me to Eliphas in his
lifetime; if she married, the land to go to sons of Eliphas,
viz: Thomas, Elisha, Sandy and Eliphas Cannon HARPER. Sons
Edgar and William, my smith tools after paying my two daugh-
ters, Lovinah CROOM and Zelphia BLACKBOURN $4.00 each.
Daughters also to have household furniture and a cow each.
Son Edgar, my Still and apparatus. To Simon CROOM, 2 Still
tubs. Granddaughter Polly CROOM, walnut chest. Executors:
Sons Edgar and William HARPER. Witnesses: Thomas and Vashel
CRAFT. Signed: Zephaniah HARPER.

Page 211. 4 November 1819. Will of Jacob PEARCE. June
          Term 1830. Wife Mary, tract land where I now
live, household furniture, etc. her lifetime. Son William,
equal share above decease of wife. Two daughters Nancy and
Sely, equal share above decease of wife. Executor: Son
William PEARCE. Witnesses: Joshua COX and Mary (X) ROARK.
Signed: Jacob (X) PEARCE.

Page 213. 26 April 1830. Will of Joseph KERNER (KORNER).
          June Term 1830. Wife (not named) (Christina,
Salem Records), house to be built by my sons and lot on Cross-
roads tract; Negro Betsy about 10 years old. Son-in-law
Apollo HERMAN, 45 acres adjoining Nordykes. Sons Philip and
John, balance Cross roads tract. Executors: Sons Philip and
John KERNER. Witnesses: Christian David KUHLN and William
WETHERS. Signed: J. KERNER. . . .
CODICIL: 7 May 1830. Instead of 45 acres to my son-in-law
          Apollo HERMAN, I give to him and his wife, Salome,
75 acres adjoining Nordyke where I now live and 25 which I
bought of John BROOKS. (5 acres not included ??).

Page 215. 13 February 1830. Will of Elizabeth REICH of
          Salem. June Term 1830. Legacies of clothing,
furniture, and money to following: My sister Catharine of
Orange County, North Carolina; Nieces Louisa, Emily, Lydia,
and Paulina REICH, Verona YATES, Jacobina ROTHROCK; My sister-
in-law Lessy REICH; Sybella REICH; My little friends Ferdin-
and BEEHLER;, Rosalie KUHLN, Frederica BOEHLER, John L.
SCHULZ, Rebecca STAUBER, Rebecca SHULZ (SCHULZ), Elizabeth
FOCKEL, Hannah SPACH and Martha BLUM; my brother in Orange
County, North Carolina. Also mentions legacy of late Brother

86

Michael. Executor: Christian David KUHLN. Witnesses:
Frederique H. BOEHLER, and Jno. Jacob BLUM. Signed:
Elizabeth (X) REICH.

Page 217. 17 September 1830. Will of William BEASON.
          September Term 1830. Wife Hannah, all property
she had when I married her; also corner cupboard, four
cheers be hern forever. Daughter Jane Mc---ROUD ??, bed and
furniture. Executor: Brother-in-law William COSNER. Witnesses: John COSNER and Nathaniel PIKE. Signed: William
BEASON.

Page 218. 1 May 1829. Will of George PRIDDY. September
          Term 1830. Wife Anna, Negro Juda, bed and furni-
ture, etc. Sons Lewis, William Pettis, George, and John,
land where I now live. Daughter Frances ABBETT, 9 Negroes
which she already has in her possession, Hampton, Charry,
Juda, Anthony, Isaac, Lee, Martha. Dick and Milly, except
Milly to come back into Estate for my sons. Daughter Jane
CARR, Negroes Jim, Nancy, Bob, Effie, Hampton and Sam.
Sons John and Pettis, Negroes Fillis and Caswell. Heirs of
my son James, "I give them nothing as I gave him his part."
Heirs of my daughter Elizabeth ABBIT, $1.00 each. Executors:
William C. COLE and John BANNER. Witnesses: Lewis (X)
PRIDDY and Henry (X) BULLING. Signed: George PRIDDY. . . .
N.B. The Negroes given Jane CARR not to belong to her hus-
     band, John CARR. Witnesses: Lewis (X) GILLY and Henry
(X) BULLING. Signed: George PRIDDY.

Page 219. 16 January 1830. Will of Elizabeth DAWSON.
          December Term 1830. Grandson Newton C. DAWSON
(son of my daughter Elizabeth DAWSON, deceased), my part land
my husband died possessed of; bed and furniture. Step-
daughter Nancy DAWSON, my wearing clothes; but Nancy share
them with my friend, Elizabeth MECUM. Executor: Newton C.
DAWSON, grandson. Witnesses: Seth HAM and Robert WALKER.
Signed: Elizabeth (X) DAWSON.

Page 220. 17 April 1828. Will of Zebulum VAUGHN. March
          Term 1831. Two Suns Pleasant and Jesse, 50 acres
lower end plantation. Sun John, 50 acres with improvement.
Wife Polly, household furniture, stock, etc. Sun Reuben, 50
acres where he now lives. Sun Elijah, 50 acres adjoining
Amer JACKSON and he and John divide with sisters (not named)
when come of age. Mentions at death of wife, Her children
to have her property. No Executor named. Witnesses: William
ROAL and John P. HALE. Signed: Zebulum (X) VAUGHN.

Page 221. 16 July 1825. Will of James WHICKER. March Term
          1831. Wife Mary, all property I possess at my
death her lifetime and to give my four youngest children:
Littleberry, Levi, Nancy, and Mary $100.00 each when come
of age. Sons Eli and Littleberry to have North part tract
of land equally. Son Levi, balance of land after death of
wife. All my children: Benjamin, Sarah HESTER, William,
James Olifent, Frederick, Susanna FRAZIER, Eli, Littleberry,
Levi, Nancy and Mary WHICKER. Executors: Benjamin and
Frederick WHICKER, sons. Witnesses: William HOLLAND and

Samuel SPACH.   Signed: James (X) WHICKER.

Page 222.   24 July 1827.   Will of John Frederick KUSHKE
          (KUSCHKE), Salem.   March Term 1831.   To Gottlieb
BYHAN, Salem, hogs, feathered creatures and vegetables for
service rendered my late wife during her illness.   Daughter
Mary COOPER, value my estate and at her death to go to her
two children, (my grandchildren), Charles and Adelaide
COOPER, Salem.   Executor: Christian Frederick MEINUNG.
Witnesses: Theodore SHULTZ (SCHULTZ) and Aberham STEINER.
Signed: John KUSHKE (KUSCHKE).

Page 223.   11 January 1828.   Will of Francis KETTNER, Senr.
          (KITNER).   March Term 1831.   Wife Elizabeth,
Negro woman Betty; furniture stock, plantation, etc.   Grandchildren: Henry and Elizabeth (children of my son Henry,
deceased, by his first wife), $10.00 each; (children of Henry
by his second wife): Nathaniel, Sally, Thomas, William,
Sanford and Ebelena and their mother Anna, money.   My former
son-in-law, John HOLLAMAN, $1.00.   Grandchildren: Thomas and
Elizabeth (wife of Willis STEWART) (Children of John HOLLO-
MAN, which are children of my daughter Elizabeth, deceased),
equal share my other children hereinafter named.   Son
Frederick, 100 acres where he now lives; at his death to his
wife Eliza during her widowhood; if she marries land equally
to my other children: Matthew, Francis, Catharine STULTZ
(STOLZ), and grandchildren Thomas HOLLOMAN and Elizabeth
Holloman STEWART.   Executor: Michael DOUB.   Witnesses: Chas.
BANNER and John MILLER.   Signed: Francis (X) KETTNER (KITNER).

Page 224.   6 November 1828.   Will of John KINNAMAN.   March
          Term 1831.   Wife Elinor, estate real and personal;
if she marry, she shall have 1/8th part.   Three sons Levi,
Phillip and Andrew, $1.00 now and full share estate be paid
12 months after my decease.   Mentions at death of wife estate
be sold and divided among my seven sons Samuel (his share to
be divided among his children); John Thomas, Walter, Zachariah
Richard, Henry and George.   Executor: John HENLEY.   Witnesses:
Squier LEDFORD, E. BROWN, and Johnathan SWAIM.   Signed: John
(X) KINNAMAN.

Page 226.   15 February 1831.   Will of Reubin SAMUEL.   March
          Term 1831.   Brother Larkin SAMUEL, 50 acre tract
I bought of Wm. WAGGONER for which I have bond on said
WAGGONER and Thomas JAMES.   To brother Larkin and my sisters
Susan and Amy, all other property and at death of last
survivor, to go to brothers Edmond and Henry.   Executor:
Brother Larkin SAMUEL.   Witnesses: Joseph W. WINSTON and
W.N. GIBSON.   Signed: Rubin (X) SAMUEL.

Page 226.   26 August 1825.   Will of John KROUSE.   March
          Term 1831.   Son George KROUSE'S 3 children Rebecca,
Susanna and Eliza, 100 acres land; also 50 acres where I now
live at decease of my wife, but George have use 100 acres
his lifetime; if his wife, Louisa, outlives him, she is to
enjoy 100 acres her lifetime.   Son-in-law John CHITTY, all
land I have given him a deed for adjoining John CONRAD.
Son Andrew, 100 acres of land.   Son-in-law Jacob MILLER, 100

acres already deeded him. Son-in-law Daniel PETREE, all
money I have advanced him and all land I have deeded him.
To Joseph CHITTY, one French Crown; having built him a
house in Viane (Vienna). Wife Dorothea, my plantation of 90
acres where I now live; at her death to be sold and divided
between son-in-laws John CHITTY and Daniel PETREE. My
daughter Hanna PETREE'S children (not named). Executor:
Peter PFAFF, Senr. Witnesses: John BUTNER and Joseph BUTNER.
Signed: John (X) KROUSE. . . .
CODICIL: 3 October 1827. Having sold some land left son-in-
        law John CHITTY, that part will void, 50 acres left
to wife for life where my house stands, at her death goes to
3 children of Louisa and George KROUSE. Witnesses: Henry
SHULLS (SCHULZ) and Jacob CONRAD. Signed: John (X) KROUSE.

Page 227. 22 February 1831. Will of Daniel WOLFF. June
        Term 1831. Children: Charity, Nancy, Eliza,
Malinda, Elizabeth, William, Samuel and Jacob, Estate
equally divided. No Executor named. Witnesses: John B.
MILLER and Solomon SPEACE (SPEAS). Signed: Daniel WOLFF.

Page 228. 10 March 1831. Will of Richard GENTRY. June
        Term 1831. Wife Rebecca, all estate lifetime or
widowhood. My minor children: Richard, Joel, Thomas, Rebecca
and John to be made equal with those who have married and left
me. My 11 Children: William, James, Ira, Nancy, Harriet,
Richard, Joel, Thomas, Rebecca, John and Eliza, equal division estate at death of my wife. Executors: Sons William
and Ira GENTRY. Witnesses: John VAUGHN and Joseph VAUGHN.
Signed: Richard (X) GENTRY.

Page 229. 6 April 1828. Will of William BOYLES, Senr.
        September Term 1831. "Being old and infirm."
Son William, Negro girl Mary. Daughter Polly (wife of John
FRANCIS), Negro woman Patsy and her youngest child Mariah.
Daughter Betsy (wife of Frederick FRANCIS), Negro girl Rilla.
Daughter Nancy (wife of Joseph BOYLES), Negro girl Esther.
Son Joel, Negro fellow Sam. Children of son Thomas, deceased,
(not named), $100.00 divided. Children of son James,
deceased, (if he has any living), $100.00 divided. Mentions
lands rented the 1st year after decease so my children who
lives in Alabama may have notice of Sale said lands.
Executors: Son William BOYLES (Jr.) and Johnson CLEMENT.
Witnesses: Wm. H. LYON, Elisha BEASLEY, and Jas. LYON.
Signed: William BOYLES, Senr.

Page 230. 21 May 1831. Will of Betsy SPRINKLE, Sr., widow.
        September Term 1831. Son Peter, all part estate
I received from my son, John SPRINKLE, deceased. Daughter
Anna Barbara HUNTER, side saddle and pewter dish, part
clothes. Son Thomas, stock, curtain, walnut bedstead.
Daughter Cloe SHORE, part clothes. All other estate sold
and equally divided between my Children: George SPRINKLE'S
children; Polly DIAL; Michael; Anna Barbara HUNTER; Peter;
Cloe SHORE and Thomas. Executor: Son Thomas SPRINKLE.
Witnesses: M. DOUB and William ANDERSON. Signed: Elizabeth
(X) SPRINKLE.

Page 230. 31 January 1822. Will of James CREWS. December
            Term 1831. "Being aged" and having given all my
children that which I allotted them except son, James, with
whom I now live, I leave all my estate to son, James.
Executor: Son William CREWS. Witnesses: Nicholas HENDRIX
and Christopher SWAIM. Signed: James (X) CREWS.

Page 230. 28 March 1825. Will of Sarah YOUNG. December
            Term 1831. Four daughters: Elizabeth JOYCE (wife
of Wm.), Mary AINSWORTH (wife of James), Martha STEPHENS
(wife of Peter) and Sarah JOYCE (wife of John), all estate
equally divided. Executor: William JOYCE, Senr. Witnesses:
Josiah TAYLOR and George BREEDLOVE. Signed: Sarah (X) YOUNG.

Page 231. 29 March 1816. Will of Gottlieb SCHROTHER, Salem.
            March Term 1832. Wife Mary Ann and my daughter
Elizabeth, estate divided equally between them. Executors:
Carl Gottlieb CLAUDER and Emanuel SHOBER. Witnesses: Abraham
STEINER, Christian WINCKLER, and Jacob ROTHHAAS. Signed:
John Gottlieb SCHROTHER.

Page 232. 5 April 1831. Will of George FISHER (FISCHER).
            March Term 1832. Eldest son John, 75 acres he
lives on. Son Thomas, 50 acres he lives on; also 20 acres
in Davidson County, North Carolina. Son-in-law Barney GAMBLE,
who has married my daughter Hannah, my homeplace where I
now live of 75 acres (branch between my place and son John,
the dividing line). Daughter Anna, two notes on John LINEBACK;
also to have possession of house I now live in. Son-in-law,
Samuel HALFORD (?) who has married daughter Elizabeth,
$225.00. Son-in-law John HIRE, who married daughter Polly,
$225.00. To Philip VOGLER, $25.00. Executors: Son John
FISHER (FISCHER) and son-in-law John HIRE. Witness: Christian HEGE. Signed: George FISHER (FISCHER).

Page 233. 3 February 1832. Will of Adam WAGGONER. June
            Term 1832. Wife Nancy, all estate real and
personal her lifetime or widowhood. Children: John, Philip,
Mary, Seth, Susan, Joel B., Betsy, Joshiah, Elijah L.,
Margaret WAGGONER, estate divided equally at death of wife.
Executor: wife Nancy. Witnesses: William STURGES and Jacob
(X) BRINKLEY. Signed: Adam (X) WAGGONER.

Page 233. 30 April 1832. Will of George TAYLOR. June Term
            1832. To two daughters of Polly S. VAWTER: Julia
Madison and Alpha Monroe VAWTER, balance of estate after
debts paid reserving half land where house and plantation in
which we now life to Alpha Monroe VAWTER and both girls to
maintain their mother as long as she is single. Executors:
Bradford VAWTER and Daniel REICH. Witnesses: Nathaniel
ALSPAUGH and John M. VAWTER. Signed: George TAYLOR.

Page 234. 14 May 1832. Will of Mercy WILKERSON. June Term
            1832. Daughter Emila (wife of John HAMMOCK), all
my estate real and personal. Other daughter Milly, already
received her part. If Emila die without issue, estate to
go to my brother Joel PARISH of Alabama and his children.
No Executor named. Witnesses: Charles BANNER and John (X)

SNOW. Signed: Mercy (X) WILKERSON.

Page 235.   15 July 1831. Will of Joseph SCALES.   June Term
            1832. Son Absalom, tract by name "Sandy Ridge"
where I now live of 1,033 acres including dwelling house and
Mill (tract deeded me by Nathaniel SCALES, Senr.); also
Negreos Hark, Selph, Alex, Sr., Nan, Sr., Lonnon, Jerry, Sr.,
Jerry, Jr., Lucy, Hiram, Nan, Jo, Frank, Ally, Bill, Sr.,
Mariah and Lett. Son-in-law Peter HAY and my daughter Sally,
his wife, ½ my two tracts by name "Halls Place and land
bought of David DALTON, Sr.; both tracts of 880 acres (land
deeded me by David DALTON and John HUGHES); also Negroes
Daniel, Rhode, Adaline, David, Jr., Moses, Delph, John,
Charlotte, Buck, Luce, Jr., Lorella and Pitt. Son Absalom,
other half Halls Place of 880 acres said Absalom to hold
land for children of my daughter Jane SCALES (wife of
Nathaniel) and for use Jane, but free from her present husband
or any future husbands; also Negroes Alford, Abram, Harrison,
Nick, Abram, Sr., Milly, Peter, Charles, Brice, Alse, Look,
Bill, Jr., Frank, and Mary in trust for Jane. Executors:
Son Absalom SCALES and son-in-law Peter HAY. Witnesses:
Wm. H. LYON and Richard MILLS. Signed: Joseph SCALES.

Page 238.   18 February 1828. Will of Isaac PFAFF, Senr.
            September Term 1832. Wife Mary Margarette,
mansion house and support from plantation. Son Christian,
plantation where I now live, 130 acres; also 21¼ acres Muddy
Creek adjoining Peter PFAFF; also my interest in Still, etc.
Daughter Rebecca SAILER, 73 3/4 acres land. Daughter Mary
Margarette KRIGER (KRIEGER), equal share my estate. Executors: Brother (blank) PFAFF and son Christian PFAFF. Witnesses: Peter PFAFF and Chas. BANNER. Signed: Isaac PFAFF,
Senr.

Page 239.   12 June 1831. Will of Micajah FRANCIS. December
            Term 1832. Sons Coleman and Milton, my land
equally divided; Milton to have dwelling house where I now
live; Coleman to have house where he is now living. Wife
Elizabeth, residue estate. Daughter Nancy, household
furniture, heifers, etc. Four other daughters: Polly
COOMER (COMER), Elizabeth COX, Diana JONES and Lucy COOMER
(COMER), residue estate divided equally after death of wife.
Executor: Son Coleman FRANCIS. Witnesses: Jno. SIMMONS,
John FRANCIS, and William SHELTON. Signed: Micajah (X)
FRANCIS.

Page 240.   11 November 1832. Will of Thomas NEAL. December
            Term 1832. To William McMILLION, stock, rifle
gun, cow, my claim in land, crops cory and rye and oats, etc.
Executor: Winston CARTER. Witnesses: Walter ALLY and Adam
MITCHELL. Signed: Thomas NEAL.

Page 241.   29 August 1832. Will of William Lewis BENZIEN,
            Salem. December Term 1832. Wife Christina
Charity (married N. SNYDER), all my estate until children
reach age maturiey (children not named). Executor: Revd.
Theodore SCHULZ. Witnesses: J.C. BECHLER and John
CHRISTIAN. Signed: Wm. Lewis BENZIEN.

Page 241. 20 February 1832. Will of Peter HAIRSTON. Decem-
          ber Term 1832. Daughter Ruth S. HARISTON, all my
estate, both land and Negroes, etc; also Gilbeys daughter
now with her mother, Nelly, at the Yadkin; Sophia to be
brought home to be with relations; if Ruth dies before her
husband, Robert HAIRSTON, then half above be divided between
Robert HAIRSTON and my granddaughter, Agness J.P. HAIRSTON's
children, (not named). Mentions tract called David MURPHEYS
200 acres and Jonathan BARNETTS 200 acres to be given to
Gilblass and Gilchrest (?). Granddaughter Agness J.P.
HAIRSTON, my Pittsylvania Estate, both real and personal.
Great-grandson Peter W. HAIRSTON, all my Yadkin Estate.
Wills that Sally BLAGG nor "none of her children" be separat-
ed, but remain and live with my daughter Ruth S. HAIRSTON
and at her death to go to granddaughter, Agnes J.P. HAIRSTON.
Executors: Daughter Ruth S. HAIRSTON, Robert HAIRSTON,
Agness J.P. HAIRSTON, and Samuel HAIRSTON. Witnesses: John
PEPPER, David WELSH, John TERRY, and George MARTIN. Signed:
P. HAIRSTON.

Page 243. 14 November 1831. Will of Thornton P. GUINN,
          Senr. (GWYN). March Term 1833. Daughter Nancy
E. when she comes of age. Mentions Negro fellow Jack which
Absalom B. GUINN took to Tennessee; Bond on Duke A. GUINN.
My children: Absalom B., Thornton P., Manoah H., Anne D.
MOORE, tract where I now live North side Dan River, equally
divided. Wife Anne, lend her land South side Dan River
during lifetime; also Negroes: Cloe, Vilate, Rody, Caroline
and Wilson, she is to furnish my minor children with bed
and furniture. Daughter Polly E. HAMPTON, Negro girl Dilce.
Son Duke A., Negro Patrick. Son Absalom, Negro Gluster.
Son Thornton P., Negro Peter. Daughter Bethania P. BOSTICK,
Negro Isaac. Son Manoah H., Negro Gabriel. Daughter Anne
D. MOORE, Negro Dinah. All Negroes above mentioned already
in possession legatees. Daughter Christina F. GUINN, Negro
boy Lewis, furniture stock, household dishes. Son David
B. GUINN, Negro boy George, etc. Daughter Susannah R.
GUINN, Negro Charles, etc. Daughter Nancy E. GUINN, stock,
household furniture. Mentions balance of land and Negro
Ellis. Executors: Son-in-law John B. HAMPTON and sons
Thornton P. GUINN, Jr. and Manoah H. GUINN. Witnesses: A.B.
DALTON, Silas WATSON, and I.E. GENTRY. Signed: Thornton P.
GUINN.

Page 247. 15 November 1832. Will of Isaac BARR. March
          Term 1833. Mentions he is a Revolutionary War
Pensioner. Daughter Elizabeth, money oweing me from U.S.
at my decease; also residue estate except following bequeaths.
To William BARR, Nancy GREGORY, John BARR, Polly OWENS, Isaac
BARR, Sally COOMER (COMER), and Joshua BARR, $25.00 each.
Executrix: Daughter Elizabeth BARR. Witnesses: Chas. BANNER
and Elizabeth (X) BARR. Signed: Isaac (X) BARR.

Page 248. 11 June 1832. Will of Rice BROWN, Citizen.
          March Term 1833. Wife Nancy, 1/3 land where I
now live including dwelling house. Son George, ½ remainder
of my land. Daughter BROWN, other half my land. To Elizabeth HUTCHERSON and my daughter Polly HUTCHERSON, bed and

furniture. No Executor named. Witnesses: John PRESTON and
Azariah HUTCHERSON. Signed: Rice (X) BROWN.

Page 249. 2 August 1830. Will of Asa EARLY. March Term
1833. Wife Polly, all my lands and tenements
waters Big Yadkin near Old Richmond and at her death, divided
between my two children. Two children, Samuel and Mary.
Executor: Wife Polly EARLY. Witnesses: William STONE and
William M. HARRISON. Signed: Asa EARLY.

Page 250. 7 June 1831. Will of Thomas BUTNER. March Term
1833. My 15½ acres adjoining Nathaniel SNIPES
and John L. HAUSER Heirs, the house and lot where I now live
in Bethabara be sold and money equally divided among my five
children: Thomas, Anna Rachael (wife of Michael REICH),
Elizabeth Johanna, Christian HARMON and Maria. Executors:
Son Thomas BUTNER (Jr.) and Joseph BUTNER. Witnesses: John
C. BUTNER and Samuel G. FOGLE. Signed: Thomas (X) BUTNER.

Page 250. 25 October 1828. Will of William PANTHER. March
Term 1833. Wife Easter, all estate lifetime or
widowhood; then estate to be sold. Sons William and Daniel,
$20.00 each. Daughters Nancy and Susanna, bed, furniture,
cow, cotton wheel when come of age or marry. All my children: Jacob, John, William, Daniel, Sarah, Barbara, Susanna,
and Nancy, also Christian LEATHERMAN to share with them.
Executor: Thomas PADGET, Junr. Witnesses: Thomas ROMINGER
and Daniel WEISNER (WESNER). Signed: William (X) PANTHER.

Page 251. 1 April 1833. Nuncupative Will of John VEST,
deceased. Probated June Term 1833. In his own
home where he had resided many years, requested following
before John CLAYTON and John LAURANCE. Wife Elizabeth,
property left with her so she may raise my younger children
and at her death estate divided equally among children.
Sons George and William continue to occupy plantation.
John VEST departed this life on 29 March 1833. Signed: John
CLAYTON, William PARKS, and John LAURANCE.

Page 251. 31 June 1824. Will of Samuel KRAMSCH. June Term
1833. Wife Susanna Elizabeth, lifetime estate.
Two daughters Louisa Charlotte and Christina Susanna, estate
divided at death of wife. Executor: Wife Susanna Elizabeth
KRAMSCH. Witnesses: John C. BLUM and F.H. SHUMAN (SCHUMANN).
The Testator, not being able to sign, declared above his last
true Will.

Page 252. 20 February 1833. Will of Maria Rosina FOCKEL,
Salem. June Term 1833. Sisters Paulina FOCKEL
and Lydia FOCKEL and Elizabeth STAUBER, silver, etc. My
cousin Emily STOCHR (STOHR), bed, etc. provided she continue
living with my parents. Mother Ann Dorothea FOCKEL, unbrella,
etc. Father Christian FOCKEL, balance cash I have at my
decease. Brother Henry FOCKEL, chest, silver, my German
Bible. Executor: Charles F. BAGGE, Salem. Witness: Samuel
G. FOGLE. Signed: Maria Rosina (X) FOCKEL.

Page 253. 15 February 1833. Will of Abraham STEINER. June

Term 1833. Wills body to Physicians and Surgeons
of Salem in case die of disease that inspecting my body would
help others. My four children: Mary, $1,000.00 including
my shares in Cape Fear Navigation Co. stock. Daughter Sarah,
$1,000.00 including my 6 shares in State Bank of North
Carolina. Son Charles Abraham, his note $750.00 plus $300.00.
Daughter Elizabeth, $1,000.00 including my 4 shares Bank Cape
Fear and my pianoforte. To the orphan girl, Matilda HINE,
who is bound to me shall be put under care of my daughter
Sarah for her apprenticeship; also $10.00 to her. To John
C. BLUM, Esq., in trust for Salem Library and Reacing Co.,
all my volumes and loose papers. Executor: Charles F. BAGGE.
Witnesses: John C. BLUM and John Jacob BLUM. Signed:
Abraham STEINER. . . .
CODICIL: 15 February 1833. Four shares stock in Bank of U.S.
I have acquired since above will to go to daughter
Elizabeth. Witnesses: John C. BLUM and John Jacob BLUM.
Signed: Abraham STEINER.

Page 256. 28 July 1826. Will of Abel SHIELDS. September
Term 1833. My children: John, Mary, Sarah, Rachel
Rubin, Ann and Deborah, $1.00 each. Wife Grace, residue of
my estate. Executrix: Wife Grace SHIELDS. Witnesses: David
HENDRICKS and Anthony WRIGHT. Signed: Abel SHIELDS.

Page 257. October 1824. Will of Abraham TRANSAU, Senr.
September Term 1833. Funeral to be in manner
United Brethren (Moravian). Wife Eva, remain in full posses-
sion of my house and lot in Bethania as long as she lives.
Six children: Philip, Abraham, Solomon, Mary Elizabeth, Mary
Magdaline, and Philipina, residue estate equally. Executors:
Son-in-law John C. BLUM and son Philip TRANSAU. Witnesses:
John Jacob BLUM and Isaac BONER. Signed: Abraham TRANSAW.

Page 258. 4 September 1830. Will of Rudolph CHRIST, Salem.
September Term 1833. Wife Anna Christina, dwell-
ing house and Weaver Shop lifetime. Youngest son Traugott
Frederic, wearing clothes and $100.00, etc. Daughter Anna
Elizabeth, pianoforte, silver spoons, etc. Son Jacob
Rudolph, weavers loom, silver spoons. Mentions tract land
500 acres on Panther Creek be sold and money placed on
interest; also bonds, notes and book accounts be sold;
mentions sale of 2,500 acres of land in Tennessee 1828 to
John C. BLUM. Executors: Daniel C. WELFARE and William L.
BENZIEN. Witnesses: Theodore SHULTS (SHULZ) and Abraham
STEINER, Junr. Signed: Rudolph CHRIST.

Page 260. 19 January 1833. Will of Martha BARNER (BONER).
December Term 1833. Daughters Judah and Patsy,
56 acres including house and orchard where I now live.
Daughters Edney STONE, Christine STONE and Rebecca MOORE,
1/3 remaining land. Three granddaughters: Polly, Judah and
Betsy MOORE (3 eldest daughters of Rebecca). Son John, $10
and no more. Son Horatio, $1.00 and no more. Daughter
Rebecca MOORE, $1.00 and no more (?). Money arising from
sale of my property divided 6 ways, viz: 1st daughter Patsy;
2nd daughter Judah; 3rd daughter Edney; 4th daughter
Christina; 5th part divided between Patsy and Sally SIMMONS;

6th part between Judah MOORE, Polly MOORE and Betsy MOORE.
Executor: William STONE. Witnesses: P.T. KERBY and Jacob
BUTNER. Signed: Martha (X) BARNER (BONER).

Page 261.   15 August 1831. Will of Charles REAVES. December
            Term 1833. Wife Obediance, lifetime claim estate
including dwelling house; 2 Negroes Isaac and Lucy. Daughter Susanah A. CREWS, have given her Negro man Squire,
furniture, horse bridle, etc.; she to have Negro girl Luckey.
Son George, Negro boy Jacob, furniture stock in his possesion
now; he to have Negro man Archer. Son William, 1 bond on
James BRUCE; judgements from Martin SHELTON, John BITTING,
Mr. KIZER and William BOYLES. Daughter Catharine BROWN,
furniture and Negro girl Martha. Mentions son William having
gone (contrary to my whishes) visiting at house of Henry
TILLEY and would not take my advise and break off with that
family; if he should abstain from them and not marry in said
family William to have estate at death of my wife. Executors:
Son George REAVES and William C. COLE. Witnesses: Richard
HILL, Wm. DEATHERAGE, and John James PAYNE. Signed: Charles
REAVES. . . .
CODICIL: 25 October 1833. Revokes part of Will leaving
            estate at death of wife to son, William. Gives
son-in-law Thomas BROWN, $100.00; remainder to go to son,
William, if he will take advise of my son George, son-in-
law Matthew CREWS and Thomas BROWN and forsake the place
mentioned in Will and not marry there; also revokes Executor-
ship of Wm. C. COLE and gives full Execcutorship to son, George
REAVES. Witness: Wm. C. COLE. Signed: Charles REAVES.

Page 263.   (No date). Will of Hanah SHAUB (SCHAUB). (As
            translated by Emanuel SHOBER). December Term 1833.
Legacies to the following: Daughters Maria Magdalena and
Lena; Betsy SHAUB (SCHAUB); Susana, Salome and Catharine
GERBER; (Goddaughter) Henrietta; Christopher; Samuel SHAUB
(SCHAUB); my son Jacob. Mentions riding habit given her by
brother Fredrick. No Executor named. Witness: Jacob WARNER.
No Signature.

Page 264.   25 August 1832. Will of Benjamin REICHEL. March
            Term 1834. Wife Mary $1,000.00 her lifetime when
it will fall to my children. Seven children: Clara Cornelia,
Edward Henry, Sophia Henrietta, William Cornelius, Angelina
Wilhelma, Amelia Charity, and Ernestine Theophela, $300.00
each. Mentions books and property equally divided and
pianoforte kept for younger children. Begs Directors of
Moravian Society in Salem and Bethlehem to provide for widow
and care for education of children so sons Edward Henry and
William Cornelius will be sent to Nazareth Boarding School
to qualify for minestry in our church; wife guardian of
children. Executors: Revd. Theodore SHULZ and Revd. Abram.
STEINER. Signed: Benjamin REICHEL. No witnesses. (F.C.
MEINUNG swore to handwriting of said Benjamin.)

Page 265.   6 January 1833. Will of Thomas BRANDON. March
            Term 1834. Wife Jane Allen BRANDON, $350.00 now
in Thomas BURTONS hands; also all my estate. Executor:
Wife Jane Allen BRANDON. Witnesses: J. JARVIS and Benjamin

(X) PEDICOTE (PEDDYCOARD). Signed: Thomas BRANDON.

Page 265. 4 November 1833. Will of Elisha LAWSON. March
        Term 1834. Wife Mary, 100 acres where I now live
lifetime and widowhood; then equally divided among my children. Children: Ambrose, Elisha, Sealy, Dosia (wife of Thomas
NICHOLSON), Nancy (wife of George COLLINS), and Patsy (wife
of John SISK). Wife Mary, residue of my estate; if she
remarries to go to son, Elisha. Son-in-law Thomas NICHOLSON
to pay other heirs $20.00 for horse now in his possession.
Executors: Wife Mary LAWSON and son Ambrose LAWSON. Witnesses: John BANNER and Josiah LEAKE. Signed: Elisha (X)
LAWSON.

Page 267. 6 January 1825. Will of Thomas GOODE. March
        Term 1834. Daughter Polly (wife of Wesley JEAN)
and her children, $1.00. Mentions Negro Amy to be free.
Grandsons Thomas and William GOODE (sons of my son Henry,
deceased), balance of my estate. Executors: Brother William
GOODE and Charles BANNER. Witnesses: Chas. BANNER, John (X)
CODEL and Nancy (X) CODEL. Signed: Thomas GOODE.

Page 268. 10 January 1834. Will of Henry HARTT. March
        Term 1834. Wife Franky, all my estate for bene-
fit of my children in raising and educating them; my boys
stay with their mother and work farm. Children: Nancy,
Wyatt, Martin, John, Martha C., Floyd, Hambleton, Henry, and
Thomas. Executors: Wife Franky HARTT and son Wyatt HARTT.
Witnesses: Con. HARTT and John WEBB. Signed: Henry HARTT.

Page 269. 5 April 1834. Will of Elizabeth GREEN (KROEHN).
        June Term 1834. Grandchild Eliza GREEN (married
to Kyer JOHNSON), $1.00 and no more. Grandchildren Caty and
Susan GRINDER, $1.00 each. Daughter Anna, bed and everything
that belongs. Daughters Christina, Anna, Catharine, Hannah,
and Salome, wearing clothes. All my children: (above named
daughters) and Frederick and Philip, balance of estate
equally divided. Grandchild Elizabeth STANARD, my Flax
Wheel. Executor: John SIDES. Witnesses: John FIDLER
(FIEDLER) and S. Thomas PFOHL. Signed: Elizabeth (X)
GREEN (KROEHN).

Page 270. 8 June 1833. Will of George LAGENAUER. June
        Term 1834. Wife Catharine, forever, all property
and furniture (except land she got of her father's estate)
brought with her at our marriage. My Heirs: Philip; Elizabeth
Catharine; children of my daughter Salome, deceased, 1 share
each. Son Philip, land he now lives on; Negro Milly.
Daughters Elizabeth (wife of Samuel RIED) and Catharine
(wife of John CLAUSE (CLAUSS)), my first survey of land of
17 acres. Children of my daughter Salome: Joshua, Phebe,
Catharine, Lucinda and Salome SCHNEIDER, 100 acres called
Richards Place adjoining 17 acres above. Mentions giving
these children Negro at decease of their father, Philip
SCHNEIDER. Daughter Catharine, Negro Rachel. To my Heirs:
Negroes Betty and her children David and old Charles.
Appoints son Philip, trustee for daughter Elizabeth (wife of
Samuel RIED) and John CLAUSE (son-in-law) as guardian of

children of daughter Salome, deceased. Executor: Son Philip
LAGENAUER. Witnesses: C. NISSON and Emanuel SHOBER. Signed:
George (X) LAGENAUER, Senr.

Page 272. 5 November 1829. Will of Lewis David Von
        SCHWEINETZ (SCHWEINITZ) of Bethlehem, Northampton
County, Pennsylvania, late of Salem, North Carolina. Probated 5 December 1829. To Revd. Wm. Henry Van VLECK, now
of City of New York, all lands in Pennsylvania, New Jersey,
North Carolina, George, Ohio, Rhode Island, and Maryland I
die seized of. To Niece and adopted child: Agnes Maria
CLUGS of Lancaster, $500.00. Wife Amalia Louisa and children
(not named here), bonds, certificates etc. in Europe not
yet paid over in right of my deceased mother or in my right
or any relative in Germany. Mentions wife educating children, but does not name them. To Academy of Natural Licences
at Philadelphia of which I am a correspondent, whole of my
Botanical Collection. Executors: William Henry Van VLECK,
New York, Revd. Thedore SCHULTS (SCHULZ), of Salem, Johann
Christian BECHLER, John Fredr. STADEFER of Bethlehem,
Pennsylvania, and Revd. John Gottlieb HERMAN (HERRMANN) of
Nazareth, Pennsylvania. Witnesses: Owen RICE, J.F. RANCK,
and Jacob RICE. Signed: Lewis David Van SCHWEINTZ. . . .
Probated 14 February 1834 Northampton County, Pennsylvania;
George HESS, Jurn., Register, Probate of Wills.

Page 277. 6 April 1833. Will of Robert HILL. September
        Term 1834. Wife Martha, all estate her lifetime
and at her death to be distributed as follows: Son Robert,
Negro Damon. Son Joel, Negro Lorenzo. Daughter Martha
HAYNES, Negro Thomas. Son John, all land I own; Negro
Prince, clock, blacksmith tools, etc. Granddaughter Selena
HILL, Negro Fanny and sorrel filly. Children: Caleb,
Susannah SAMUELS, Elizabeth MATTHEWS, Robert, Martha HAYNES,
Joel, children of my deceased daughter Francis DAVIS and
John, residue of estate divided equally. Executors: Sons
Joel and John HILL. Witnesses: Hampton BYNUM and Gilbary
PHILLIPS. Signed: Robert HILL.

Page 278. 13 October 1834. Will of John FREEMAN. September
        Term 1834. Wife Elizabeth, 1/3 part estate
lifetime and widowhood; Negroes Lucy and Rachel. Son William,
land and property already received. Daughters Hulda, Agnes,
Mary, Ellender, $100.00 each. Son John, all land and pro-
perty I have lent wife; Negro Eli. Executor: Wife Elizabeth
FREEMAN and son John FREEMAN. Witnesses: Thomas CARR,
Rachel CARR, and William PEGG. Signed: John (X) FREEMAN.

Page 279. 5 October 1827. Will of James MARTIN began 13 May
        1827, probated December Term 1834. Wife Martha,
all her dower of Negros from her first husband: Rose and her
2 children Scat and Heriot, 2 Negro girls Lize and Charity,
Negro man Ned; also plantation where I now live of 640 acres
with my chief Mansion house on Snow Creek; 320 acres on Mill
Creek; 420 acres adjoining my home tract adjoining William
MOORE, Senr.; in all 1,380 acres her lifetime or widowhood.
Two sons Edmund Loftin and John Julius MARTIN, above land
at decease of wife; also son John Julius to be educated with

college education. Wife, My Negroes her lifetime: Cuff, Jack the shoemaker, Aaron, Zack the blacksmith, Brown, Francis, Rachel and her children, Mary, Elley, Dolly, Sheriff, Crece and her children Melea, June, Louisa, Grace and her children, Virgil and Kite, Edde and her children John and Anthony, all the old Negroes Yankey, Betsy, a bounty claim in Tennessee of 800 acres between Wolff and Hatcher Rivers being part 5,000 acres divided between old Colo. James HUNTER, Major Pleasant HENDERSON, old Thos HENDERSON, deceased and myself. Mentions Executors to sell 300 acres on Beaver Island Creek in Rockingham County adjoining Stokes Line. Son Henry, all my part bounty land claims to support Iron Works, reserving ½ Grist Mill, ½ Forge lately repaired by Hugh MARTIN and his son William; they having use of it for 20 years without paying any rent. As to legacies I gave my first Children: Sally HENDERSON, Hugh MARTIN, Anna LEAREY, Polly ROGERS and Alen MARTIN (since dead), Fanny HUNTER and James MARTIN, have given more than to last children. Makes reference to will made 15 April 1825 in which gave son James, my Negro Jack the shoemaker who is so old do not consider him a gift. Executors Wife Martha MARTIN and son James MARTIN, Jr. No witnesses: Signed: J. MARTIN. . . .
CODICIL: 22 September 1833. Son Henry MARTIN is becoming very disapated and ungrateful to me, I therefore revoke all legacies made to him in my Will and give him the horse and saddle he now rides; if he reforms, my wife may give him Forge and bounty land as before mentioned. Signed: J. MARTIN. . . .Proved by Andrew BOWMAN, Charles BANNER, and Jeremiah GIBSON as handwriting of said James MARTIN.

Page 281. 15 September 1834. Will of Nathaniel HENDRIX. December Term 1834. Wife Elizabeth, Negro Adam and Grace; household furniture, etc., $40.00 cash. To Daniel ROBERTSON (son of James ROBERTSON), colt, furniture, tools. Executor: George BROOKS. Witnesses: Lewis MICKEY, Joseph J. CONRAD, and John BRUNER (BRUNNER). Signed: Nathaniel HENDRIX.

Page 282. 3 August 1834. Will of Chrisanna CRITENDON. December Term 1834. Daughter Polly (wife of John KING), money in trust. To John CRITENDON "who was my husband and absconded from my bed and board several years past and for that reason the Gen'l. Assembly of North Carolina granted me a divorce", $1.00. In case daughter Polly dies without issue, estate to go to John HAMPTON and wife Polly and not to John KINGS relations. Executors: Emanuel SHOBER and Charles BANNER, Fielder DAVIS and Robert (X) HAMMOCK. Signed: Chrisanna (X) CRITENDON.

Page 283. 18 January 1834. Will of Maria Magdalene RIGHTS. March Term 1835. My Executors to place an engraved Marble Tombstone for the Tomb of late husband, John RIGHTS, from money arising from a bond given me by Jacob and Abraham CONRAD, now in hands of my son Matthew's Executors; balance money be divided among my 5 children. Son John and his children, 1/5 bonds I've signed for said John to Theodore SHULTS (SCHULZ). Daughter Johanna Elizabeth (wife of Godfrey OEMAN (Oehmann)), 1/5 bonds signed for said

98

daughter to Theodore SHULTS (SCHULZ). Grandchildren: Susan, Zacharias and Constantine RIGHTS (children of my deceased son Matthew), 1/5 above bonds. Daughter Lulanith (wife of Gottlieb LINEBACK), 1/5 above bonds. To Lucy (wife of son John), Edwin and Hannah (children of son John), furniture, etc. To Anna (wife of son Joshua) and Lewis (son of son Joshua), silver, etc. Executors: Frederic C. MEINUNG and son Joshua RIGHTS. Witnesses: Christian David KUHLN and Henry R. HERBST. Signed: Maria Magdalina (X) RIGHTS.

Page 285.   27 September 1834. Will of Colly PHILLIPS. March
              Term 1835. Daughter Agnes, when comes of age;
money arising from sale of estate, furniture. My Brothers
Francis and Owen D. TATE, above money if my daughter dies
young. My sister Polly (wife of Abraham BOLEJACK), above
furniture if daughter dies young. Also sister Polly to
rear daughter Agnes. Executor: Brother Francis TATE.
Witnesses: William HUNTER and Thomas SPRINKLE. Signed:
Colly (X) PHILLIPS (female).

Page 286.   30 April 1835. Nuncupative Will of Caty REDMON,
              deceased. June Term 1835. Before James DEARING,
J.P., Catharine REDMON made oath she was at house of said
Caty and heard her tell her children (not named) she wanted
Polly FULTON (called Mary FULTON) "to come in as one of my
own children." Signed: Catharine REDMON and James DEARING,
J.P. . . .Probated on oath Catharine REDMON and Malinda
FLYNT.

Page 287.   4 December 1831. Will of John KING. June Term
              1835. Wife Polly, Negro girl Amelia, all my
plantation, tools, furniture. Brother David, Negro Tom and
his wife Mary and children Lewis, Charles, Henry, blacksmith
and coopers tools and rifle. Brother George KING, Slaves
Jacob, Joseph and Abraham. Brother Harbert KING, Slaves
Reubin and Robert. My other brothers, if living in any
State or Territory of U.S., $1.00 each and no more. Sister
Elizabeth JOYCE, $1.00. Executors: Wife Polly KING and
Tandy MATTHEWS, Senr. Witnesses: C. BANNER (Charles) and
John F. POINDEXTER. Signed: John KING. . . .
CODICIL: March 13, 1935. Land I bought of John SNOW, Senr.
              be sold to pay my debts. Witnesses: William
WALKER and Tandy MATTHEWS. Signed: John KING.

Page 288.   2 April 1835. Will of Barbara KIGER. June Term
              1835. Son John Harmon KIGER, stock, household
furniture for his care of me in my old age. Executor: Son
John Harmon KIGER. Witnesses: L. BOLEJACK and Charles KING.
Signed: Barbara (X) KIGER.

Page 289.   19 August 1835. Will of Ann P. WOLFF. September
              Term 1835. Brothers Samuel and Jacob WOLFF, my
interest in lands coming to me as heir my late father, Daniel
WOLFF and $125.00. My mother, Martha WOLFF; Brother William
W. WOLFF: Sisters, Charity CONRAD, Martha Malinda and Pamela
Elizabeth WOLFF, residue of my estate. Niece Mary Ann
(daughter of brother Wm. W. WOLFF), bureau and sidesaddle.
Niece Martha Ann CONRAD (daughter of Charity CONRAD); silver

spoon. My Mother, Negro Violet. Executors: Brothers Samuel and Jacob H. WOLFF. Witnesses: A.H. SHEPPERD and John B. MILLER. Signed: A.P. WOLFF.

Page 290. 22 February 1813. Will of George CARVER. September Term 1835. Sons George and Joseph, my plantation and land of 248 acres (except 2 acres for meeting house and burial ground). Daughter Christina, furniture, stock, loom for keeping my house. Daughter Polly (wife of Benjamin ELROD), $10.00. Personal property sold and divided equally among daughters Betty (wife of Stephen ELROD), Betsy, Anna, Aga, and Christina. Executors: Sons Joseph and George CARVER. Witnesses: J. BUTNER and Henry FIDLER (FIEDLER). Signed: George (X) CARVER.

Page 291. 25 January 1826. Will of Mary Eve DOUB (DAUB), widow. September Term 1835. All personal estate be sold among my children, except wearing clothes to be divided between daughters M. Elizabeth and E. Mary DOUB. Six sons and 2 daughters: Namely "according to age": Henry, William, Jacob, Joseph, Elizabeth, Michael, Mary, and Peter. To Alvira and John W.W. DOUB, orphans of John DOUB, deceased, one part of my estate with my above named children. Executors: Sons Henry and Michael DOUB. Witnesses: Daniel SPAINHOUR, Jacob SPAINHOUR, and H.G. ANDERSON. Signed: Mary E. (X) DOUB.

Page 292. 6 March 1835. Will of Benjamin CLEMENTS. September Term 1835. To Heirs of 2 deceased daughters, Susan COLE and Letty TUCKER, the four Negros (not named), already received; also beds and furniture. My youngest infant daughter Nancy John, 4 Negroes Lewis, Larkin, Spencer, and Louisa; bed and furniture; $1,000.00 now in hands Absalom SCALES, Esq. if Nancy John dies young, above legacy to the heirs of two deceased daughters above named. Mentions land on waters Burchstone Creek and Dan River divided between heirs above deceased daughters: Letty's 2 children and Susan's 8 children. Wife (not named), lifetime claim plantation I live on, stock, household furniture; also lend her Negroes Buck and Charlotte. Executors: Wm. C. COLE and John GRIFFIN. Witnesses: John S. PATTERSON and Charles R. GRIFFIN. Signed: Benjamin CLEMENTS.

Page 294. 7 October 1829. Will of Edmund TILLEY, Senr. December Term 1835. Son David, Negros Martin and Malinda. Mentions Negro Becky and Jim and all my land and household furniture be sold and divided equally among my children (not named). Executors: David TILLEY and Matthew R. MOORE. Witnesses: Thomas MARTIN and Phebe TILLEY. Signed: Edmund TILLEY.

Page 295. 19 August 1835. Will of Jacob LEWIS. December Term 1835. Wife Elizabeth, all estate for her lifetime or widowhood; then be sold and equally divided among my children. Children: Moses, Noah, James, Peter, John, Hasten, and Matta. Executor: William VOSS. Witnesses: Thomas CAMPBELL and Daniel POWERS. Signed: Jacob (X) LEWIS.

Page 296. 30 May 1834. Will of Samuel FODRAL. December
          Term 1835. Wife Malinda, land, Negroes Betsy,
Rhoda and their children and Daniel, etc. Children: Jeremiah,
Palina, Martha, Susannah, William, John, George, and Mary
Eliza, above estate death or marriage of wife. Mentions
children coming of age and getting an education. Daughter
Susannah (over and above), $5.00. Granddaughter Mary Ann
SMITH, $5.00 having given son-in-law Henry SMITH (who married
my daughter Jincy, now deceased), their part my estate.
Executrix: Wife Malinda FODRAL. Witnesses: John BANNER and
Elisha BANNER. Signed: Samuel (X) FODRAL.

Page 297. 11 May 1835. Will of Sarah THOMASON. December
          Term 1835. Niece Sarah SNIPES, side saddle.
Niece Elizabeth LAWNER, skillet, 600 Sligh, 700 sligh, chairs,
etc. Sister Elender SNIPES, ½ residue of my estate. Executor: William WALKER. Witnesses: Elizabeth (X) WALKER and
Hugh PATTERSON. Signed: Sarah (X) THOMASON.

Page 298. 1 August 1833. Will of Waomy DAWSON. December
          Term 1835. Nephew Newton C. DAWSON (son of my
sister Elizabeth DAWSON, deceased), 1/3 part 100 acre tract
and all my movable property. Executor: Newton C. DAWSON.
Witnesses: George FULP, Sr. and George V. FULP. Signed:
Waomy (X) DAWSON.

Page 299. 23 June 1835. Will of Joseph HUTCHERSON. Decem-
          ber Term 1835. Wife Nancy, 1/3 stock, full right
of my dwelling house and land I now live on for her maintenance during life or widowhood. Son Peter, above at death or
marriage of wife. Executrix: Wife Nancy until son, Peter
reaches age 21; then he be sole Executor. Witnesses: A.
SCALES and Wm. T. JOYCE. Signed: Joseph (X) HUTCHERSON.

Page 300. 4 September 1835. Will of Samuel KROUSE. Decem-
          ber 1835. Wife Anna Maria and son William Thomas,
carry on tanning business in Bethabara under direction of
Executors until Wm. Thomas reaches age 21; then he is to have
1/3 part tannery and house and lot; also rifle. Son John
Edwin, 1/3 tannery and house and lot and a watch, shot gun,
$12.00. Executors: John HINE and John C. BUTNER. Witnesses:
Joseph BUTNER and John BUTNER. Signed: Samuel KRAUSE.

Page 301. 13 May 1833. Will of Henry RIPPEL, "being in
          advanced years." March Term 1836. Wife Elizabeth,
remain on place where I now live and enjoy benefits during
widowhood. Grandchildren: (children of my daughter Sarah,
deceased), wife of John LEIGHT, $2.00. Son John (if living),
one part (if dead) to go to children of my son Henry. Son
Christian, one part. Son Martin (if living) one part (if
dead) to children of my daughter Susannah, 70 acres adjoining
his land, blacksmith tools. Son Henry, one part. Daughter
Susannah (wife of John ADER), one part. Daughter Elizabeth
(wife of Henry KIGER), one part and Loom. Executor: Son
Martin RIPPEL. Witnesses: Jacob SHULTS (SCHULZ) and F.C.
MEINUNG. Signed: Henry RIPPEL.

Page 303. 9 January 1836. Will of Julianna Catharine HEIN,

(HINE). March Term 1836. Daughter Susannah, 21 acres and house where I live, household furniture. Grand-children Juliana, large bed, bedstead and flax wheel. Grandson William CORNELIUS, my cow. Granddaughter Malvina, chest. Grandson Nathaniel, small bed. Daughter Catharine, Dutch oven. Daughter Susanna SANDERS, shall hold in trust for her children as their bequeaths. Executor: Gottlieb BYHAN. Witness: N. BYHAN. Signed: Julianna Catharine (X) HEIN.

Page 304. 19 March (no year). Will of James B. FROST. June Term 1836. Wife Louisa, $66.00, my horse Brutus, bed, six prints (including portraits), she is to give each of our children $50.00 out of settlement of my fathers estate. My little children: Elizabeth and James; literary work "Ladys Book" and "The New York Mirror". Mentions 100 acres bought of Joshua FREEMAN. Executor: Brother-in-law John H. WINSTON. Witnesses: A.B. RUTLEDGE and John GOLDING (GOLDEN). Signed: James B. FROST.

Page 305. 23 May 1836. Will of Joshua COX, Junr. June Term 1836. To Lettitia WATSON, 100 acres off of lower end of my tract. To James WATSON, all my stock. Sister Nancy, $20.00. To my sisters both living and heirs of those deceased, balance of my land. Executor: Richard COX. Witnesses: Thomas MARTIN and Matt R. MOORE. Signed: Joshua COX (Junr.). . . .
CODICIL: 23 May 1836. 1/7th land to living sisters; 1/7th part to heirs sisters, deceased. Signed: Joshua COX (Junr.).

Page 306. 3 August 1836. Nuncupative Will of Richard HILL. September Term 1836. On above date said Richard called Samuel HILL, Junr. and John NORTON to write his will. 15 August 1836, being third day after his death..."My Negroes be hired out and my Southern Plantation be rented until my debts are paid." Wife Nancy, have use rest plantation for her support and childrens support until youngest becomes of age (children not named). Mentions Negro girl Mary or Caroline. Signed: Samuel HILL, Junr. and John NORTON.

Page 307. 16 June 1836. Will of Dudley GATEWOOD. September Term 1836. Wife Tempy, 1/7 part money arising from sale of estate. Children: George, Mordicea, Elizabeth and John, $1.00 each. Six children: William Elijah, Nancy, Mary, Robert, and Richard, 1/7 part money arising from sale of estate. Daughter Anna AMOS and her heirs, all part left to my wife if any remain at wifes death. Executor: Son William GATEWOOD. No Witnesses. Signed: Dudley GATEWOOD. Proved by oath William M. WALL and Washington AMOS who swore to signature of said Dudley GATEWOOD.

Page 308. 21 August 1834. Will of Henry SAMUEL. September Term 1836. Wife Elizabeth, all my estate after debts paid. Executrix: Wife Elizabeth SAMUEL. Witnesses: Larkin SAMUEL and Jos. W. WINSTON. Signed: Henry SAMUEL.

Page 308. 6 July 1836. Will of Charles CHITTY. September

102

Term 1836. Son Charles, southmost part of my
plantation where I now live adjoining Thomas FISHER of 52
acres. Daughter Catharine (wife of Conrad ROMINGER), 16
acres including building where she lives adjoining land of
Charles. Daughters Mary (wife of Andrew SPAUGH (SPACH)),
Elizabeth (wife of Jacob SPAUGH (SPACH)), and Lydia (wife of
Thomas SHORES), balance of my land equally divided. Lydia
to have my loom. Horse to be sold to buy tombstones for me
and my wife. Executors: John J. CHITTY and George NADINGS
(NADING,NOEDING). Witnesses: Gasper TODD and Martin PIPPEL.
Signed: Charles (X) CHITTY.

Page 310. 11 April 1835. Will of Jacob FISHEL. September
            Term 1836. My widow (not named) to live on
plantation her widowhood. Sons Solomon (northern part
plantation, 15 3/4 acres adjoining Fleet LONGWORTH) and David
(southern part plantation, 61 3/4 acres adjoining Solomons
corner adjoining James WILLIAMS). Executors: Sons Solomon
and David FISHEL. Witnesses: Theodore SHUTS (SCHULZ) and
F.C. MEINUNG. Signed: Jacob FISHEL.

Page 311. 21 November 1831. Will of Thomas DUNCAN "being
            far advanced in years." September Term 1836.
Daughter Anna KERNS' son William, 5 shillings. Daughter
Rachel LYSLE, Negro Margaret already received. Daughter
Rhody, what Charity will bring when sold. To James DUNCAN,
Negro Balaam and his part land. To Eady STONE, Negro Patsy
(to be sold). To Mary FLETCHER, Negro girl Lucy already
secured. To Dicy FLETCHER, Negro girl Alsy. To Judy YOUNG,
deceased, 150 acres I now live on. To Rebecca WELCH, Negro
Emily. To Russell DUNCAN, Negro John, ½ of 100 acres below
and adjoining my old plantation to be sold and other half
to James DUNCAN. Granddaughters Elizabeth and Rachel WELCH,
2 beds and furniture. Son of James WELCH mentioned; appointed James WELCH guardian of Russel, my son. Executor: James
DAVIS, Senr. Witness: Wm. A. MITCHELL. Signed: Thomas (X)
DUNCAN. . . .
CODICIL: 6 January 1832. Negro girl Alsey be given grand-
            daughter Marthy YOUNG. Also land mentioned be given
James and Russel DUNCAN, I now give the whole to Russel and
at his death, Russels part to grandson, James York WELCH and
James DUNCAN shall receive no more of my estate as he receiv-
ed his share ($12.00) in fall of 1831. Witnesses: Henry
MARTIN, Senr., Jno. J. MARTIN, Thomas NEAL, Asa WOOD, and
Matthew WOOD. Signed: Thomas (X) DUNCAN. . . .
May 16, 1834. I, Thomas DUNCAN sold James RYERSON (RIERSON)
Negro Emily which I gave Rebecca WELCH, to Rebecca $300.00
instead of Emily. Witness: William DAVIS, Jr. Signed:
Thomas (X) DUNCAN.

Page 314. 17 May 1832. Will of John WRIGHT, Senr. December
            Term 1836. Daughter Isabella, ½ land called
Hickman Place, cows, furniture, 1/3 grain, etc. Son Joseph,
other half Hickman land. Rest of my children: Daughter Nancy
LARIMORE'S bodily Heirs, son, James T.; Daughter Margaret's
bodily heirs, son John F.; daughter Mary McANALLY, residue
of my estate divided equally. Executors: James T. WRIGHT
and Jesse McANALLY. Witnesses: Benjamin (X) MORGAN, Lenoah

MORGAN and Solomon MORGAN. Signed: John WRIGHT.

Page 315. 16 July 1836. Will of William B. JOYCE. December
         Term 1836. Wife Elizabeth, be comfortably support-
ed out of my estate; Negro woman Chain. All my Legatees:
Sons Elemuel, William, James, Perrin, Hamilton, and Calvin;
Daughters Naomi, Fanny, and Lethele. Son Perrin, Negro Lewis.
Son Hamilton, Negro John. Daughter Naomi, Negro Arminda.
Daughter Fanny ENGLAND (now dead), her part to her two sons
when arrive age 21 (not named). Executors: Elemuel JOYCE
and Hamilton JOYCE. Witnesses: James JOYCE, Calvin JOYCE,
and Perrin JOYCE. Signed: Wm. B. JOYCE.

Page 316. August 1834. Will of John SELL. December Term
         1836. Wife Rachel, all estate after following
bequeaths taken. Daughter Sarah FRAZIER (wife of Lowel
FRAZIER), $1.00. Son William, all estate left at death of
wife. Executor: William SELL. Witnesses: Thompson SMITH
and John H. SWAIM. Signed: John SELL.

Page 317. 6 August 1822. Will of Mary COX. March Term 1837.
         Three sons, Joshua, Jesse and John, all my Negroes.
Daughter Mary HALBERT, $400.00 provided she gives up land her
father died possessed of. Daughter Catharine COX, 20 shill-
ings. Daughter Nancy McKINNEY, 20 shillings. Executors:
Sons Joshua and Jesse COX. Witnesses: Joshua COX, 3rd,
David TILLEY, and Alexander KING. Signed: Mary (X) COX.
CODICIL: 6 June 1831. To my son John COX, now deceased, I
         revoke all his legacy except $1.00. Witnesses:
David TILLEY, Joshua COX, 3rd, Richard COX, and Alexander
KING. Signed: Mary (X) COX.

Page 318. 25 December 1836. Will of John STULTS (STOLZ).
         March Term 1837. Wife Temperance, the place
where I now life and plantation where widow SNIPES now lives,
during life or widowhood, etc. Son Absalom STULTS, $5.00 in
addition to what he received. Son Jonathan, ¼ of a share of
my estate. Son Philip, ½ share of my estate. Daughter
Levinah (wife of Lewis HAUSER), ½ share of my estate.
Grandchild by my daughter Lucy NICHOLS and Eli HENDREN, ½
share. Daughter Marryann (wife of Jonathan MARKLAND), ½
share. Heirs of my daughter Temperance, ½ share. My granddaughter Maryann (of Absaloms firs wife), $10.00. Five
youngest children: David, Elisha, John, Daniel, and Elizabeth,
to have full shares each to School and raise them. Mentions
having bought shares of Peter and Abraham SHAMEL and after
death "old Mrs. SHAMEL" Executors collect and divide said
shares. Executor: Frederick H. SHUMAN (SCHUMANN). Witnesses:
Lewis MICKEY and Henry SHOUSE. Signed: John STULTS (STOLZ).
CODICIL: 30 December 1836. Wife to have property for life
         and full share of balance of my estate with my
youngest child. Witnesses: J. BUTNER and Christian BUTNER.
Signed: John STULTS (STOLZ).

Page 320. 27 January 1837. Will of Peter SHORE (SHOR, SCHOR).
         March Term 1837. Wife Christina, to live on
plantation as long as remains widow; Executors to rent out
land; wife have household furniture, stock, etc. Son Benjamin,

25½ acres where I now live and 19 acres on head Casper STOLZ
Mill Pond. Son Jacob, 80 acres where I live at death of
wife. Son John Henry, 40 acres South corner of my plantation;
Executors to sell plantation bought of Theodore SHULTS
(SHULZ). My children: Mary (wife of Henry FULK), Elizabeth,
Benjamin, Jacob, Joseph, and John Henry, 1 share each residue
of estate. Executors: Sons Benj. and Jacob SHORE. Witness-
es: John C. BUTNER and Christian BUTNER. Signed: Peter (X)
SHORE.

Page 321. 2 July 1836. Will of Susannah GREEN (KROEHN,KROHN).
            March Term 1837. My brothers and sisters: Daniel,
Samuel, David and Joseph ZIMMERMAN; Elizabeth GREGORY, Sally
BEROTH, Catherine FISHEL and Margaret PETREE, $1.00 each;
also $1.00 to heirs of Christina SHULTS (SCHULZ) and heirs
of Christian ZIMMERMAN. To Philip LAGENAUER, my black woman
Alse. To Frederic GAMBOLD, note I hold on him,$150.00. Gives
cash to sons (not named) of John GAMBOLD. To Christian
NISSEN, house clock; Samuel RIED'S daughter Katherine, $400;
Christina LANIUS, $5.00; Treasurer of Freedland Church, $5.00;
Frederic and John GAMBOLD, residue of my estate divided
equally. Executor: Friend William SPURGEON. Witnesses: John
CLOUSE (CLAUSS) and Elizabeth (X) RUDE (REUDE). Signed:
Susannah (X) GREEN.

Page 323. 19 April 1837. Will of Jacob SCHAUB. June Term
            1838. Negro Mary to be sold and her children sold
with her. Wife Maria Salome, furniture, china, silver and
support from estate lifetime. Daughter Betsy, bed and
furniture, etc. Five children: Samuel, Rebecca (wife of
Elisha SPAINHOUR), Elizabeth (Betsy), Holly (Mary, wife of
John Henry WALDRAVEN), Jacob, residue estate. Executor:
George F. WILSON. Witnesses: Peter PFAFF and Samuel STRUPE
(STRUB). Signed: John Jacob SCHAUB. . . .
CODICIL: 9 May 1837. Concerning sale of Negro Mary and
            children; Negro boy Charles to be sold separately.
Witnesses: M. DOUB (DAUB) and Samuel STRUPE (STRUB). Signed:
John Jacob SCHAUB.

Page 224. 6 March 1837. Will of John William Jacob COOK
            (KOCH). June Term 1837. To friend Lewis LIVEN-
GOOD, 50½ acres in Davidson County; also balance of property.
Executor: John HINE (son of Fredr. HINE). Witnesses: Jacob
LIVENGOOD and Philip SNIDER. Signed: John Wm. Jacob (X) COOK.

Page 325. (No date). Will of Joseph COLLAR. June Term 1837.
            Wife Sarah Martha. Children (not named) to be
cared for and educated, my two plantations adjoining my home
tract (by name Adam FULKS old place and Daniel FULKS place)
be rented. No Executor named. Witnesses: Drury BOYLES and
Alex BOYLES. No signature. (Written at bottom of page:
Revoked at September Term 1837).

Page 326. 13 April 1834. Will of Simon CROOM. June Term
            1837. Wife (not named), all my estate except my
land for life or widowhood. Children: John, Elizabeth and
Patsy, above estate at death or marriage of wife. Son John,
plantation where I live at death or marriage of wife, Rifle

gun. Daughters Elizabeth and Patsy, land adjoining John
CROOM, Senr. No Executor named. Witness: Jno BLACKBURN.
Signed: Simon (X) CROOM.

END BOOK III

WILL BOOK IV

(1837--1864)

Page 1. 17 April 1837. Will of Charles Frederic BAGGE,
         Salem. September Term 1837. Wife Anna Maria,
$5,000.00. Daughter Rebecca Matilda SHULTS (SCHULZ), $10,000.
00; several tracts of land: 2,000 acres Muddy Creek from
Fredr. Wm. MARSHALL to my father Traugott BAGGE 1774; 400
acres purchased of Gottlieb SPACH on Neetman Creek; 1,937
acres my father bought of John RIGHTS; 178 acres in Davidson
County, North Carolina bought of John and George HANES.
Daughter Antoinetta Louisa BAGGE, $10,000.00; 2,000 acres
near Germanton bought of Squire LEDFORD; 22 acres bought of
Thomas LLOYD; 11 acres Davidson County, North Carolina bought
of Adam BOYER: 200 acres Surry County bought of John RANKE.
Daughter Lucinda Frederica BAGGE, $10,000.00; 20 shares
Capitol Stock of Cape Fear Navigation Company. Mentions
when youngest daughter reaches full age. To Children William
HERTEL: William, Benjamin Cornelius, Ellen Malvina, and
Elizabeth, $100.00. To Ministers to preach Gospel, interest
from $500.00. Wife Anna Maria, my house, lots in Salem
during widowhood shared with children and she be guardian
of minor children. Executors: John Jacob BLUM, Storekeeper

106

and Frederic C. MEINUNG. Witnesses: John C. BLUM and Levi
V. BLUM. Signed: C.F. BAGGE.

Page 4. 15 March 1837. Will of Milly WILSON. September
        Term 1837. Brother Malkegah, to raise my son,
Obediah WILSON (being 8 years old 18 May next). Executor:
Brother Malkegah WILSON. Witness: Joseph MARTIN. Signed:
Milly (X) WILSON.

Page 5. 26 September 1837. Will of Silas ANGELL. Septem-
        ber Term 1837. Brother Joseph and his wife and
children (not named), for my affection for them, all of my
estate. Executor: Brother Joseph ANGELL. Witnesses: Thomas
CARR and Robert F. CARR. Signed: Silas (X) ANGELL.

Page 6. 23 June 1837. Will of Jacob DOUB (DAUB). September
        Term 1837. Wife Susannah, my plantation where I
now live during life and widowhood; also land bought of
Jacob SCHAUB, etc. Son John Boyd DAUB, above at wifes death;
horse. To William THOMAS, stock at wifes death. Son Daniel,
½ my lower plantation; horse. Son David Westley, other half
plantation; horse. Four daughters Elizabeth, Rebecca,
Susannah and Alvira Mary Eve, all property my wife does not
want to be sold and money equally divided; $50.00 each.
Two sons under age: John Boyd and William Thomas, stay with
mother and work farm. Two youngest daughters: Susannah and
Alvira Mary Eve, to have schooling. Land to be divided
between my four sons. My children: Elizabeth, Rebecca,
Daniel, David Westley, John Boyd, Susannah, William Thomas
and Alvira Mary Eve, share equally. Executors: Brother
Michael DOUB and 4 sons (above named). Witnesses: Jos.
DOUB, John T. HOLDER, Jacob SPAINHOUR, and Elijah SPAINHOUR.
Signed: Jacob DOUB (DAUB).

Page 8. 25 August 1837. Will of Reuben SHIELDS. December
        Term 1837. Wife Elizabeth, house and maintenance
from plantation lifetime or widowhood; balance crops go to
grandson, Elisha FIELDS, who lives with me; wife also have
furniture, stock, etc., but not my land. Grandson: Elisha,
my land; if die without issue, land to grandson, Andrew
SHIELDS. Sons Abel and Samuel, $1.00 each and no more.
Daughter Lydia (wife of Isaac BEASON), $1.00 and no more.
Other Heirs: William, Benjamin, Susannah TEAGUE, Jerusha
IDOL, Elizabeth PAYNE and my granddaughter Mary IDOL, money
from balance of my personal property when sold, divided
equally. Executor: David HENDRIX. Witnesses: Roberson (X)
STAFFORD and David MATTHEWS. Signed: Reuben SHIELDS.

Page 8. 17 October 1837. Will of William SPURGIN. December
        Term 1837. Wife Margaret, all my land except my
Sawmill; also Negro boy Adam; $50.00; a house forever.
Two sons Joseph and William, rent from Sawmill for 10 years
for their education. My children: Christina, Sarah, Phebe
Jane, Joseph R., and Wm. J., residue of estate divided
equally along with wife. Executors: Wife Margaret and
Jacob FORGUSON. Witnesses: A. WILLIAMS and Sarah WILLIAMS.
Signed: William SPURGIN.

Page 9.   6 February 1836.   Will of Christopher STANLEY
          (STANDLEY).   December Term 1837.   Wife Martha,
lifetime and widowhood, 80 acres I now live on South side
Buffalow Creek including dwelling house.   Daughter Margaret
Elliot, above land at death of wife and 55 acres North side
Buffalow Creek including Mill and dwelling house where she
now lives adjoining Daniel HUTCHERSON.   Son Thomas, 50 acres
where he now lives both sides road leading by A. SCALES and
waters of Buffalow Creek; at his death to his wife, Elizabeth;
at her death to grandson, Christopher; also $50.00 to Thos.
Son William, 138 acres Buffalow Creek adjoining Nathaniel
SCALES where he now lives but land to remain in hands of
John BANNER.   Son John, $100.00.   Daughter Alley COALSON,
$100.00.   Daughters Martha RITENHOUSE, Elizabeth SMALLMAN,
Tabitha VICKERS, Nancy JAMES, and Polly AMOS, $1.00 each.
Executor: John BANNER.   Witnesses: A. SCALES, John L. COLE,
and Wm. PADGET.   Signed: C. STANLEY. . . .
CODICIL: 18 September 1836.   Wife to have $50.00 paid by
          Executors.   Witnesses: A. SCALES, Nathaniel SCALES,
and William PADGET.   Signed: C. STANLEY.

Page 11.   1 June 1831.   Will of Mary RAY, widow of George
          RAY.   December Term 1837.   Youngest daughter Ruth
(wife of Wm. OAKS and with whom I now live), any and all
Estate.   Names Negroes Lille and Starling.   Daughter Anna
(wife of John BARR), 50¢ and no more.   Daughter Rebecca
(wife of William BARR), 50¢ and no more.   Daughter Elizabeth
(wife of John VEST), 50¢ and no more.   Executors: Daughter
Ruth OAKS and son-in-law, William OAKS.   Witnesses: John
CLAYTON, Proctor B. FLYNT, and Fountain W. FLYNT.   Signed:
Mary (X) RAY.

Page 12.   21 July 1826.   Will of Jacob LANIUS.   December Term
          1838.   Wife Anna Catharine, 118 acres where I now
live adjoining Jacob LANIUS, Eli PHILLIPS and Levi PHILLIPS;
stock, Negro Sela with her child Susan MORGAN.   My children:
Jacob, George's Heirs, Henry, John, Elizabeth BUTNER, Salome,
Magdalene SWAIM and Kosina SWAIM'S Heirs.   Executors: Wife
Anna Catharine LANIUS and son Jacob LANIUS.   Witnesses:
Samuel R. HUBENER and Levi PHILLIPS.   Signed: John LANIUS.

Page 13.   (No date).   Will of Edmund TILLEY, Senr. produced
          in Court said Will was removed for trial (as
recorded on page 294, Will Book 3, Stokes County) and now is
ordered recorded.   December Term 1837.

Page 15.   3 December 1837.   Will of Thomas TUTTLE.   March
          Term 1838.   Wife Catharine, land I now live on for
life or widowhood, cattle, sheep, horses, hogs, household
furniture, farming tools, etc.   All my children (not named),
above equally divided at death of wife.   Executrix: Wife
Catharine TUTTLE.   Witnesses: S. BOLEJACK and William TUTTLE.
Signed: Thomas TUTTLE.

Page 16.   19 December 1837.   Will of Christian Frederick
          DENKE.   March Term 1838.   Wife Maria, all property
including my botanical Prints; at her death $2,000.00 is to
be paid to agents of Heathern Missions United Brethren

(Moravians). Executors: Wife Maria DENKE and C.D. KUHLN. Witnesses: Charles BRIETZ and Abraham STEINER. Signed: Christian Fredr. DENKE.

Page 17. 5 May 1836. Will of Leonard SCOTT. March Term 1838. Wife (not named), 1/3 all my land including house and barn, bottom land; Negroes except those mentioned, furniture, etc. Son Austin, life with my wife on her third land; balance be tended by the other boys. Grandson Paten OWEN, to be equal heir as his mother, Polly OWEN, my daugther would have been had she lived. Son Austin, two shares as Valentine has deceased. Sons Samuel, Jesse, Leonard and Charles, horse, money and furniture each. Daughter Polly OWEN, deceased, furniture. Son Henry, horse, money and furniture. Son John, colt, money, 15 acres land adjoining LEDFORD'S field. Daughter Nancy HAUSER, bed furniture and Negro Haley and money. Daughter Elizabeth PHILLIPS, bed, furniture, Negro Malinda, money. Executors: Son Leonard SCOTT and Samuel HAUSER. Witnesses: R. A. POINDEXTER, Charlotte POINDEXTER, and Thomas SPRINKLE. Signed: Leonard SCOTT.

Page 20. 4 June 1829. Will of Joseph BANNER, Senr. June Term 1838. Son Charles, 5 shillings (he having has his share). Daughter Charity BRIGGS, lend her lifetime, Negro Lucy. Grandsons: Charles, Seth and Banner PEPLES (sons of my daughter Ruhamer PEPLES), Negroes Ben and Rose. Daughter Mary GRIGG, 5 shillings (she having had her share). Daughter Sarah McANALLY, Negroes Jenny and Vina. Son Joseph, Negro girl Edy and Jay, 150 acres adjoining land where I now live including house and improvement. Mentions 315 acres including Muster Ground South side Dan River be sold. Wife Sarah, balance of land. Executors: Son Joseph BANNER and son-in-law Charles McANALLY. Witnesses: Reuben D. GOLDING (GOLDEN) and Shadrack MORRIS. Signed: Joseph BANNER, Senr.

Page 22. 13 April 1838. Will of Thomas BUTNER. June Term 1838. Wife Mary Elizabeth, household furniture, house and lot where I now live and give a bond to Theodore SHULTS. Executor: John C. BUTNER. Witnesses: N. BYHAN and Herman BUTNER. Signed: Thomas BUTNER.

Page 23. 27 October 1835. Will of Lewis WAGGONER. June Term 1838. Son-in-law Godfrey ODUM, $150.00. Children: Spencer, Joseph, Sally (wife of Benjamin COFER), and Delphia, residue of estate. Executor: Salathiel STONE. Witnesses: J.C. STONE and Salathiel STONE. Signed: Lewis WAGGONER.

Page 24. 18 August 1832. Will of John WILKINS, Senr. June Term 1838. Son John Jr., Negro girl Abigail. Son-in-law Benjamin HUTCHERSON and Wife Delila, Negro Sook and her child Clary. Son-in-law Richard VERNON and wife Nancy, Negro boy Mingo. Son Jeremiah WILKENS, Negro Daniel. Son Thomas WILKENS, $100.00. Son-in-law Jeremiah HUTCHERSON and wife Elizabeth, $100.00. Wife Sarah, whole estate during lifetime. Sons William and George WILKINS have none of estate whatsoever. Executor: Absalom SCALES. Witnesses:

Lemuel and Perrin JOYCE and Daniel HUDSON. Signed: John (X) WILKINS, Senr.

Page 25. 23 December 1836. Will of Christian Thomas
          PFOHL (translated). June Term 1838. Wife Elizabeth
(M.n. FOCKEL), my sole heir. Four sons: Samuel Thomas,
Theodore Christian, Gotthold Benjamin, and Charles Kenatus,
$25.00 each. Three daughters: Dorothy Elizabeth, Charlotte
Frederica, Caroline Sophia, $25.00 each. Executors: Wife
Elizabeth PFOHL and sons S. Thomas and T. Christian. Wit-
nesses: Theodore SHULTS (SCHULZ). Signed: C. F. P. . . .
(Translated from German language by Theodore SHULTS (SCHULZ),
Emanuel SHOBER and John C. BLUM.)

Page 27. 19 June 1835. Will of Gottlieb SHOBER "being old".
          September Term 1838. Lot in Salem, including
dwelling, Book Store with Postoffice be sold private sale;
also private Library sold within family. Daughter Hetwin
Elizabeth, $4,000.00 and trinkets and servant, Enoch.
Daughters Paulina and Teresa, whatever trinkets above daughter Elizabeth wishes to divide. Son Emanuel, his bond to me
$3,000.00 and Negro woman Nancy (wife of Enoch) but if Nancy
and Enick be legally liberated and promise to Remove to
Liberia, Africa, they shall be free; also land in Surry and
Stokes County. To Rebecca (widow of my deceased son Nathaniel), $100.00. To Rosina CLAUDER and Elizabeth LINEBACK,
$100.00 each. To Stokes County Sundy School Union, $10.00.
All my children: Emanuel, Paulina Herman, Theresia WOLLE,
Hetwin Elizabeth SHOBER, children of Johanna ZEVELY, and
children of Nathaniel SHOBER. Mentions anything being
obtained from his land in Maryland from Nantucket Indians
as recorded in Dorchester County 1795 to go to son Eamnuel.
Executors: Son Emanuel SHOBER and Christian BLUM. Witnesses:
John VOGLER and Alex. C. BLUM. Signed: Gottlieb SHOBER.
CODICIL: 19 June 1835. Proposes sending out ministers,
          creating a society for said purpose, and wills that
Executors give $100.00 a year for same. Witnesses: John
VOGLER and Alex. C. BLUM. Signed: Gottlieb SHOBER.

Page 31. 3 August 1833. Will of Verona REICH. December
          Term 1838. To three nephews: Phillip, Emanuel
and Edward REICH (children of Christopher REICH, deceased);
Niece Catharine (wife of David CLEWELL) to be divided between
her son, Eugene CLEWELL and daughter Anette; Henrietta and
Louise REICH; Sybella (wife of Phillip REICH); brothers:
Lewis and wife (not named), John, Benjamin (land in Orange
County, North Carolina), $50.00 each. To sister Catharine,
friend Maria Elizabeth (wife of Christian BLUM); niece Any
(wife of Joshua RIGHTS); Chrissy (wife of Emanuel REICH);
Polly WAGAMAN; Barbara SCHULTS, money. To little friend,
Ema (daughter of Philip and Sybilla REICH), bed and furni-
ture now in care of Hanah VOGLER, widow. Executor: C. D.
KUHLN of Salem. Witnesses: John P. REICH and Sibylle C.
REICH. Signed: Verona (X) REICH.

Page 32. 2 December 1835. Will of John WARD. December
          Term 1838. Wife Rachel, remain on my plantation
durning natural life, $50.00. Children: Betsy GEORGE; Mary

110

GEORGE; William; Rebeca JACKSON; Jacob; Heirs of John WARD, deceased; Anna H. DUNCAN; Ebenezer W.; Sally WILLIAMS; Mitchell; Rachel PATTERSON and Judah L. RICHARDSON, one share each. Executors: Son William WARD and son-in-law Charles DUNCAN. Witnesses: John HILL and John T. BLACKBURN. Signed: John WARD.

Page 34. 17 November 1828. Will of Timothy ROARK. March
           Term 1839. Wife Mary, house built for Jesse
ROARK with 38 acres land her lifetime; stock, furniture, etc.
Son William, balance tract except small parcel sold to Amer
JACKSON; stock, blacksmith tools. Balance be divided with
my four children (not named). Executors: Wife Mary ROARK
and son William ROARK. Witnesses: William PEARCE, Senr. and
Rual ROARK. Signed: Thmothy ROARK.

Page 35. 26 November 1838. Will of William TEAGUE, Senr.
           March Term 1839. Wife Elizabeth, 100 acres east
end where I live; stock, furniture, etc. Youngest son
Elijah, above land at decease of wife and balance of land I
now live on. Sons William, Isaac, and Elijah, shop tools
equally divided. Six daughters and two eldest sons: Elizabeth
TEAGUE, Phebe ROBINS; Hanna DRANCH (?); Martha PITTS; Anna
McCOLLUM; Sarah TUCKER; Elizabeth HEIGHT; William and Isaac
TEAGUE. Executors: Eldest son William TEAGUE and youngest
son Elijah TEAGUE. Witnesses: Moses SMITH and Jacob SMITH.
Signed: William TEAGUE, Senr.

Page 37. 1 November 1836. Will of Christian WINKLER, Salem.
           March Term 1839. Son William Parmenio, my house
and lot, Bakery and Confectionary with all utensils of copper,
iron, glass, wooden and earthern kind for sum $1,600.00
divided among my five children: Christian Henry; William
Parmenio; Mathilda Amalia (wife of Jacob SIEWERS); Lewis
Benjamin; Henrietta Angelica (youngest daughter); also
household furniture, personal effects, etc. Executors: Son
Chr. Henry WINKLER and son-in-law Jacob SIEWERS. Witnesses:
Benjamin WARNER, Jacob F. SIEWERS, and William P. WINKLER.
Signed: Christian WINKLER.

Page 38. 15 December 1836. Will of Rebecca HARTMAN, Salem,
           Spinster. March Term 1839. Legacies to: Rebecca
and Belinda FETTER (daughters of Jacob FETTER); Dorothea
CHRISTMAN (wife of Jacob CHRISTMAN); Niece Benigna FETTER;
sister Elizabeth CHRISTMAN; Niece Rosina KRAUSE; sister
Hannah EBERT; Caritas BENZIEN; nieces Henrietta and Sophia
FETTER; four daughters (not named) of my niece Benigna FETTER;
nephew Peter FETTER (my German Bible); nephew Augustus FETTER
(German Hymn Book); Jacob CHRISTMAN; Sally STEINER and
Frederick BECHLER. Executor: John VOGLER. Witness: Isaac
BONER. Signed: Rebecca (X) HARTMAN.

Page 40. 16 September 1819. Will of Henry SHORE (SCHOR),
           Bethania. June Term 1839. "Having attained ad-
vanced age." Children: Henry; Mary (wife of John HANES);
Magdalina (widow HAUSER); Elizabeth (wife of John Christian
LEHMAN); Mary Barbara (wife of Simon Peter HAUSER), money
arising from sale personal property; Mary Barbara's to be

held in trust for her children. To seven legitimate children (not named) of deceased son Peter, $10 each. To three children of deceased son Jacob, namely: Peter, Christian and Polly SHORE, $10 each. To son Henry and son-in-law John Christian LEHMAN (for trouble they had with me in my old age), 150 acres each out of 1,000 acres I own on Obine River in Tennessee; remaining 700 acres sold and money divided among five above living children; also 250 acres near Yadkin River. To son-in-law John C. LEHMAN, Grist Mill near Bethania for $400.00. Wills old Negro woman Frank to be set free. Executors: Son Henry SHORE and son-in-law John C. LEHMAN. Witnesses: Michael HAUSER and Samuel STRUB. Signed: Henry SHORE. (Translation from original which is in German, signed Christian LASH.)

Page 42. 17 April 1837. Will of Charles Frederick BAGGE, Salem. (This will is recorded on pages 106 and 107 of Vol. IV.

Page 45. 26 November 1838. Will of William TEAGUE, Senr. (This will is recorded on page 111 of Vol. IV.

Page 47. 15 June 1839. Will of Solomon HAUSER. September Term 1839. Wife Elizabeth, all real estate, half land and Mill, known as Sadler's Mill, personal estate, Negro Enoch and at wifes decease to go to children of my brothers and sisters (none named). Executor: George F. WILSON. Witnesses: Martin HOLDER and Lewis MICKEY. Signed: Solomon (X) HAUSER.

Page 48. 3 May 1838. Will of John VANCE, Senr. September Term 1839. Son William, land where I now live (purchased of Seth COFFIN) at decease of wife. Daughter Mariah MARSHALL, $20.00. Wife Lucreacy, plantation as above; stock, household furniture and at her death divided equally between sons and daughters (not named). Executor: Son John VANCE. Witnesses: George BROOKS, John H. LOW, and Bennet FRAZIER. Signed: Jon VANCE.

Page 49. 6 July 1839. Will of Catharine BLUM. September Term 1839. To be buried according to custom of United Brethren Church. Son John Henry, land middle fork Muddy Creek (by deed from Theod. SHULTZ (SCHULZ), agent of Lewis D. SCHWEINITZ, to my late husband John H. BLUM) for $137.50; stock, crops, etc. Daughter Elizabeth, above paid by John Henry household furniture, crops, stock, etc. Four sons: David, Jacob, John Phillip, and John Henry, residue of above sum and crop, stock, household furniture, etc. Executors: John Jacob BLUM, friend and relation. Witnesses: John C. BLUM and Isaac BONER. Signed: Catharina (X) BLUM.

Page 50. 19 September 1838. Will of Henry WALLER. December Term 1839. Wife Nancy and son Squire James, land I now live on including house and he to maintain her her lifetime. Children: Elizabeth (wife of Isaac SPEACE (SPEAS)); Nancy (wife of Jonathan SPEACE); Henry J.; Mary

(wife of Thos. W. DAVIS), 2/3 estate. Three daughters:
Rebecca, Nancy and Elizabeth, money from note I have on
son-in-law Thos. W. DAVIS for $300.00. No Executor named.
Witnesses: Wm. A. LASH and Thos. B. LASH. Signed: Henry (X)
WALLER. . . .
CODICIL: 4 October 1838. Household furniture divided between
           four daughters at death of wife; to son Squire,
my riding saddle. Witnesses: Wm. A. LASH and Thos. B. LASH.
Signed: Henry (X) WALLER.

Page 52. 1 December 1832. Will of Thomas GARTH, Albermarle
           County, Virginia. 3 November 1834. Son Jesse
W., $1.00 having advanced him his share. Children: William,
Willis, Frances and Elizabeth, all estate; Elizabeth's
part of $500.00 to be held by Executors. Mentions being
security along with Wm. GARTH and James MICKIE for Thomas
K. CLARKE (husband of daughter Elizabeth) for hire certain
Negroes (not named). Executors: Son Willis D. GARTH and
William GARTH. Witnesses: T.B. DYER, Robert DYER, and W.W.
TOMPKINS. Signed: Thomas GARTH. . . .
Albermarle County, Virginia: Ira GARRETT, Clerk, probated
3 November 1834; Wm. D. MERRIWEATHER, Magistrate. . . .
Stokes County, North Carolina, December Term 1839; recorded;
R.D. GOLDING (GOLDEN), Clerk.

Page 55. 28 July 1837. Will of Bryson BLACKBURN. March
           Term 1840. Wife (not named), all estate. Son
William, 26 acres to maintain my widow. Children: William,
Robert, Anna FAW and granddaughter Selena FAW, residue of
estate. Executors: Sons William and Robert BLACKBURN and
son-in-law Daniel FOY (FAW). Witnesses: Edger HARPER and
John BLACKBURN. Signed: Bryson (X) BLACKBURN.

Page 56. 19 October 1839. Will of Horatio HAMILTON. March
           Term 1840. Daughter Mary HOLLAND (wife of John
HOLLAND of Salem), plantation I now live on Middle fork
Muddy Creek adjoining widow BUTNER, George HEGE and others
of 250 acres; also Negro John and $250.00. Daughter Sarah
FISHER (wife of George FISHER), 102 acres Muddy Creek for-
merly owned by Michael MILLER, deceased, adjoining Valentine
MILLER: also 96 acres Sparks Creek, Davidson County, North
Carolina adjoining Christian HEGE, John SPACH, Jr., and John
FISHER; also Negreos Bill, Anna, and Annas child, Caroline.
Daughter Elizabeth VOGLER (wife of Phillip), Negro Lewis and
Matilda. Three grandchildren: Drusy, Horatio and Lucy
PEDACORD (PEDDYCOART), children of daughter Elizabeth VOGLER
by her former husband (not named), increase of Negroes Lewis
and Matilda. Two grandchildren: Charlotte VOGLER (wife of
Timothy) and Geo. H. HAMILTON (children of son Samuel, de-
ceased), 290 acres Sparks Creek in Davidson County, North
Carolina (formerly land of John MILLER, deceased) adjoining
David WISENER; Charlotte also to have Negro girl Maria and
Geo. H. HAMILTON to have Negroes Allen and Daniel. Execu-
tors: Son-in-law John HOLLAND and Timothy VOGLER. Witnesses:
Jacob SCHOLTZ (SCHULZ) and George FOLTZ (FOLZ). Signed:
Horatio HAMILTON.

Page 58. 30 May 1838. Will of Thomas WHITE, Manchester,

Deaborn County, Maryland. Wife Elizabeth, 1/3
estate. My lawful children (not named), any property left.
No Executors named. Witnesses: Daniel ROBERTS and William
HARRISON. Signed: Thomas (X) WHITE. . . .
Dearborn County, Indiana,   11 July 1838. Mark M. CRACKEN
appointed Administrator of Estate of Thomas WHITE, deceased;
James DILE, Clerk.
Stokes County, North Carolina. June Term 1840. Above will
presented for probate and ordered recorded. R. D. GOLDING
(GOLDEN), Clerk.

Page 60.   10 January 1840. Will of Benjamin BANNER, Senr.
          June Term 1840. Two daughters, Mary Martin and
Sally BANNER -- and my three sons: Phillip, Joseph and
Benjamin BANNER, all real and personal estate divided five
equal ways. Son Henry BANNER, 50¢ and no more. Executors:
Daughter Mary Martin and son Philip BANNER. Witnesses:
Matthew CREWS and John CLAYTON. Signed: B. BANNER.

Page 61.   7 April 1840. Will of Richard FLYNT. June Term
          1840. Three children: Mary, Malinda and John J.
FLYNT, cow, bed and furniture each. Wife Elizabeth, residue
of estate. Executor: Son Joseph FLYNT. Witnesses: Samuel
CLARKE, Lewis VEST and Elijah NELSON. Signed: Richard (X)
FLYNT.

Page 62.   9 July 1840. Will of Mary SMITH, Salem. September
          Term 1840. Buried according to rites United
Brethren (Moravian). Legacies to: Nieces Anna (wife of
Phillip RIED of Indiana), Elizabeth (wife of Jacob RIED of
Indiana), Sally (daughter of Phillip and Anna RIED); nephew
Benjamin SMITH of Ohio; Catharine FAIRCHILD (daughter of
Christian SMITH, deceased); Eliza (daughter of Jacob and
Elizabeth RIED); Henry SMITH of Ohio; Hannah SPOONHOWER;
Salem Sisters House; Magdalena ROTHHAS; Catharine SCHAFFNER:
Mary Eliza SPACH; Molly REICH; Henry SCHAFFNER; Barbara
SCHOTT: Justine STOCKBURGER; Magdelena TRANSAU; Barbara
LINEBACK; Sarah LOTHROP; Gertrude SCHULTZ (SCHULZ); Henrietta
WINKLER: Margaret KRIEGER; Anna Maria GAMBOLD; Christina
KIMMEL; Polly BECKEL (BOECKEL); Pauline SCHNIDER; Aline
OEHMANN: Christina GIBBINS; families of ROTHHAAS, SCHAFFNER,
and SPACH; Betsy BIEBIGHAUS; Amelia REICH; Sally ROTHROCK:
Lepsy SPACH; Johanna STAUBER; Sally WATERSON; Belinda FETTER;
Betsy ROTHROCK (Sally's sister); Mary Ann SCHYER (SCHROYER-
SCHREIER-SCHREYER); Hannah and Christina BROESING; Lisette
BIDEL (BEITEL); Valina SCHNIEDER. Executor: C.D. HUHLN,
Salem. Witnesses: Frederica HEFFEL (HUEFFEL) and Emanuel
SHOBER. Signed: Mary SMITH.

Page 65.   3 August 1830. Will of Moses BARROW, Senr.
          September Term 1840. Wife Jemima, 50 acres,
dwelling house, spring of water, stock, household furniture,
etc. Two sons Aaron and Phillip, land, dwelling as above,
horses, etc. at death of wife. Grandson Frankling DOBSON
(son of my daughter Fanny DOBSON), above stock, household
furniture, etc. death of wife. Grandchildren: Luiza and
Susanna BARROW (children of son William, deceased), $1.00
as Wm. already received his. Grandson: Charles BARROW (son

114

of Chas. BARROW, deceased), $1.00 as Charles already received
his. Daughter Elizabeth (wife of George LINVILLE), $300.00.
Daughter Amy (wife of Wm. HESTER), $265.00. Son, Moses, land
already received. Executor: Son Aaron BARROW. Witnesses:
David LINVILLE, Senr. and Nancy LINVILLE. Signed: Moses (X)
BARROW, Senr.

Page 67. 11 July 1840. Will of William C. COLE. December
          Term 1840. Wife (not named), remain on premises
for next 10 years and school all my children as they become
of age and give each $500.00, bed, and furniture except
those who are married: Robert, Nancy (wife of Alford REVES),
Letty (wife of Andrew MARTIN). Mentions his father left
him as Agent for children of sister Elizabeth BLACKWELL.
Executors: Sons Robert B. COLE and Barizellai COLE and son-
in-law Andrew MARTIN. No witnesses given. Signed: Wm. C.
COLE. . . .Proven by handwriting on oaths William BOYLES
and Floyd WEBB.

Page 68. 9 January 1835. Will of Hannah POOR. December
          Term 1840. Son Hugh, entire estate. Executor:
John BANNER. Witnesses: Hamilton JOYCE and Austin DURHAM.
Signed: Hannah (X) POOR.

Page 69. 7 September 1839. Will of John TUTTLE. December
          Term 1840. Wife Barbara, my land, negroes, stock,
household furniture, etc. her lifetime or widowhood.
Children: Heirs of son Thomas, deceased; Michael; Elizabeth
BOLES; Mary GORDON; Heirs of daughter Anna EBERT, deceased;
Henry; John; William; Peter; James; Elijah; and Sally EASON,
equal shares at decease of wife. Executors: Wife Barbara
TUTTLE and sons Henry and William TUTTLE. Witness: Samuel
BOLEJACK. Signed: John TUTTLE, Senr.

Page 71. 21 September 1840. Will of Elizabeth FROST.
          March Term 1840. Daughter Catharine BITTING, bed
and furniture. Son-in-law John H. BITTING, residue estate
divided with grandchildren Elizabeth B. and James FROST
(children of son James B. FROST, deceased) when they come
of age. Sister Rebecca PETREE, $300.00. Executor: Son-in-
law John H. BITTING. Witnesses: Riley F. PETREE and Sarah
and J. GIBSON. Signed: Elizabeth (X) FROST.

Page 72. 15 January 1841. Will of John SPEACE, Senr.
          (SPEAS). March Term 1841. Negro girl June be
sold among my children; Negro boy Jacob be sold public sale.
Son Solomon, have $200.00 less than other children because
he left me two years ago before he was of age. Mentions
note due Adam HAUSER and debt to Abram CONRAD. My Heirs:
Henry, John, Daniel, Huronymous, Katharine and Elizabeth
(wife of William LONG). Executor: Son Daniel SPEACE.
Witnesses: Thomas MASENCUP and Isaac SHORE. Signed: John
(X) SPEACE (SPEAS).

Page 73. 14 May 1830. Will of Thomas CREWS. March Term
          1841. Wife Mary, lifetime estate. Children:
Sally JORDAN; Patsy DWIGGINS; Ashley; Polly WARREN; Masey
FRY; Usley DWIGGINS; Constant WHICKER: Betsy DEAN; Thomas;

and Milly FRY, above equally divided at wifes decease.
Milly FRY (daughter) being dead, her share to her children:
Lewis, Betsy and Patsy FRY. Mentions Negroes Jenny and
Nathan be kept in family; Nathan now belonging to son Thomas.
Executors: Son Ashley CREWS and son-in-law Solomon WARREN.
Witnesses: George LINVILLE and Jemima LINVILLE. Signed:
Thomas (X) CREWS.

Page 74. 1 September 1840. Will of John C. GIBBONS, planter.
March Term 1841. Wife Mary, plantation her life-
time (112 acres); also stock, household furniture. Daughters
Catherine, Christina, Susannah SWAIM and Elizabeth SMITH,
$1.00 each. Daughter Maryann GIBBONS, stock, bed, and furni-
ture and William GIBBONS to give her $5.00. Daughter Salome
GIBBINS, stock, bed and furniture and $10.00. Son William,
mare, farm tools, stock, plantation, etc. at death of wife.
Executors: Son William GIBBONS and son-in-law John SMITH.
Witnesses: Kelon PEDDYCORD and Caleb JOHNSON. Signed: John
GIBBONS.

Page 75. 3 February 1841. Will of Crosley BRINKLEY. March
Term 1841. Wife Rosana, land on which I now live
to maintain her her lifetime. Children (which have married
and left me): Charles, Thomas, Jeremiah, James, Willis, Mary
BROWN and Barsheby KROWS (DROUSE); (Barshaby to have 50 acres
at her mother's death taken off lower end; Willis to have
land where he now lives at mother's death). Son William, 50
acres from upper end including cabin built for James BRINKLEY;
also cow and calf. Executors: Son Thomas BRINKLEY and wife
Rosana BRINKLEY. Witnesses: James LOVILL, E.F. LOVILL, and
Benjamin PETTIT. Signed: Crosley BRINKLEY.

Page 76. 25 March 1841. Will of Barnard FARMER. June Term
1841. Wife Mary, entire estate. Son John F.
FARMER, $1.00 and no more. Grandson Clabourn SCURLOCK, $1.00
and no more. Granddaughter Judith SCURLOCK, $1.00 and no
more. Daughter Mary (wife of William CREWS). Mentions all
"my family of blacks" to be equally divided between Mary
REAVES and Mary CREWS. Executor: Peter CRITZ (KRITES,CRITES,
KREUZFUESSER, CRITESFESSER). Witnesses: Edwin SMITH and
Peter CRITZ. Signed: Barnard (X) FARMER.

Page 78. 3 May 1841. Will of Conrad NEAL. September Term
1841. Sons Asa, George, William, John, Joseph, and
Samuel, plantation I now live on, but wife (not named) to
live on it as well as daughters Polly and Nancy, above sons
to pay my son Thomas, $2.00 on their coming of age. Execu-
tors: Sons Asa and George NEAL. Witnesses: John PEPPER and
James RIERSON. Signed: Conrad (X) NEAL.

Page 79. 14 July 1841. Will of Daniel C. WELFARE (WOHLFAHRT)
September Term 1841. Wife Catharine, all property
as long as she remain my widow; if she marry, property
divided between herself and my three children (not named).
Mentions children coming of age. Executors: Wife Catharine
WELFARE, Jacob F. SEIWERS, and Charles A. COOPER. Witnesses:
David BLUM, Senr. and William HOLLAND. Signed: Daniel C.
WELFARE.

Page 80.   17 June 1841.   Will of Mary Magdalene SWAIM.
September Term 1841.   Daughters Hulda, Rachel, and
Sarah, money and furniture.   Sons Eleazar, Eli, Thomas,
money and farm tools.   Balance of estate and my portion of
my father's estate equally divided among all my children.
Executor: John SMITH, Senr.   Witnesses: David G. BODENHAMER
and Jonathan LAUNIUS.   Signed: Mary Magdaline SWAIM.

Page 81.   13 November 1833.   Will of Christian Fredrick
SCHAFF (SCHAAF).   September Term 1841.   Wife
Maria (late FRENZEL), money.   Sister (widow) Johanna Helena
BETTSVITZ, a resident lower Lusalia in Europe and in event
of her demise to her children: Charles Ferdenand and
Ernestine Henrietts.   Sister of my wife (widow) Anna GREEN
(late FRENZEL) now living Berlin (Germany?).   To widow
Christina FRENZEL (late JANIS) living in Kleenwelke, near
Bandesin, upper Lusalia in Europe.   Executor: Theodore
SCHULZ.   Witness: F.C. MEINUNG.   Signed: Christian Fredr.
SCHAFF. . . .
CODICIL: 24 January 1840.   Clothing of his wife not to be
sold at public sale, but given to indigent members
of congregation at Salem.   Witness: Samuel Thomas PFOHL.
Signed: C.F. SCHAFF.

Page 83.   2 January 1831.   Will of George KRIEGER.   September
Term 1841.   Wife Sarah, stock, household furniture,
house lifetime; also part household furniture belonging to
her at our marriage.   Granddaughter Dorothy KRIEGER, $20.00.
Children: Peter, Jacob, George, Mary, Elizabeth, Caty,
Margrit, Charity and Susannah, residue of estate equally.
Executors: John B. MILLER and Jacob CONRAD, merchant.
Witnesses: Chas. BANNER, Henry BRIGGS and John B. MILLER.
Signed: George (X) DRIEGER.
CODICIL: 5 February 1839.   All stock and sheep to wife.
Witnesses: Chas. BANNER and Owen D. TATE.   Signed:
George (X) KRIEGER.
CODICIL: 23 February 1841.   Granddaughter Dorothy BOWDEN shall
have no part of my estate; Jacob CONRAD now deceased,
appointed Francis TATE, Executor.   Witnesses: Timothy KRIEGER
and Owen D. TATE.   Signed: George (X) KRIEGER.

Page 85.   28 October 1841.   Will of David B. GUINN.   Decem-
ber Term 1841.   Son William Thornton, shot gun,
shot bag and a good education.   Wife Narcissa, half my estate
her widowhood; hire Negro boy Elis to buy wife a negro girl.
Mentions at death of his mother, his part of her estate.
My brother and sisters and my wife's brothers and sisters:
Polly E. HAMPTON, Duke A. GUINN, Absalom B. GUINN, Bethenia
P. BOSTICK, Thornton P. GUINN, Manoah H. GUINN, Ann D. MOORE,
Christina E. HAMPTON, Susannah R. PETREE, Nancy E. PETREE,
Malissa HAMPTON, John OWEN, and Nancy J. OWEN.   Executrix:
Wife Narcissa GUINN.   Witnesses: Joseph ANGEL, A.B. DALTON,
and William WETHERS.   Signed: D(avid) B. GUINN.

Page 86.   24 October 1841.   Will of John CONRAD.   December
Term 1841.   Wife Catharine, live in my house her
widowhood; my share in Mill; horse and carriage, horse.
Sons Timothy and Jonathan, keep their mother in grain, etc.

117

also to have stock and plantation where I now live. To Mary
LINEBACK, who lives with me, if she remains with my wife til
age 18 to have bed and furniture. Son Jesse, black mare he
has at his house. Children: Solomin, Christian, Joseph,
Timothy, Ephraim, Jonathan, and Susannah Rebecca PFAFF, re-
mainder of estate equally divided with their mother.
Executors: Sons Solomon and Jesse CONRAD. Witnesses: George
F. WILSON and William CONRAD. Signed: Jesse (X) CONRAD.

Page 88. (No date). Will of John STOLZ, hatter, villiage of
         Bathania. December Term 1841. To my relations:
Simon Peter STOLZ, John Jacob STOLZ, and Maria TRANSAU,
$1.00 each. Wife Christina Gertrutd, all estate. Executor:
Philip TRANSOU, Bethania. Witnesses: Elias SHAUB and
Abraham CONRAD. Signed: John STOLZ.

Page 89. 7 August 1841. Will of Nathaniel PRESTON. Decem-
         ber Term 1841. Wife Elizabeth, enjoy 100 acres
Plantation deeded me by my father; household furniture,
stock, crops; also 55½ acres land. Nine children: Martha
A., George W., John W., Nancy J., Young C., Heston E.,
Harriet J., Nathaniel and Charles R., bonds on C. BENBOW,
A. WHICKER, C. QUILLIN and Peter FULP. Executor: Son Heston
PRESTON. Witnesses: Daniel M. LINVILLE, George COOK, and
Aaron LINVILLE. Signed: Nathaniel (X) PRESTON.

Page 90. 22 September 1841. Will of Eva Barbara SHOTT
         (SCHOTT), Salem, Spinster. December Term 1841.
Brothers Solomon and Henry, $10.00 each. To Sybilla REICH,
Maria BECKEL (BOECKLE), my nurse Anna Johan SPANHOWER Of
Salem, $5.00 each. My father George SHOTT (SCHOTT). My
mother Mary SHOTT (SCHOTT). Sisters Mary SHOTT, Elizabeth
SPACH and Louisa CHITTY. Executor: Father George SHOTT
(SCHOTT). Witness: Thomas PFOHL. Signed: Eva Barbara (X)
SCHOTT.

Page 91. 2 October 1825. Will of Henry ALSPAUGH, Senr.
         December Term 1841. Wife Nancy, my land where I
live during widowhood; then be equally divided between three
youngest sons: Nathaniel, Henry, and Manuel. Son John, land
where he lives. Daughter Mary, bed and furniture, etc.
Youngest daughters Nancy and Elizabeth, bed and furniture,
etc. Executors: John ALSPAUGH and John ALFORD. Witnesses:
George TAYLOR and Polly ALSPAUGH. Signed: Henry (X)
ALSPAUGH.

Page 93. 18 July 1840. Will of Gabriel POINDEXTER. March
         Term 1842. Brother Joseph J. POINDEXTER, my pro-
perty; Negro Anderson; Negro girl Somerville. Mentions
estate of my father; also brothers and sisters, but does not
name them. Executor: Brother Joseph J. POINDEXTER. No
witnesses listed. Signed: Gab. POINDEXTER. . . .
Recorded by oaths of Wm. POINDEXTER, C.H. NELSON and Isaac
GOLDING that handwriting was that of Gabriel POINDEXTER, decd.

Page 94. 16 May 1837. Will of Elisabeth FLYNT. March Term
         1842. Sons Sandy; Heirs son James; Sanford, $1.25
each. Daughter Lucinda (wife of Jesse BRIGGS), $1.25. Sons

John, Proctor (Negro Henry), Fountain W., bed and furniture
each. Daughters Nancy and Elizabeth, bed and furniture each.
Sons William and Allen, $12.00 each. Executors: Sons William
and Allen FLYNT. Witnesses: John C. BUTNER, William OAKES,
and John VEST. Signed: Elisabeth (X) FLYNT.

Page 95. 1 April 1840. Will of Casper STOLTS (STOLZ).
        March Term 1841. Wife Mary Magdalena, Negro woman
Vetel and house to live in if she doesn't choose to live with
son, Daniel. Daughter Polly (wife of Michael HAUSER), bed
and furniture; Negro girl Lucy; land where I formerly lived.
Daughter Anna (wife of Henry SHOUSE), Negro girl Carolina and
$1,150.00 in a bond for the store. Daughter Christina (wife
of John KISER), Negro girl Mariah and plantation where they
now live. Son Daniel, Negroes Elisa, James, Calvin and
Andrew; the blacksmith shop and tools; plantation and house
I now live in, $1,150.00 and furntiure, etc. Executors:
Son Daniel STOLZ and son-in-law Henry SHOUSE. Witnesses:
E. KRAUSE and Edmond HENDRIX. Signed: Casper (X) STOLZ.
CODICIL: 12 July 1841. Heirs son, John to have $700.00 each
        when become of age. To Salomy, my daughter-in-law
land where I had her house built, her lifetime and then to
my sons Heirs: Mary and Mandy STOLZ; also land adjoining John
SPACH and John RANCK. Witnesses: Christian HAUSER and
Matthew WILKINS. Signed: Casper (X) STOLZ.

Page 97. 2 September 1841. Will of J.J. Edwin KROUSE.
        March Term 1842. Brother William, note against
him in hands of my guardian, Daniel STULTZ; my part land
undivided coming from estate of my father, Samuel KROUSE.
To Levin HINE, my shot gun. My mother Maria, all money and
notes coming to me. Executor: John HINE. Witnesses: George
F. NELSON and Joseph BUTNER. Signed: John E. KROUSE.

Page 98. 21 April 1835. Will of Elijah WEBB. March Term
        1842. Wife Susannah, land where I now reside,
stock, crops, etc., slaves: Jack, Owen, Edy, John, Elizabeth,
Phillis, Jane and Charles. To May J. STEVENS, $500.00 if
she ever marries. Executor: Major William C. COLE. Witnesses: Henry (X) MOREFIELD and Elizabeth (X) MOREFIELD. Signed:
Elijah WEBB.

Page 99. 27 February. Will of Mary K. HOLDER. June Term
        1842. Son Martin, $50.00 owing me from my deceased
husband. Daughter Susannah (wife of Daniel HAUSER), $80.00
which Daniel collected from Mr. BARBER. Executor: Joseph
BUTNER. Witnesses: Solomon PFAFF and Josiah LINEBACK.
Signed: Mary K. (X) HOLDER.

Page 101. 15 September 1834. Will of Anna Margareth KRIEGER.
        September Term 1842. Legacies to: Daniel WELLER
of Frederick County, Maryland; Elizabeth RUDY (RUEDE) wife of
Christian RUDY; Christian BICHLER, John Jacob BLUM; Frederica
BECHLER (governess Single Sisters Choir, Salem); Sister's
Poor Fund; Hanah SPACK; Anna ROTHHAAS of Salem; Elizabeth
BLUM (wife of John P. BLUM, now of Indiana); Justina STOCK-
BURGER; John, Jacob, Samuel, Daniel Jr., Joseph Henry, and
William KRIEGER of Maryland; Henry RICHSECKER (?); my nephews:

Jacob RUDY and Maria RUDY (children of Christian RUDY (REUDE);
Barbara WILHUT; Antonetta SMITH (daughter of John SMITH of
Maryland); each of my godchildren: Henrietta MOORE (wife of
Dr. MOORE of Nazareth), Elisa KRAMER, Lisetta MEINUNG,
Matilda SIEWERS, Henrietta REICH, Rebecca SHULTZ (SCHULZ),
Barbara LINEBACK and Rebecca HARTMAN; Mary WHITE; Frederica
RUEDE; Barbara FOLTZ (widow); Charles KRAMER; Sally WATERSON:
Dorothy BLUM (wife of Jacob); Hannah Elise SHULTZ (SCHULZ);
Elizabeth STOCKBURGER; Sophia Maria BLUM; Julia Sue BLUM;
Elizabeth WINKLER; Henry WINKLER: William WINKLER; Constan-
tine HERBST: and Daniel WELLER, Jr. (nephew). Executor:
John Jacob BLUM. Witnesses: John C. BLUM and Isaac BONER.
Signed: Anna Margareth KRIEGER. . . .
CODICIL: April 1839. To Mary (only daughter of Elizabeth
          and Christian RUEDE) instead of wife of Christian
RUEDE; also void legacy to Fredrica BECHLER; void Rebecca
HARTMAN legacy, instead to go to Elizabeth HERBST (widow of
Henry R. HERBST); void Mary WHITE'S legacy. Witness: John
C. BLUM. Signed: Anna Margareth KRIEGER.

Page 103.   20 April 1839. Will of John HUFF.   September
          Term 1842.   Children: Daniel, Hebeah(son), Jesse,
John, Mary, Lavina, Anna, William, Louis, Elizabeth, and
Sarah, $1.00 each.   My widow (not named), $82.00 and South
end old plantation I now live on for lifetime; then divided
between my four children: Wels, Jurdan, Margaret and David
(unless they die before they come of age).   Executor: John
HENLEY.   Witnesses: Thomas WILSON and Seth HAM.   Signed:
John (X) HUFF.

Page 104.   11 December 1841. Will of Hannah JACKSON.
          December Term 1842.   Granddaughter Lousindy
BENNETT (wife of Elisha BENNETT), household furniture, stock
and money; note on Alex. BOLES.   To William GIBSON, the old
mare and saddle, etc.   To William Green GIBSON, colt.
Executor: Alexander BOLES.   Witnesses: Martin BOLES and
William EATON.   Signed: Hannah (X) JACKSON.

Page 105.   22 February 1841. Will of James LARIMORE.   Decem-
          ber Term 1842.   Wife Leanner, lifetime estate;
then to heirs her body except my son David D. FRANKLIN to
have $75.00 more than the girls for his schooling; Daughter
Harriet HARDIN, equal share with other children so she will
not become a charge.   Mentions Negro boy Lorison be hired out
until children becomes of age (children not named); Executors
to sell my 80 acres of land in Jefferson County, Tennessee.
Executor: William WALKER.   Witnesses: Robert WALKER and
Michael J. FULP.   Signed: Jas. LARIMORE.

Page 106.   12 October 1842. Will of Matthew KETTNER.
          December Term 1842.   Wife Mary, homestead planta-
tion I now live on, including dwelling house, Negro Lucy;
household furniture, etc.   Daughters Katharine (wife of
Hamilton WILSON), Elizabeth (wife of Charles HORNEY); Philip
EBERT (son-in-law); Phebe (wife of Philip EBERT), residue
of money from sale of property equally divided.   Executor:
Frederick C. MEINUNG.   Witnesses: H.K. THOMAS and Samuel
LONG.   Signed: Matthew (X) KETTNER.

Page 108. (No date). Nuncupative Will of Sarah JARVIS.
          December Term 1842. Warren TENNISON and William
and Nancy to have cloth for clothing. Proved oath of James
JARVIS.

Page 108. 9 January 1841. Will of Lewis WOLFF. December
          Term 1842. Wife Mary, dwelling house and land
by former agreement with my son, William. Sons Frederick
and William and daughter Sally SPAINHOUR, balance of
estate divided between them. Daughter Christina and her
husband Joseph MILLER, bond on said Joseph of $25.00 plus
property already given them. Daughter Elizabeth GRIGGS,
property and money already given. Executors: Sons William
WOLFF and John B. MILLER. Witnesses: C. BANNER and William
(X) WOLFF. Signed: Lewis (X) WOLFF.

Page 110. 24 December 1842. Will of James ZIMMERMAN. March
          Term 1843. Brothers and sisters: Susan PINEGAR,
Lenah CREWS, Reuben ZIMMERMAN, Elizabeth BARROW and James
(son of brother John ZIMMERMAN). Executor: Reubin ZIMMERMAN.
Witnesses: George F. WILSON and Lenonard ZIGLAR. Signed:
James (X) ZIMMERMAN.

Page 111. 19 January 1837. Will of Henry CARTER "advanced
          in age". March Term 1843. Wife Sarah, lifetime
estate. Sons and daughters: John N., Nancy PAYNE, Mary
PAYNE'S children Winston, Anderson, and George W. Executors:
Sons Anderson and George W. CARTER. Witnesses: Wm. A.
MITCHELL and Pleasant FOY. Signed: Henry CARTER.

Page 112. 13 April 1835. Will of Reubin ZIMMERMAN. March
          Term 1843. Wife Elizabeth, lifetime estate.
Heirs of deceased son, John, $1.00 and no more. Five
children: James, Reuben, Susanna, Leanna, and Elizabeth,
Negroes (not named) divided equally; also estate at death
of wife. Executor: Son Reubin ZIMMERMAN. Witnesses: Jas.
Z. BROWN and John W. ZIGLAR. Signed: Reuben (X) ZIMMERMAN.

Page 114. 1 March 1836. Will of Anna BOYER. June Term
          1843. Son Joseph, plantation, stock, household
furniture, etc. Bible. Daughter Lydia, wearing apparel, etc.
No Executor named. Witnesses: Jno. BLACKBURN, Philip
WHITMORE, and Elizabeth (X) HARPER. Signed: Anna (X) BOYER.

Page 115. 24 September 1842. Will of Elizabeth CROOM. June
          Term 1843. All estate divided equally between
Lydia FRY, Mary FRY, John FRY, and Eliza FRY (Jacob FRY'S
children); also my interest in land of brother John CROOM to
go to above children. Executor: Jacob FRY. Witnesses:
David DOUTHIT, Eve McIVER, and John FLETCHER. Signed:
Elizabeth (X) CROOM.

Page 116. 2 March 1843. Will of Frederic KETTNER (KITNER).
          June Term 1843. Wife Elizabeth, remain on planta-
tion; household furniture etc.; Negro man Cases. Brother
Henry's children (not named), $1.00. Brother Matthew's
children (not named), $1.00. Sister Catharine, $1.00.
Brother Francis, $1.00. Be buried at Carver's Meeting House

as will my wife be, with common Tombstones. To Emily S.,
Sarah, Elizabeth and Titus MILLER (children of George),
personal estate at death of my wife. Executor: George MILLER.
Witnesses: John LIVENGOOD and Branch (X) BOWER. Signed:
Fredric (X) KETTNER.

Page 117. 30 March 1843. Will of Thomas PLUMMER. June
          Term 1843. Wife Elizabeth, lifetime estate for
support of my children until they come of age (children
not named). Executor: John B. HAMPTON. Witnesses: John
HILL and Joel F. HILL. Signed: Thomas PLUMMER.

Page 119. 15 March 1843. Will of Johanah SPONHOUER
          (SPAINHOUR, etc.), Salem. June Term 1843.
Buried rites of church of United Brethren whose member I am.
Three sisters: Elizabeth REICH, Gertrude SMITH and Catharine
CONRAD, money left after my funeral. Mentions late Mary
SMITH, deceased. To Rebecca CONRAD and Lydia LINEBACK (late
CONRAD) stepdaughters of my sister Catharine. Nieces:
Carolina REICH and Amelia WINKLER (late REICH), daughters of
my sister Elizabeth; and Charlotte and Louisa SMITH, daugh-
ters of my sister Gertrude. To Sarah SIDDELL and my God-
child, Caroline GOSLEN (late STOCKBURRGER). Executor: E.A.
VIERLING and S. Thomas PFOHL. Signed: Anna Johanna (X)
SPONHOUR.

Page 120. 23 November 1839. Will of Elizabeth ELDRIDGE,
          Martin County, Indiana. November Term 1840.
My children (not named), equal portion of my estate except
daughter Paulina's share which shall be divided between her
children (not named) as they come of age. No Executor.
Witnesses: James SHORSEY and John (X) WESTMORELAND. Signed:
Elizabeth ELDRIGE. . . .Levi A. ELDRIGE appointed Administra-
tor of Estate of Elizabeth ELDRIGE, November Term 1840,
Martin County, Indiana. Rufus BROWN, Clerk; J.W.P. LOVE,
Probate Judge.

Page 122. 11 February 1843. Will of Sarah STOCKBURGER.
          June Term 1843. Children to remain with my
Mother and Brother Silas, until of age, Rachel F., Sarah E.
and Mary A.E. STOCKBURGER. Executor: Silas PHILLIPS.
Witnesses: David RIDINGS and Jno. BLACKBURN. Signed: Sarah
(X) STOCKBURGER.

Page 123. 9 January 1843. Will of Jacob SHORE (SHOR).
          June Term 1843. Having been married twice, my
first wife being sister of Henry HAUSER, deceased and daughter of Peter HAUSER, Senr., deceased. To present wife Mary
(daughter of Joseph HAUSER, deceased), Negro man Elijah I
bought of Jos. HAUSER; plantation where I now live. Children by wife Mary: Angelina, Permelia, Augustine, Edwyn and
Edward Henry and to a son my wife had before our marriage
by name, Ephraim HAUSER. Son Levi, half my plantation where
he now lives. Requests all estate be sold and equally
divided between all my children (not named) by first and
second wives. Executor: John B. MILLER. Witnesses: Emanuel
SHOBER and Hubert EBERT. Signed: Jacob (X) SHORE. . . .
CODICIL: 4 June 1843. Wife Mary's legacy from her father,

Joseph HAUSER, Senr. to her and her children; notes against Alen FLYNT, Isaac HAUSER and John L. SHORE. Witnesses: George F. WILSON and Daniel BUTNER. Signed: Jacob (X) SHORE.

Page 126. 10 December 1830. Will of Magnus HULTHIN.
September Term 1843. To friend Theodore SCHULZ, all estate, including money and Stocks, etc. Mentions Stocks in State Bank of North Carolina and Cape Fear Navigation, New Bern Bank and money from same be used in Missions of United Brethren, for support of aged Ministers of U.B. Church and education of children known as Wachovia Sustentation Deacony. Executor: Theodore SCHOLZ. Witness: Daniel C. WELFARE. Signed: Magnus HULTHIN.

Page 128. 24 July 1843. Nuncupative Will of Chadwick VAWTER.
September Term 1843. On 15 July 1843 at house of Chadwick VAWTER he said: Wife Susanna and son William and youngest son Josiah to give bond to Mr. SCHULZ for money he owed on land including mansion house. Son Sparks, tract of land where Sparks lives. Other children: George T., William, Josiah, Paulina, Matilda and Sophronia. Chadwick VAWTER died 19 July 1843. Signed: Daniel REICH and Bradford VAWTER.

Page 129. 2 June 1841. Will of John Adam FISCHEL, farmer
and tradesman. September Term 1843. Wife Catharine (formerly ZIMMERMAN), all estate. Brothers John Henry; Conrad; Daniel and Phillip; children of deceased brother Jacob; Solomon and David, $1.00 and no more. Children of deceased sisters (not named): John and Daniel KREUZFUSSER; Catharine BECKEL; Jonathan and Daniel MILLER; Tobias BECKEL; Mary Margareth ROTHROCK and Thomas SHORE, $1.00 each and no more. Executrix: Wife Catharine FISHEL and George HEGE, friend. Witnesses: George FOLTZ and Henry SCHULTZ. Signed: John Adam FISHEL.

Page 131. 9 April 1835. Will of Winifred BLACKBURN.
December Term 1843. Daughter Mary, furniture, Negro girl Fanny. Son Gabriel W., furniture. Son Samuel S., furniture; Negro boy Peter. Mentions Negroes Eliza and her child and girl Martha BETHUNE. Executor: John B. BLACKBURN of Townfork. Witnesses: Temperance (X) STIGNER and Caleb H. MATTHEWS. Signed: Winifred BLACKBURN.

Page 132. 19 October 1843. Will of Gabriel W. BLACKBURN.
December Term 1843. My Mother Winifred BLACKBURN, all of my estate. Executrix: Mother Winifred BLACKBURN. Witnesses: Wm. A. LASH and Beverley JONES. Signed: G. W. (X) BLACKBURN.

Page 133. 18 July 1839. Will of William CLAMPET. December
Term 1843. Children: Hannah WILLARD; Elizabeth BODENHAMER; Dinah SHIELDS Heirs: Richard; Sarah WIER; William; Ruth HARREL; and Cloe HARREL, $1.00 each having already received. Daughter Mary CLAMPET, furniture, stock, etc. Wife Ruth, remainder estate lifetime. Son George, above estate at death of wife. Executor: Son George CLAMPET. Witnesses: John H. SWAIM and Hiram STAFFORD. Signed:

William CLAMPET.

Page 134. 1 November 1842. Will of Charles Gottlieb CLAUDER.
          December Term 1843. To Lydia TRANSAU, $24.00 and
walnut table for her attention to me and my deceased wife.
Son H. Gottlieb, $25.00 and residue estate. Executor:
Emanuel SHOBER. Witnesses: John VOGLER and Hubert EBERT.
Signed: Charles Gottlieb CLAUDER.

Page 135. 10 October 1842. Will of Frances GORDON. Decem-
          ber Term 1843. Sister Stacy GORDON, all my
interest in estate of my father, John GORDON, deceased,
because she is my favorite. Executor: Levi FISHER. Witnesses: Wm. S. KEY and Jefferson FISHER. Signed: Frances (X)
GORDON.

Page 136. 10 October 1843. Will of Robert HESTER. December
          Term 1843. Wife Sarah, all estate except 25 acres
during widowhood; if marries to have only a child's part.
Eldest daughter Susannah, as long as she remains single, 25
acres of land West of my dwelling house where my son, William
builed a house and lived when he first married. Daughter
Polly WALKER (wife of James WALKER), $5.00. Daughter Phebe,
$81.35. Son John, $81.35. Youngest son Elijah, $81.35.
Other children: William Lucy LINVILLE, Martha SWAIM, Faith
LINVILLE, and Ann WALKER. Executors: Son William HESTER
and son-in-law Milton H. LINVILLE. Witnesses: William
WALKER and Thomas WALKER. Signed: Robert HESTER.

Page 138. 3 August 1843. Will of David LINVILLE, Senr.
          December Term 1843. Son John, all my part tract
known as Aaron LINVILLE Heirs or Wm. and David LINVILLE and
comes together with part I bought of my sister Elizabeth
MOORE (widow of Alexander MOORE of Tennessee). Son Haywood,
30 acres West part tract purchased of Harmon CREWS, adjoining Allen WICKER, Moses LINVILLES old line, but my wife
Nancy to have ½ fruit each year. Son Emanuel, residue of
my estate, but my wife have 1/3 including dwelling house her
widowhood. Mentions that son Haywood was kicked in head by
a horse (in infancy) and is a lunatick; appointed wife
Nancy and son Emanuel, his guardians. Son Milton H., land
already received. My unfortunate daughter: Elizabeth (wife
of E. Ronson ROBERTSON), $1.00. Wife Nancy, stock and crops,
etc. Daughters Martha, Juliana and Juranda, bed and furniture and cow each. Mentions all children to get $600.00
from estate William MOORE, deceased, equally divided among
them. Our daughters: Hannah HUTCHINGS (HUTCHENS), Martha,
Juliana and Juranda, any part estate wife wishes them to
have. Executors: Wife Nancy LINVILLE and son Milton H.
LINVILLE. Witnesses: S. HESTER and John HESTER. Signed:
David LINVILLE, Senr. . . .
CODICIL: 3 August 1843. If son Haywood dies without issue,
          his share to go to son Emanuel. Wife Nancy is to
help daughter Elizabeth ROBERTSON with provisions if necessary. Witnesses: S. HESTER and John HESTER. Signed: David
LINVILLE, Senr.

Page 141. 2 September 1843. Will of Simon STULTS (STOLZ).

December 1843. Wife Sarah, all estate if she remains unmarried until youngest son, Alfred becomes 21 years old. Children: Parmenius (male), Welhelmina, Amelia and Alfred, residue estate shared equally. Executor: J.G. LASH. Witnesses: Adam SNOW and Elias SCHAUB. Signed: Simon STOLZ.

Page 142. 25 October 1841. Will of Christian LASH. March Term 1844. Wife Anna, 1/3 estate, including house and lott in Bethania. Children: Elizabeth CONRAD (widow Jacob CONRAD), Sarah TRANSAU (wife of Solomon TRANSAU), William S., Lewis C., Thomas B., and Israel G., residue of estate equally divided; Executors take charge share of my unfortunate son, Lewis C. Daughter Philapina (wife of Abraham CONRAD), already received during lifetime of her former husband, John H. HAUSER. Executors: Sons Wm. A., Thos. B., and Israel C. LASH. Witnesses: Michael DAUB and Elias SHAUB (SCHAUB). Signed: J. Christian LASH.

Page 144. 2 October 1843. Will of Solomon DEEN. March Term 1844. To Elizabeth SMITH (wife of Moses SMITH); Heirs of Wm. DEEN; Heirs of Fredrick DEEN; Mary FRAZER (wife of Jeremiah FRAZIER), each equal share after paying my son, Archelous DEAN $10.00. Executors: Son-in-law Moses SMITH and Jeremiah FRAZER. Signed: Solomon (X) DEEN (or DUN).
*NOTE: This could also be DUNN or DUN, the signature is definitely DUN or DEEN, the name in the probate is definitely DEAN, spelled with an A. Witnesses: John WATSON and John LOWREY.

Page 145. 25 May 1830. Will of William KNOTT. March Term 1844. Wife Tabatha, all my lands as long as she remains my widow and no longer; also other estate if she be willing to share property with my Negroes Jack, Molly and Manoah. Three daughters Elizabeth HUTCHINGS (HUCHENS), Jane KNOTT and Polly HUTCHINGS. Grandson James KNOTT (son of William), ½ my lands East of Blews Creek adjoining Solomon WARRENS and Guilford County line. Grandsons Julian Manoah Hampton KNOTT and John KNOTT (children of Charles G. KNOTT), other half above land adjoining Phillip JENA, LINVILLE and James HOLBROOK. Son Sterling, ½ land on West adjoining LINVILLE, CRIM and line to be run between Sterling and his brother Henry; also a cow and as Sterling is a lunatick, I request William be his guardian. Son Henry, one cow. Executors: Wife Tabitha KNOTT and son William KNOTT. Witnesses: D. LINVILLE and George LINVILLE. Signed: William (X) KNOTT.

Page 147. March 1840. Will of Elizabeth VIERLING, Salem. March Term 1844. Burial according to rites Church United Brethren. To Edward RICE of Bethlehem, Northampton County, Pennsylvania, Silver Divider. My grandchildren: Sanford, Romlus, Edmund, Lewis and Gideon SHULTZ; William and Samuel Benjamin VIERLING; Anglica, Amelia and Ernestine REICHEL; Martha, Carolina and Charlotte SHULTZ (SCHULZ); Ernestine, Caroline and Eliza VIERLING: Stasia MIKSCH; Sophia and Owen KRAMER; Edward, William, Clara, and Sophia REICHEL; and Louisa SHULTZ (SCHULZ), Silver and Bibles.

To friend, Sophia FETTER (VETTER). Daughter Eliza (wife of Charles KRAMER). Children of daughters: Elenor SHULTZ (SCHULZ), deceased and Frederica REICHEL, deceased. Sons Ernest and Theophilus. Daughter Caroline (wife of John MIKSCH) of Bethlehem, Pennsylvania. Executor: C.D. KUHLN. Witnesses: Charles COOPER and Lewis BELO. Signed: Martha E. VIERLING.

Page 149. 2 June 1838. Will of James WILLIAMS. March Term 1844. Wife Lavinia, remain on plantation lifetime; use of household furniture, stock, etc. for her comfort. Children of Jenny LOWDER (wife of Jonathan LOWDER) and Polly STANDIFER (wife of William STANDIFER), $10.00 to buy them clothing. Daughters Nancy, Barbara, Rebecca, Catharine and Lavinia, residue of estate divided equally and not be sold without consent of daughter Nancy. Executors: Theophilus VIERLING and Jacob SIEWERS. Witnesses: Jno. HILL and Isaac GOLDING (GOLDEN). Signed: James WILLIAMS.

Page 150. 17 August 1838. Will of Hezekiah ARNOLD. June Term 1844. To John B. HAMPTON of Townfork, all estate in trust; trusting he will divide with poor traveling Methodist preachers. Executors: John B. HAMPTON and Thornton P. HAMPTON. Witnesses: John VAUGHN and Joseph VAUGHN. Signed: Hezekiah ARNOLD.

Page 151. 15 May 1844. Will of Daniel FAW (PFAW). No probate given. Wife Any, all estate. Son William above estate at death of wife. Mentions "all my Heirs". Executors: Wife Any FAW and B.A. WIESNER. Witness: Jacob FAW. Signed: Daniel (X) FAW. . . ."No Will" written on bottom of page, no probate given.

Page 152. 13 August 1841. Will of Eve HEGE, Davidson County, North Carolina. June Term 1844. Wills all estate except that which is in possession of Son, Christian, be equally divided between three daughters: Elizabeth, Christina, and Catharine. No Executors named. Witnesses: Henry A. SHULTZ and Jacob F. SIEWERS. Signed: Eve (X) HEGE. Handwriting proven by oaths J.F. SIEWERS and F.C. MEINUNG.

Page 152. 3 October 1825. Will of John Joachim HAGEN. June Term 1844. Burial in custom United Brethren Church. Wife Susanna, all estate unless she marries; then to be equally divided between wife and surviving children (not named). Son Francis, my house and lott in Salem. Requests the Court to appoint Administrator of Estate. Witnesses: John C. BLUM and John LICK. Signed: John J. HAGEN.

Page 154. 29 March 1844. Will of Joseph LASLEY. June Term 1844. Wife Nancy, lifetime estate. Seven children: John B.; Menoah; Harriet J. VAWTER; Frances A.R.; Joseph W.E.; Ivy W.; and Ira (?), estate divided equally at death of wife. Mentions children coming of age and land in Kentucky divided equal. Executors: Sons John E. LASHLEY and Menoah LASHLEY. Witnesses: W.A. MITCHELL, A. MITCHELL, and Thomas M. SCALES. Signed: Joseph LASHLEY.

Page 155.   26 May 1844.   Will of John NULL, Senr.   June Term
            1844.   "Beloved Companion", Catharine, home
plantation and personal property.   Eight equal shares: John,
Jr., Isaac, Polly BECK (wife of Wm. BECK), Fanny KAPP (wife
of John KAPP), Betsy MOODY (wife of Nathaniel MOODY), and
William.   Two remaining shares and plantation where my son
Henry lives be given my friend, Henry SHOUSE.   Bond held
against son, John for $800.00 be considered his share.
Executors: Henry SHOUSE and William BECK, Jr.   Witnesses:
Geo. F. WILSON and John CLAYTON.   Signed: John NULL.

Page 156.   1 January 1841.   Will of William YOUNG, Senr.
            June Term 1844.   Wife Mary, her maintenance dur-
ing her life.   Son Benjamin, 45 acres Northeast end where I
now live.   Daughter Rebecca MABE and (her husband John MABE),
50¢ only as she has received 75 acres.   Executors: Libba
HOOKER (possibly a double given name) and Mary YOUNG, daughters.   Witnesses: Chas. BANNER, Martin (X) TILLEY, and
Polly (X) YOUNG.   Signed: William (X) YOUNG.

Page 158.   23 May 1844.   Will of John VAWTER "advanced in
            years".   June Term 1844.   Wife Elizabeth, all
estate during natural life.   Son James M., $50.00 and furni-
ture.   Granddaughters Mary E. and Sarah J. FAGG, $150.00.
Children: James M., Eliza SCALES, and Elizabeth LASLEY,
estate death of wife.   Executors: Thomas M. SCALES and Wm.
A. MITCHELL.   Witnesses: Solomon HARDY, B. RICHARDSON, and
Michael (X) POWERS.   Signed: John VAWTER.

Page 160.   14 February 1840.   Will of John T. BLACKBURN.
            September Term 1844.   Wife Margaret, my homestead,
ten Negroes (not named), all estate her lifetime; my undivid-
ed interest my father's tract on Townfork which my brother
Madison and I bought to be divided at death of my Step-
Mother; also 39 acres Blews Creek.   Mentions his land on Dan
River and when his children become old enough to be sent to
school.   Also percent of estate to go to Heirs of body of
Bethenia BLACKBURN (sister of my wife), Mary Jane WALL (sis-
ter of my wife), William and Martha FLYNT (children of Joseph
M. FLYNT, deceased); Heirs of my brothers Madison, A.B. and
William BLACKBURN and of my sister, Elizabeth BOSTICK.
Executors: Wife Margaret BLACKBURN and John B. HAMPTON.
No witnesses given.   Signed: John T. BLACKBURN. . . .Hand-
writing proven by oath of Madison BLACKBURN, T.H. NELSON,
Wm. A. LASH, John P. SMITH, George LINVILLE and Isaac
GOLDING (GOLDEN).

Page 163.   27 May 1833.   Will of James DAVIS (Senr.).
            September Term 1844.   "Man of advanced age."
Wife Margaret, all lands from Duckling Shoals Creek Side
River, including Mansion House, household furniture, Negroes:
Tony, Lewis, Mose, Winny, Leah, Nell, Delpha, Theny, and Mart;
at death of wife to be sold and divided among my now surviving
children; also to wife, stock, Blacksmith tools, Still, etc.
Daughter Elender DEARING, deceased, her share equally divided
among her children (not named); Negro Charles.   Son William,
to carry on business of plantation to mutual advantage of
he and his mother, land North side Dan River where son James'

land begins, 550 acres I purchased where Winston CARTER now
lives; Negro Isom. Son James, all lands on Dan River he has
not now a title to, mouth Duckling Shoal near new cabbin
built for Patsy SOUTHERN; also land Big Snow Creek where John
MITCHELL formerly lived; also furnace tract bought of Peter
HAIRSTON; also Mills on river adjoining Henry WADKINS; land
on Snow Creek bought of Constantine LADD, deceased; 200
acres Duggin Place; Negroes Charles and Thomas. Daughter
Rebecca DEARING, balance Wadkins tract. Sister Elender
McDANIEL, son James to pay her 1/3 LADD land's worth.
Daughter Mary SALMON, above already received, Negro Luckey I
bought of her husband, John SALMONS and Negro boy Salem.
Daughter Jame COVINGTON, Negroes Edmond and Boyles. Daugh-
ter Rebecca DEARING, above already received, all Wadkins
Plantation where she and her family now lives; Negro girl
Amer. Daughter Betheny EASON, above already received; Negro
girl Agge and Negro boy Green. Daughter Anna EASON, above
already received, Negro girl Elvira and boy Stokes. Daugh-
ter Margaret CARTER, above already received, Negro girl
Sal and child Leah. Granddaughter Minerva DAVIS (daughter
of my daughter Margaret CARTER), Negro Jesse and woman
Cressa ro remain in hands of my son William, as her guardian
until she becomes of age. To each of my daughters, equally
500 acres on Obine River in Tennessee under deed Judge James
MARTIN (son of Colo. James MARTIN). Executors: Wife Margaret
DAVIS, Jeremiah GIBSON, and Hampton BYNUM. Witnesses: W.A.
MITCHELL and Charles McANALLY. Signed: James DAVIS (Senr.).
CODICIL: (No date). At death of wife, Margaret, son William
to have all that remains on plantation. Witnesses:
W.A. MITCHELL and Charles McANALLY. Signed: James DAVIS
(Senr.).

Page 168. (No date). Will of Elizabeth McANALLY. Note:
this will incomplete, no date and no probate date.
Daughter Mary BOOTHE, 42.19 for benefit of her and her four
youngest children. Eldest son, Charles, 5 shillings. 2nd
daughter Ruhamer WRIGHT, $181.00. Son John McANALLY'S
surviving sons (not named), $400.00 divided equal. Heirs
Jesse McANALLY, $200.00. Daughter Elizabeth ......
Here the will stops.

Page 169. 29 August 1843. Will of Dorothy Elizabeth PFOHL,
Salem. September Term 1844. Legacies to: Mother
Elizabeth PFOHL. Sisters Frederica and Sophia PFOHL.
Sisters-in-law Ann Elizabeth PFOHL (late SCHROTER), Anna
Susannah PFOHL (late MUCKE). Nieces Clementine, Louisa and
Julia PFOHL. Nephews Lewis, Augustus, Christian, Edward,
and Willifm PFOHL. To Selma SPACH (daughter of David and
Frederica SPACH) and Maria HEIN. Executor: Brother Samuel
Thomas PFOHL. Witnesses: Thomas T. BONER and Joshua BONER.
Signed: Dorothea Elizabeth PFOHL.

Page 171. 4 December 1838. Will of Reubin ZIMMERMAN, Junr.
September Term 1844. Be buried in same graveyard
with my Mother; my coffin be of cherry plank worth $12.00;
my tombstone worth $12.00 or $14.00 like Mother's. All right
in estate of my father and all my estate divided equally
among brothers and sisters: James; Susannah (widow Leonard

PENNIGAR of Tennessee), Leannah (wife of Levi CREWS), and
Elizabeth (wife of Philip BARROW). Executors: James
ZIMMERMAN, Susannah PINNEGAR, Levi CREWS, and Philip BARROW.
Witness: D.B. BUTNER. Signed: Reubin ZIMMERMAN.

Page 173. 9 September 1844. Will of Augustine CREWS.
December Term 1844. Wife Elizabeth, 100 acres
taken from 2 tracts; household furniture, farm tools, balance
of estate divided among children (not named). Two sons
James and Thomas, all my lands, but equal value to each
daughter. Executors: Wife Elizabeth CREWS and brother Levi
CREWS. Witnesses: Coleman JENKINS and Wm. (X) MARSHALL.
Signed: Augustine CREWS.

Page 174. 12 December 1844. Will of Edward EDWARDS, Senr.
December Term 1844. Household furniture, tools,
stock, crops except bed be sold. Son Daniel, 1 bed; 50 acres
and house where I now live. Children: John and Jane (wife
of Peter MOSER), $1.00 each. Children William, Daniel,
Edward and Elizabeth (wife of Henry KIGER), debts oweing me
equally divided. Son Joseph, $110.00 as he has already
received share. Daughter Polly (wife of Joseph BOLES), land
adjoining BOLES, LEE and WALL. Grandson, John Edwards (son
Johns youngest son), land where he now lives adjoining
Edward H. EDWARDS, Rider tract. Grandson Henry MOSER (son
of daughter Jane and Peter MOSER), 50 acres land. Daughter
Elizabeth KIGER, land East side Little Yadkin below bridge,
but John BOOSE to tend land for two years. Three sons
William, Daniel and Edward have all remainder land equally
divided, but if Daniel bring Frances LOWRY in it or have
her live with him, he shall forfeit his share. Mentions
Edward, Junrs. sons coming of age, but does not name them.
Executors: Edward H. EDWARDS and Henry KIGER. Witnesses:
Michael SPAINHOUR and John FRY. Signed: Edward EDWARDS, Senr.

Page 176. 21 May 1841. Will of John SHORES (SCHOR), Senr.
December Term 1844. Wife Elizabeth, share all
estate with children. Ten children: Anna (wife of Henry
SPECE(SPEAS)); John; Children of daughter Elizabeth, deceased,
she was married to John B. MILLER; Mary (wife of Daniel
SPECE); Henry; Catharine (wife of George HAUSER); son Jacob's
children, he being dead; Sarah (wife of Samuel B. STAUBER);
Solomon's children; and Isaac. Son John, land where he now
lives Southwest side Yadkin River, Surry County, 203 acres.
Son Henry, 175 acres land he now lives adjoining above tract.
Son Jacob's children, land where Jacob lived at his death,
112 acres both sides Mill Creek and Speas Creek; tract bought
of George MASSENCUP. Son Isaac, my homestead where I live;
purchased of Wm. ELDRIDGE and his wife on Mill Creek of 426
acres. To Rebecca SHORES (widow of my son Solomon, deceased),
shall live in Mansion house where she now resides as long as
she remain his widow. My three grandchildren (children of
Rebecca and Solomon), Israel ALEXANDER, John H. and William
Turner SHORES, share equal with my other children. Executors:
Son John SHORES and John B. MILLER. Witnesses: Thomas
MASENCUP and Lewis LINEBACK. Signed: John SHORE. . . .
CODICIL: 7 October 1844. Mentions deaths of Henry, Jacob
and Solomon SHORE; Henry's widow, Susannah live on

land as long as she remains his widow and then land to his children (not named here); also same with Susannah, widow of Jacob and Rebecca, widow of Solomon. Witnesses; M. DAUB and Samuel STRUPE (STRUB). Signed: John SHORE.

Page 180. 26 January 1841. Will of Philip SIDES (SEIZ). December Term 1844. Daughter Elizabeth (widow of Henry SPACH, deceased), who now lives with me to have plantation where we live and end her widowhood, to be sold and money divided between my children and my grandchildren (not named). Executor: Brother John SIDES. Witnesses: John C. BLUM and Philip LAGENAUER. Signed: Philip SIDES.

Page 181. 17 October 1842. Will of James WAUGH. December Term 1844. Daughter Susan L. WEBB and her children: Slaves I let her have at her Marriage: Molly, Jim, Patience and her two children Sidney and Betsy Ann; also 10 shares Capitol stock Bank Cape Fear; if Susan remarries, property held in trust by my son, Jesse A. for her children. Daughter Eliza COURTS and her children, slaves given her at her marriage, Chiney and her children Alleck and Bill; also 10 shares in Cape Fear Bank, at her death in trust by Jesse A. for her children. Son Jesse A., in trust for use of children my deceased daughter Mary M. WAUGH: James, Samuel, Susan and Victoria, slaves let Mary have at her marriage: Nelly and Beven, 10 shares Bank Cape Fear Stock. Son Jesse A., in addition to what he already has received all lotts with their improvements in Wilkesboro, Wilkes County, North Carolina, all notes and bonds I hold on him; 10 shares Stock Bank Cape Fear. Wife Eliza, residue my property; if she remarries, she is to have only 1/5 part; the 4/5 to my three children and children of my deceased daughter Mary. Executors: Wife Eliza WAUGH and son Jesse A. WAUGH. Witnesses: George MOCK and Jacob FORGUSON. Signed: James WAUGH.

Page 183. 13 March 1843. Will of Jonathan SWAIM "living on waters South fork Muddy Creek, Blacksmith." December Term 1844. My ten sons and one daughter: by my first wife: Jesse, William, Levi, Moses, Jonathan, Michael, David, Silas, Alford and Edah, to be raised out of my estate. Wife Eva, land where I live and all I possess as long as she bears my name and at her decease to be sold and equally divided between my three youngest daughters: Drusilla, Catharine and Milly. Executor: Peter TRANSAU. Witnesses: Samuel STEWARD and Moses SWAIM. Signed: Jonathan SWAIM.

Page 184. 23 December 1844. Will of Andrew BOWMAN, Germantown. March Term 1845. Daughter Mary, confirm all I have given her. Daughter Ann W., same; also mahogany bedstead and bed formerly her sister Martha's; also Negro girl Elizabeth. Son-in-law Constantine L. BANNER, Esq., in trust for my daughter, Margaret, remaining mahogany bed so man she married (John L. MOO(?)) will never have control. No Executors or witnesses named. Signed: Andrew BOWMAN. Proved by J.L. BITTING, Isaac GOLDING (GOLDEN) and L.B. BANNER.

Page 185. 3 September 1844. Will of Christian BRIETZ.

March Term 1845. Buried in United Brethren Custom. Son Levin R., house where I reside and house clock. Daughter Lisetta L., 10 shares Cape Fear Bank Stock; forte piano. Grandson, James F. BRIETZ, 10 shares Cape Fear Bank Stock. Son Charles, $1,000.00. Executor: Son Charles G. BRIETZ. Witnesses: William Wesley PETREE and William C. STRUPE (STRUB). Signed: Christian BRIETZ.

Page 186. 4 February 1845. Will of Juble L. DALTON. March Term 1845. Wife Margaret P., all my estate and out of same she give my ony child Franklin Webb DALTON a good education; if she remarries she is to have none of my estate. Executor: Wife Margaret P. DALTON. Witnesses: William WITHERS and Nancy (X) DAILEY. Signed: Jubal L. DALTON.

Page 187. 13 December 1838. Will of Barbara FOLZ. March Term 1845. Burial custom United Brethren Church. Daughter Anna, personal property, debts owing me and money in hand, house and lott. Children: Polly WAGEMANN and George FOLZ to have $10.00 each before above legacy given Anna. No Executor given. Witnesses: George HEGE and Emanuel REICH. Signed: Barbara (X) FOLZ.

Page 188. 1 March 1844. Will of Conrad KREUSER. March Term 1845. I have divided one-half my parental legacy among my natural brothers and sister; I do not consider them in this last Will. To friend, Charles LEVERING of Bartholemen County, Indiana, $874.00; principal bond owing me by said Charles. To friends: Gilbert BISHOP, Catharine HECKEDORN, John Nathan BLUM, Alexander BLUM, Sophia M. BRIETZ (wife of Levin BRIETZ), Julia BLUM, various amounts of money. To S. Thomas PFOHL as Warden Salem Congregation, money. To Theodore SHULZ, agent of Missions of United Brethren, $800.00. To American Bible Society, $400.00; my clothes to be given to poor Brethren in Church. To Benjamin WARNER, Philip LAGENAUER, and Samuel R. HUEBENER. Executors: John Jacob BLUM and his son John Nathaniel BLUM. Witnesses: Benjamin WARNER and S. Thomas PFOHL. Signed: Conrad KREUSER. CODICIL: 10 January 1845. Catharine ERNST who has lived in my family for sometime shall remain in my house with Mrs. Catharine HECKEDORN. Witnesses: Benjamin WARNER and S. Thomas PFOHL. Signed: Conrad KREUSER.

Page 191. (No date). Will of Charles SHUTT (SCHOTT). March Term 1845. To George, Frederick, John and Christian SHUTT; Anderson NICKOLSON; Nancy SMITH (formerly Nancy HICKS now wife of Wm. SMITH); Anna NICKOLSON (wife of Anderson); Nancy NICKOLSON (daughter of Anderson). Executor: Anderson NICKOLSON. Witnesses: Davis G. BODENHAMER and Thomas J. WILSON. Signed: Charles (X) SHUTT (SCHOTT).

Page 192. 7 February 1845. Will of Anna SHOUSE. March Term 1845. My little girl Maranda, all money I have on hand. To Leanna and Lucinda SHOUSE, my wearing clothes. Executor: Michael HAUSER. Witnesses: Geo. F. WILSON and Davis B. BUTNER. Signed: Anna (X) SHOUSE.

Page 193. 12 March 1845. Will of Harmon BUTNER. June Term
          1845. Daughter Elizabeth, household furniture and
$50.00. Balance estate be sold and divided among my child-
ren (not named). Executor: Son David B. BUTNER. Witnesses:
David G. BODENHAMER and Edward KROUSE. Signed: Harmon (X)
BUTNER.

Page 194. 10 December 1844. Will of Travis BARBER. June
          Term 1845. Son John, 40 acres in Pulaski County,
Illinois on Ohio River. Wife Amy, all remaining estate and
at her death equally among children: Isaac, John, Sally,
Travis, Thomas, Elizabeth, Adaline, and James. Executors:
Daughter Elizabeth BARBER and son Isaac BARBER. Witnesses:
J.P. VEST and Proctor B. FLYNT. Signed: T. BARBER.

Page 195. 14 May 1844. Will of William FAW. June Term
          1845. Brothers, Mother and Sisters, all profits
arising from my plantation until brother Lemuel becomes of
age; then plantation to go to Lemuel. Brother Calvin.
Sisters Nancy and Margy FAW. Executors: B.A. WEISNER and
Abraham FAW. Witnesses: Jacob FAW and Thomas HANES. Signed:
William FAW.

Page 196. 19 January 1844. Will of William GRIFFITH, Senr.
          June Term 1845. Wife Susannah, dwelling house,
furniture lifetime; then among children. Son Wm. R. Jr., my
plantation of 138 acres and sawmill. Daughter Patsy, beds
and furniture. Sons George, James, and Wm. R.; Daughters
Margaret, Mary and Martha. Children of son Adam that he
would have received had he lived. Executor: Son Wm. R.
GRIFFITH. Witnesses: N.L. WILLIAMS and John BRINKLEY.
Signed: William (R.) GRIFFITH.

Page 197. 31 March 1845. Will of Amos MARSHALL. June Term
          1845. Wife (not named), widowhood estate.
Executor: J.W. GIBSON. Witnesses: James M. FULP and Robert
W. GIBSON. Signed: Amos (X) MARSHALL.

Page 198. 16 March 1845. Will of David SPAINHOUR. June
          Term 1845. Wife Catharine, house where I live
and 50 acres lifetime; then to go to Joel SHOUSE (Husband
of my daughter Franky) who are to maintain my wife her
lifetime. All stock, tools, Stills and Utensils, household
furniture, etc. sold and money divided among children.
Children: Franky (wife of Joel SHOUSE), Abraham, Charlotte,
Jeremiah, and Isaac. Executor: Son Isaac SPAINHOUR. Witnesses: M. SPAINHOUR and J. SPAINHOUR. Signed: David
SPAINHOUR.

Page 199. 12 August 1845. Will of Leonard ZIGLAR. Septem-
          ber Term 1845. Wife Elizabeth G., one-half plan-
tation, Negros Elisha, Lewis, Rachel and her two children,
stock, household furniture, etc. Mentions house and land
bought of Daniel STOLZ, lot bought of L.G. HADEN. Executors:
John HILL and James Z. BROWN. Witnesses: Geo. F. WILSON and
C.B. ZIGLAR. Signed: L. ZIGLAR.

Page 200. 8 July 1834. Will of Ephraim STRUPE (STRUB).

September Term 1845. Wife Salome and my children remain on land where I now live her lifetime; after son Eugene Samuel reaches 21 years, he is to have land. Other two children Florina Rebecca and Lavina Rosina. Brother Samuel STRUPE (STRUB) to be guardian of 3 children. Executor: Brother Samuel STRUPE (STRUB). Witnesses: E. C. LEHMAN and Levi GEORGE. Signed: Ephraim STRUPE (STRUB).

Page 202. 1 December 1845. Will of Sarah W. BANNER. December Term 1845. Legacy left me by my father to go to my nephews and nieces (children of my brother Benjamin BANNER): Wilson, Adaline, Marcrum(?) and Catharine BANNER. Executor: John CLAYTON. Witnesses: Wm. W. TERRY and B.F. FOLGER. Signed: Sally (X) BANNER.

Page 202. 10 August 1845. Will of William BOYER. December Term 1845. Son Decatur, 63 acres I received from my father's estate, he to pay his sisters $100.00 when youngest comes of age. Mentions Decatur coming of age. Negroes be hired out until daughter Lavinia is of age. Mentions Whiskey to be sold as well as balance of estate. My children: Decatur, Lavinia, Caroline, Olly and my youngest daughter I leave to my brother-in-law, John HARPER and my sister, Catharine to name. Executors: Brother John BOYER and brother-in-law John HARPER. Witnesses: Jno BLACKBURN and William HARPER. Signed: William (X) BOYER.

Page 204. 24 September 1845. Will of Solomon CONRAD. December Term 1845. Beloved Companion Mary: stock, crops, household furniture. Plantation sold and money paid to Mary anually. Executors: Solomon PFAFF and Jesse CONRAD, brother. Witnesses: George F. MILLER and William CONRAD. Signed: Solomon CONRAD.

Page 205. 28 April 1843. Will of Jacob FOLTZ (FOLZ). December Term 1845. Wife Elizabeth, 74 acres where I now live, stock, household furniture; she is to sell enough to provide for children under (not named). Son Madison, land at death of wife. Executor: Gasper TODD. Witnesses: Samuel R. HUEBENER and Charles FULLER. Signed: Jacob FOLTZ (FOLZ).

Page 206. 16 November 1843. Will of Robert HUTCHENS. December Term 1845. Wife Elizabeth, all my land to dispose to children as she sees fit. Negro girl Easter, stock, household furniture, etc. Son John $1.00 and no more. My nine Heirs: Enoch, Mary, Libby, Griner, Robert, Elender, Elizabeth, Smith, and William, money sale of residue estate equally divided. Executor: Aaron LINVILLE. Witnesses: Daniel M. LINVILLE and John BRATTAIN. Signed: Robert (X) HUTCHENS.

Page 208. 12 December 1845. Will of Fruel (Fuel?) CREWS. March Term 1846. Wife Aley, 1/3 land including Manchion dwelling, tools, household furniture, Salt, etc. Four children: Hannah L., Dorothy F., Tyra G., and Robert H., money from sale residue estate divided equally with wife Aley. Executor: John LOWRY. No witnesses. Signed:

Fuel CREWS. . . .Handwriting proven by oath of Robt. WALKER, Levi WHICKER, and Henry W. MARSHALL.

Page 209. 30 December 1835. Will of William GARDNER. June Term 1845. Wife Abigail, one bed and furniture; $1,000.00 arising from sale of residue estate. To Charles STARBUCK and wife Ruth, 1/3 part. To Philip KERNER and wife Judith, 1/3 part. To Charles and Philip in trust for my daughter Anna STARBUCK (wife of Benj. STARBUCK), 1/3 part. Designates Charles STARBUCK and Philip KERNER as sons-in-law. Executors: Charles STARBUCK and Phillip KERNER. Witnesses: J.A. HARGRAVE, Geo. C. MENDENHALL, and John F. KERNER. Signed: William GARDNER.

Page 211. 24 March 1842. Will of Margaret MILLER. June Term 1846. Daughters Elizabeth SPACH, Nancy BODENHAMER, and Catharine LEHMANN, clothes. Sons Michael and Francis, clothing. Children of John MILLER, Jacob MILLER and deceased daughter Rosa WERNER, clothing. Executor: J.G. LASH. Witnesses: Thomas B. LASH and Adam SNOW. Signed: Margaret (X) MILLER.

Page 212. 14 August 1845. Will of Martin RIPPEL. June Term 1846. Wife Christina, lifetime claim plantation, household furniture, etc.; Negro man Jacob and my old man Lade. Brothers John, Christian and Henry, $1.00. Nephew Edwin LEIGHT and his sister Sarah (wife of Edmund TUCKER), $1.00 each. Sisters Susana AEDER (ADER) (wife of John ADER); Elizabeth (wife of Henry KIGER (GEIGER)), $1.00 each. To Solome ZIMMERMAN, Christina GLADFETTER (GLATTFELDER, daughter of George) and Eliza MILLER, now living with us, equal share money arising from sale at death of wife. Executor: Francis FRIES. Witnesses: John M. STAFFORD and H.K. THOMAS. Signed: Martin RIPPEL.

Page 214. 18 August 1846. Will of John c. BURKHARD(T). September Term 1846. Legacies of personal properties to: Grandchild Maria Elizabeth BUTNER (daughter of John and Charlotte Frederica BUTNER). My three children Christian Frederic, Charlotte Frederica (wife of John BUTNER), and Caroline Beata BURKHARD. Executors: Son Christian Frederic BURKHARD and John BRIETZ. Witnesses: F.C. MEINUNG and Alex. MEINUNG. Signed: John C. BURKHARD.

Page 216. 22 August 1846. Will of Edward CREWS. September Term 1846. Wife Jane, lifetime claim estate, then sold and divided between my father, brothers and sisters. Requests that George LINVILLE, Geo. V. FULP, and Aaron BARROW lay off years supply for wife. Executor: Milton H. LINVILL. Witnesses: L. HESTER and John HESTER. Signed: E. CREWS.

Page 217. 28 June 1846. Will of Jesse OWEN. September Term 1846. Wife Polly, lifetime claim, two tracts 253 acres where I now live in Stokes County and where my son Lewis lives (200 acres) in Patrick County, Virginia I bought of Wm. BOYLES. Children: Lewis, Betsy, Mary, Lucy, Franklin, John, Lockley, and Floyd, money arising from sale of estate at death of wife; equally divided. Mentions if any child

tries to break Will, he or she be cut out of Will entirely!
No Executor named. Witnesses: Joseph BISHOP, J.W. BARR,
John BEASLEY, and John FLIPPIN. Signed: Jesse (X) OWEN.

Page 219. 27 April 1846. Will of Emanuel SHOBER, Salem.
September Term 1846. Wife (not named) (Anna
Married name HANES-Moravian Records), my house and lott in
Salem I occupy, household furniture, $5,000.00, etc. Son
Charles, above house and lott at death of wife; Grandmother
SHOBER'S Bible. Son Francis, house and lott corner Main
Street now occupied by my sister (not named); old German
Bible. Mentions all his lands to his sons when reach maturity;
most land came to him by Will of father (not named) Hicks and
Harris land in Surry County exempt from above. Mentions
land purchased from Mr. SHULZ adjoining E. VIERLING and John
WATERSON and lott on Blews Creek Road, each of children to
have $8,000.00. Two daughters not named. To Chas. F. KLUGE,
all my factory stock. To Salem Poor fund, $100.00. To Thos.
C. PFOHL, $200.00 to keep public square in proper condition.
Executors: Charles E. and Francis E. SHOBER, sons. No wit-
nesses. Counsel: Jno. A. GILMER. Signed: Emanuel SHOBER.
Handwriting proven by oath August T. ZEVELY, James T.
MOREHEAD and John F. POINDEXTER.

Page 223. 7 September 1845. Will of Revd. Charles A. Van
VLECK, Greenville County, Tennessee. Wife
Christina Susan, personal estate for use in rearing my
children. Brother Wm. H. Van VLECK, assist wife if she needs
him. Executors: Dr. Alex. WILLIAMS, Jacob HOWARD, and wife
Christina Van FLECK. Witnesses: Valentine LANIER and James
BRITTON. Signed: Charles A. Van VLECK. . . .Certificate
of Probate from Greenville County, Tennessee, 4 May 1846.
Geo. W. FOUTE, Clerk. Charles GOSS, Chm. Co. Ct. Stokes
County, North Carolina, September Term 1846, ordered recorded.

Page 225. 20 December 2838. Will of Joseph BOLEJACK.
December Term 1846. To Charlotte JARREL (daughter
of my deceased brother John BOLEJACK), two bonds on Elijah
JARREL. Other six children of my deceased brother John:
James, William, John, Polly, Joel, and Elizabeth, $150.00
equally divided. Sister Mary Ann BOLEJACK, 75 acres South
side Townfork adjoining John KIGERS Mill branch, Betty
SIMMONS spring branch, during her lifetime; then to my great
nephew William Asberry BOLEJACK; also to Mary Ann my Negro
Lucy and $200.00. Sister Elizabeth FRANCIS (wife of Wm.
FRANCIS), $200.00. Brothers Samuel and Matthew, $150.00
each. Executor: Great nephew Wm. Asberry BOLEJACK. Witnesses: Isaac S. GIBSON and Jno. F. POINDEXTER. Signed: Joseph
BOLEJACK.

Page 227. 23 September 1846. Will of Mary MARTIN. December
Term 1846. Brothers Philip and Joseph BANNER;
lifetime home on my land and dwelling. Brother Benjamin
BANNER, my land and Negro girl Eda, Old Jenny, Harman and
Mariah and keep them together. Executor: Brother Benjamin
BANNER. Witnesses: John CLAYTON, Senr., Abner PRYOR, and
Wilson C. BANNER. Signed: Mary (X) MARTIN.

Page 228. 20 December 1846. Will of Thomas CREWS. December Term 1846. Wife Mary, household furniture; support from money arising from sale estate and at her death equally divided between my children (not named). Executors: Sons James B. CREWS and Levi CREWS. Witnesses: Leonard G. HEYDEN and Jonathan CREWS. Signed: Thomas (X) CREWS.

Page 229. 25 March 1843. Will of Samuel STANLEY. December Term 1846. Son Frederick, $183.00. Son Jacob, land North ditch running through my farm. Two daughters Celia and Mary F., bed and furniture, money and cow each. Wife Jane, land South above ditch and all personal property. Executor: Jeremiah FRAZER. Witnesses: John LOWRY and Moses and James EVANS. Signed: Samuel STANLEY.

Page 230. 26 March 1846. Will of Fredrick SPACH. December Term 1846. Wife Lucy, lifetime claim plantation, dwelling house, personal property. Children: Alexander, Samuel Benton, William, Jane and Bethany (female), residue of estate equally divided when come of age. Executor: John REICH. Witnesses: Wm. L. ATWOOD and Emanuel ALSPAUGH. Signed: Frederick SPACH.

Page 232. 11 September 1846. Will of Lucinda SALMON. March Term 1847. All estate sold (except Negroes: Old Phebe and girl Henrietta) and divided between son, John D. SALMON and daughter Paulina S. SMITH (old Phebe to Paulina) Granddaughter Martha T. SAMUEL (wife of Hampton SAMUEL), Negro girl Henrietta and a skillet. Executor: Isaac S. GIBSON. Witnesses: Jno. HILL and Jno. F. POINDEXTER. Signed: Lucinda SALMON.

Page 233. 10 April 1842. Will of Joel TILLEY. March Term 1847. Wife Elizabeth, $125.00; Negroes Harry and Sary; stock, household furniture lifetime claim homestead. Son Thomas Jefferson, land he lives on in Surry County; line between him and John TUTTLE (who married my daughter Elley (Ellen) TILLEY). To John TUTTLE and wife Elley (my daughter), land where they live in Surry County, if John TUTTLE pay after my death $50.00 to my son Aaron B. TILLEY; also to John and Elley, Negro girl Mary. Son Aaron B. TILLEY, 600 acres where he lives in Stokes County; also note of $50.00 on John TUTTLE and $50.00 on Moses TILLEY; also Negro James. To Silas TUCKER and my granddaughter Frances TUCKER, 500 acres in Stokes where I now live at death of my wife; also Negro Jacob. Son Moses TILLEY, land he lives on in Surry, line between him and John FRANCIS (who married Nancy TILEY). To John FRANCIS and wife (my daughter Nancy), land in Surry County adjoining John TUTTLE and Moses TILLEY; also Negroes Sarah and Jenny. Mentions two Negroes Matilda and Henry to my three sons. Executors: Son Aaron B. TILLEY and grandson-in-law Silas TUCKER. Witnesses: James LYON and Martin and Ephraim SIMMONS. Signed: Joel TILLEY.

Page 235. 4 October 1846. Will of John H. BITTING. June Term 1847. Wife Catharine, Negro woman Lucinda and yellow girl Lidea (Lucinda's daughter); 100 acres Freeman

place on Neatman Creek where Wm. P. PULHAM lives; any estate
for her use and use my children as common property and she
settle in some village so as to educate my children and
during lifetime my father I prefer she live near him; also
934 acres where I now live and 700 acres known as Scott land
adjoining to be sold. Mentions being guardian to Heirs of
Joseph HOLLAR; Bond on Riley F. PETREE; Noah MARSHALL; Will
of Joseph WAGGONER, deceased; Negroes Will and Martin. Son
John, be education well and graduate at Chapel Hill and
(son?) Nicholas have same. Daughters Elizabeth, Mary Ann
and Louisa, obtain education. Executors: John F. POINDEXTER
and Joseph A. BITTING, brother. Witnesses: Reubin D.
GOLDING (GOLDEN) and Riley F. PETREE. Signed: Jno. H.
BITTING.

Page 238. 21 March 1837. Will of George McKNIGHT. June
         Term 1847. Wife Polly, all property she brought
with her at our marriage; also provisions, etc. Children of
William McKNIGHT: Sally and Alge, $5.00 if they sign legal
conveyance 63 acres land to the Moravians. Son Adam, equal
share personal estate, already received land. Children of
my daughter Rachel, deceased (who married Obediah VEST) (not
named). Daughter Polly NORMAN, equal share in land with my
three sons. Son Joshua, land where he lives. Son George,
63 acres where he lives. Mentions 5 slaves but does not
name them. Executors: Sons George and Joshua McKNIGHT.
Witnesses: John BUTNER and Silas PHILLIPS. Signed: George
McKNIGHT.

Page 240. 3 May 1847. Will of Harmon REDMON. June Term
         1847. Sister Elizabeth FLYNT, 50 acres where she
lives to be surveyed by Philip DAVIS and Griffin FLYNT.
Phillip DAVIS be guardian to my unfortunate son Gabriel
REDMON his lifetime and at Gabriel's death said DAVIS have
entire estate. Brothers Joseph and John REDMON and sister
Elizabeth FLYNT, equal division money arising from sale of
slaves (not named) except woman Crissa who has been given
to Phillip DAVIS. Executor: Phillip DAVIS. Witnesses: Jno.
HILL, Benjamin ZIGLAR, and William ZIGLAR. Signed: Harmon
(X) REDMON.

Page 241. 24 December 1846. Will of John SPAINHOUR. June
         Term 1847. Wife Elizabeth, lifetime claim all
estate. Son (youngest) John, 190 acres where I now live on
Barker's Creek at decease of wife if he pay other children
(not named). Executor: H.G. ANDERSON. Witnesses: Abraham
KRIEGER and Constantine B. ANDERSON. Signed: John (X)
SPAINHOWER.

Page 243. 6 February 1847. Will of Barbara LEINBACK of
         Salem. December Term 1847. To Eugene CLEWELL
(son of David CLEWELL), bed and linen, etc. To Anetta
CLEWELL (daughter of David CLEWELL), clothes, etc. To
David CLEWELL, his note of $25.00. To Dorothy CLEWELL (wife
of David CLEWELL), furniture and china. Brother Joseph
LEINBACK, his note for $25.00. Legacies to: Frederica
CHITTY (wife of Traugott CHITTY); Rebecca STAUBER; Sick Nurse
of Salem Sisters House; Treasurer Bible Assoc. Salem;

Treasurer Home Missions Society, Salem; Catharine SCHAFFNER
(wife of John SCHAFFNER); sister-in-law, Susan LEINBACK (wife
of Joseph) and three daughters (not named) of Joseph; nieces:
Sarah FETTER (wife of Peter FETTER), Maria HALL (wife of
John HALL) and Caroline GOSLIN (wife of Wm. GOSLIN); my step-
sister, Elizabeth HAUSER (widow Solomon HAUSER) of Betheny;
Henrietta BRUNNER (wife of Henry BRUNNER); Louisa ALBRIGHT
(wife of Henry ALBRIGHT), both of Nazarith, Pennsylvania;
God-children: Adelade CHITTY (daughter of Traugott CHITTY),
Francis SCHAFFNER (son of Henry), Jane WELFARE (daughter of
Daniel), Paulina MICKE (wife of John), and Elizabeth Lane
(late BRENDEL); Frederica HUFFEL; Catharine GIBBONS; Anna
Maria GAMBOLD; Gertrude SCHULZ, Sarah LATHROP; Sally WATER-
SON; Elizabeth BLUM; Hannah and Christina BROSING: and my
stepsister, Lea WARNER (wife of James). Executor: Dr.
Christian David KUHLN. Witnesses: S. Thomas PFOHL and
Abraham STEINER. Signed: Barbary (X) LINEBACK.

Page 246. 12 November 1847. Will of Lewis REICH. December
          Term 1847. To Charles Wm. BUTNER, my horse. To
C.W. BUTNER, Jesse STYERS and my mother (not named), that
coming to me from my father's estate. Brother Timothy,
Clothes. Executor: John A. STYERS. Witnesses: Willis
LAURANCE and Samuel J. STYERS. Signed: Lewis (X) REICH.

Page 247. 24 September 1846. Will of Henry SCHULZ, Senr.
          December Term 1847. Grandson Edwin Theodore
SCHUTZ, 195 acres where I live but to pay Louisa Elizabeth
and Julie Antoinette Mandeville SCHULZ $100.00 each when
they come of age. Daughter-in-law Rebecca SCHOLTZ (widow
of my son-not named), a home on my land her widowhood.
Executor: Martin HOLDER. Witnesses: Jacob (X) KRAUSE and
Peter (X) MARSHALL. Signed: Henry (X) SCHULZ.

Page 248. 4 September 1847. Nuncupative Will of Thomas A.
          GRIGG. March Term 1848. Wills that Anderson I.
GRIGG settle all his debts and residue estate go to said
Anderson. Test: Eliza A. GRIGG and Cornelia GRIGG.

Page 249. 22 October 1847. Will of Robert WALKER. June
          Term 1848. Son William, $25.00 as he has already
received considerable amount of money; 100 acres land and
Negro boy Tom. Daughter Nancy (wife of Joseph BRIGGS), Negro
boy George and girl Amy. Daughter Mary (wife of Clayton
VANHOY), Negro Caroline and land I bought of Vincent BROWN,
both of which she has already received. Daughter Ruth (widow
of Martin W. VANHOY), 63½ acres where she lives; Negro Phebe
and her child Clarissa. Daughter Ann Elizabeth (wife of
Hugh LOWRY), Negro Bill and girl Viletta which she already
has. Son Robert L., Negro Silas, $175.00, the Mill and its
land. Wife Martha, old Negro Nathan and woman Matilda and
boy Henry Clay, household furniture, stock, 1/3 home tract
of 502 acres including dwelling. Executors: Sons Robert
L. and William WALKER. Witnesses: C.H. MATTHEWS and Jno. F.
POINDEXTER. Signed: Robert WALKER.

Page 251. 29 November 1836. Will of Jacob CONRAD, a
          Citizen of Stokes County. September Term 1848.

Son William, stock, tools, 4 tracts of land, 191½ acres.
Son Frederic, money from William. Daughter Mary Susannah
(wife of Solomon HOLLAR), money from William. Granddaughter
Burrella Elvira, money from William. Mentions 191½ acres
land bought 1/11/1812 from Chr. CONRAD Heirs, also 46 acres;
46½ acres from State 12/24/1796; also 7 acres; also Oil Mill.
Executor: Son William CONRAD. Witnesses: Wm. A. LASH and
Geo. F. WILSON and Daniel HAUSER. Signed: Jacob (X) CONRAD.
CODICIL: 22 March 1848. Granddaughter not to have share
        until age 18; son Frederic to pay sum to William.
Witnesses: Geo. F. WILSON and Martin HOLDER. Signed: Jacob
(X) CONRAD.

Page 253. 6 May 1846. Will of Elizabeth CRISSMANN, Salem.
        September Term 1848. Grandson Peter FETTER,
$250.00. Daughter Benigna FETTER (wife of Jacob), household
furniture, linen. Granddaughter Belinda FETTER, furniture,
$75.00, etc. Son-in-law Jacob FETTER, $10.00 and table.
Son James, furniture. Daughter-in-law Dorothy (wife of
James), furniture. To Augusta and Charles FETTER; Rebecca,
Olivia, Laura and Sophia ROMINGER; Sophia and Henrietta
FETTER; Fr. and C. BENZIEN. Mentions house and lot in
Liberty one mile North of Salem where I now live be sold at
death daughter Benigna and money divided between her and her
nine children: Belinda, Thomas, Rebecca, Peter, Augustus,
Sophia, Henrietta, Henry and William FETTER and house be
kept in good repair by Jacob FETTER. Executor: John VOGLER.
Witnesses: E.A. VOGLER and A.C. HEGE. Signed: Elizabeth (X)
CRISSMANN. . . .
CODICIL: 15 May 1846. Son James draw interest on $100.00
        during life then divided between his children:
Abner, Arlis, Allen and Henry.

Page 255. 5 December 1839. Will of Mary ROMINGER. Septem-
        ber Term 1848. To Jacob SHORE, personal property
and land on South Fork Creek. No Executor. Witness: W.L.
SWAIM. Signed: Mary (X) ROMINGER.

Page 256. 26 December 1846. Will of Elisha MEREDITH.
        December Term 1848. Wife Sarah, lifetime claim
all estate; then sold and divided among my Heirs. Son
Jonathan, $1.00; Heirs of my daughter Assineth HITHCOCK; her
son Elisha, $2.00; her grandson Edward Westley SMITH, $1.00;
my daughter Mary, $50.00. Executor: Son-in-law Richard
STANLEY. Witnesses: Geo. W. BOWMAN and John ROSS. Signed:
Elisha MEREDITH.

Page 257. 4 August 1847. Will of Francis FULTON. March
        Term 1849. Estate to be sold and money divided
equally among my children: Dicy REDMAN, Samuel, Francis,
Allen, Joel, Fewel (son) and Elisha, each have 1/10th part.
Grandson Noah WELSH, 1/10th part. Grandchildren living in
Tennessee that my daughter Elizabeth bore William WORD, a
note on their father for $18.00. Four grandchildren (child-
ren of daughter Milly and William ABBOTT) not named, 1/10th
part. Son Joel to be guardian of grandchildren under age
18. Executor: Son Fewel FULTON. Witnesses: Martin REDMAN
and B.F. POWERS. Signed: Francis FULTON.

Page 259.   9 May 1849.   Will of Jeremiah GIBSON.   December
          Term 1849.   Wife Sarah, room in my house which we
occupy and furniture, etc. during her life; then to son, J.
S. GIBSON; also Negro Lovina and her 2 children James Rufus
and Maria.   Granddaughter Olivia G. GIBSON (now Olivia G.
STEDMAN), 400 acres Buffalow Creek I bought at Joshua
BANNERS sale; also house and lott upper end Germanton in
Stokes and Forsyth Counties; also land I bought of Dr. John
PEPPER, Saray GIBSON and M.T. BENTON; also slaves Catharine
and her two children Caroline and Anderson, Jefferson and
wife Venus and their children Milton, Harriet, Wiley, Nancy
Elizabeth and Smith; Negro Henderson; also to Olivia $5,000.
00; if Olivia Gertrude dies without issue; land, negroes and
money remaining shall go to my son Isaac G. GIBSON.   Execu-
tor: Son Isaac G. GIBSON.   Witness: none.   Signed: J. GIBSON.
Proved by oath of Matthew R. BANNER that will was found
after death of said GIBSON among valuable papers and effects.
Handwriting proved by Matthew R. BANNER, John and Joel H.
HILL, Marshall T. BENTON and Reubin D. GOLDEN.

Page 260.   9 February 1849.   Will of Susanna EATON.   December
          Term 1849.   Granddaughter Camilly Catherin EATON
(daughter of James), cow and calf.   Grandson James Morven
EATON (son of James), bed and furniture.   Executor: James
EATON.   Witnesses: Alex. KING and William KING.   Signed:
Susanna (X) EATON.

Page 261.   10 November 1846.   Will of Jesse FRY.   June Term
          1850.   Wife Massey, tract land where I live; Negro
Martha, household furniture.   Three grandchildren James M.,
Nancy E., and Irvin Asley Thomas CRUMPLY, 100 acres above
land East end after wifes death.   Daughter Lucinda PETREE
(wife of Wm. W.), slaves Esther and her children Gideon, Ann
and Olivia.   Son Lewis M., 218 acres where he lives on
Oldfield Creek, slaves Emanuel and Mary.   Daughter Martha
MORRIS (wife of Lewis), house she lives in and 10 shillings.
Executors: Son Lewis M. FRY and son-in-law Wm. W. PETREE.
Witnesses: M.T. BENTON and John F. POINDEXTER.   Signed:
Jesse FRY.

Page 263.   18 November 1840.   Will of Leonard ZIGLAR.   June
          Term 1850.   Wife Nancy, all estate for her comfort
and that of my four daughters Elizabeth, Anna, Susannah and
Mary; also Negro girl Sarah and all other estate except land;
at death daughters land to go to son James ZIGLAR.   Executor:
Son James ZIGLER.   Witnesses: Thos. C. PLUMMER and John G.
HILL.   Signed: Leonard ZIGLAR.

Page 264.   26 June 1850.   Will of Thomas KING.   September
          Term 1850.   Executor sell my slave Sam and all
my property.   Brother Geo. L. KING, $1.00.   Sisters Nancy
ASHWORTH and Polly C. HANBY, estate equally divided.   Executor: John W. BITTING.   Witnesses: Thos. M. PUCKETTE and
Anthony L. BITTING.   Signed: Thomas KING.

Page 265.   8 November 1848.   Will of Thomas BROWN.   December
          Term 1850.   Wife Catharine, land where I live
known as Charles EVANS tract; also small tract I bought of

James DAVIS including my Mansion House; also Negro Jack, furniture, etc. To children (not named) of my eldest daughter Polly and her husband, John IRON, $50.00 as Polly received when married. Seven daughters Elizabeth THOMAS, Catharine REDMAN, Jaby JAMES, Jincy PADGET, Caroline COVINGTON, Sally SMITH and Nancy BROWN, equal share residue estate. Executor: Samuel FULTON, Senr. Witnesses: George and Asa NEAL. Signed: Thomas (X) BROWN.

Page 267. 20 March 1846. Will of John L. BITTING. March Term 1851. Wife Martha, house and lot where I live and lately bought of Dr. A(ndrew) BOWMAN; also land on Buffalow; $1,500.00; Negro Mary, household furniture, etc. Son Samuel L., horse, $2,000.00, beds and furniture, mentions wife of Samuel but does not name her. Daughters Elizabeth and Ann Gertrude, $2,000.00 each and if marry, bed and furniture when come of age, $500.00 toward schooling. Children: Polly GOLDING (GOLDEN), John H., Walter R., Joseph A., Samuel Lewis, Martha E. and Ann Gertrude, the last 7 equally, but Polly GOLDEN to have chest where I keep the key; Jesse COX is to be allowed to live on his land 5 more years and if pays for it, Jesse to have title. Executors: Calep H. MATTHEWS and John H. BITTING and Reuben D. GOLDING (GOLDEN). Signed: J.L. BITTING. . . . CODICIL: 28 September 1848. John H. BITTING has died since making my will; his children to have his share; Samuel has received his share of $2,000.00. Appointed Walter F. BITTING Executor in place of John H. Witnesses: None. Signed: J.L. BITTING. Handwriting proved by John W. GIBSON, Marshall T. BENTON and Wm. A. LASH.

Page 269. 26 September 1846. Will of Bethenia EASON. March Term 1851. Daughter Susannah TUTTLE (wife of Peter TUTTLE), Negro boy Tom and all my estate. Son-in-law Peter TUTTLE, Negro Warren. Executor: Son-in-law Peter TUTTLE. Witnesses: Isaac GOLDEN, H. MILLER and John H. PETREE. Signed: Bethenia (X) EASON.

Page 270. 31 July 1848. Will of Sarah FRANCIS, Pensacola, Florida. 4 September 1849. Daughter Evoline Elizabeth FRANCIS, slaves: Armistead, Zene (his wife), Zene's daughter Eliza; two girls Harriet and Ann (daughters of Peggy); also house and lot on Romana Street between P Y. WESTRA and Franciscus CORNMYNS; also half household furniture and half cattle in Escambia County. Daughter Balsura (formerly wife of Francis TAPIOLA), Negro woman Chaney, Hailey, John (son of Chaney), Frank (son of Peggy), house and lot on Palifora Street, she to pay my son William Madison FRANCIS $400.00; also remaining half of furniture and cattle. Daughter Angelina CUMMINGS of Pensacola; Negro Jesse and wife Peggy, Jane, Rhoda, Elizabeth and Mary Margaret. Son Wm. Madison FRANCIS, Negro Peter, Maria, Malissa and Emily, 50 acres in Monroe County, Alabama; also tools and cattle. Mentions lands she inherited in North Carolina be sold and proceeds divided among above children. Executors: Charles EVANS and Owen M. AVERY, both of Pensacola. Witnesses: E.W. DARR, J.W. HALL, and John BROSNAHAM. Signed: Sarah (X) FRANCIS. . . .

CODICIL: August 1849. Having sold Negro Zene and her daughter Eliza and bought man Dick, said Dick is will to
daughter Evaline plus $200.00 in money. Witnesses: Joseph
SCIRRA, Geo. WALKER, and Francis BONIFAY. Signed: Sarah (X)
FRANCIS. . . .
4 September 1849. Escambia County, Florida, Admitted for
probate by oaths Chas. EVANS and Owen M. AVERY; F.E. dela RNA,
Clerk; Charles EVANS, Probate Judge; Charles DOWNEY, Secre-
tary of State; Thomas BROWN, Governor of Florida. Stokes
County, North Carolina, December Term 1851, recorded.

Page 275 is blank.

Page 276. 8 January 1851. Will of Benjamin BOLES. June
Term 1852. Negroes Lewis, Mary and her two
children Martha and Lucella be sold privately to pay debts
and funeral expense. Lewis, Mary and children to choose
master and David LEAKE have refusal; also sell Negro Cynthia
and land on road from Red Shoals to Mrs. Catharine TUTTLES;
also land called dower tract on road from Red Shoals to old
Academy. Wife Nancy, balance estate her lifetime; then to
my children (not named). Son Thomas Jefferson BOLES, shotgun.
Executors: Reuben D. GOLDING (GOLDEN) and Isaac S. GIBSON.
Witnesses: John PEPPER and Jas. A. PEPPER. Signed: Benjam.
BOLES.

Page 278. 2 September 1847. Will of Samuel FLIPPIN. September Term 1852. Wife Mildred, property she owned
at our marriage, towit: Negro girl July; horse, household
furniture, trunk; also loan her my plantation or a part
adjoining Henry PELL, Lewis B. BANNER, John C. FLIPPIN,
Presley GEORGE, the Mill and JESSUPS line; also Negro
Druery and Sarah; stock, provision, household furniture, etc.
Daughter Mary A. ATKINSON, 150 acres land west of FLIPPINS
and BANNERS Mill where Presley GEORGE lives; also land where
ATKINSONS live on road from Edmund WALLERS to George ROGERS,
said land being in Patrick County, Virginia, waters Peters
Creek. Son Joseph T., land where he lives adjoining land
willed Mary A.; stock, blacksmith tools, etc. Son John C.,
413 acres lately deeded him; also set blacksmith tools. Son
Raleigh W., land he lives on in Patrick County, Virginia on
Peters Creek; Son Samuel M., land he lives on; part old
Lyon tract. Daughter Nancy M. BANNER, 294½ acres known as
old Brick House tract adjoining Henry PELL and Jesse McKINNEY.
Daughter Martha J. GEORGE, 552 acres adjoining Lyon tract
recently deeded to Martha J. and Presley GEORGE. Daughter
Lea W. FRANCIS, land adjoining Henry PELL, near my barn to
Patrick County and Germanton road adjoining tract willed
Mary A. Mentions land adjoining Branxton ATKINSON and
JESSUPS Mill, his half interest in saw and grist Mills be
sold and money equally divided among heirs. My brother
John FLIPPIN, Senr., 200 acres where he lives; at his death
to be sold and divided; leaves legacy to John FLIPPIN (son
of John Sr.) when becomes of age. Executor: Lewis B. BANNER.
Witnesses: Wilson FULTON, G.W. JESSUP, and Meredith PELL.
Signed: Samuel FLIPPIN.

Page 284. 25 July 1848. Will of Thomas SHIPP. June Term

1853. Son Martlett, bed and furniture. Grandson
Albert McKajor SHIPP, horse, bed and furniture. Balance
estate be sold except "my two auld Negroes Keer and Lewis."
Daughter Nancy JOINER. Two grandsons Wm. Thomas SHIPP and
Albert McKager SHIPP. Mentions 1,600 acres land, plantation
he lives on, stock, furniture. Also money owing friend
Alexander KING. Executors: Hampton BYNUM and Alexander KING.
Witnesses: G.W. JESSOP and Albert R. KING. Signed: Thomas
SHIPP.

Page 286.   28 December 1844.   Will of Joel TUCKER, Halifax
            County, Virginia.   Recorded December Term 1853.
Two sons Gabriel W. and Benjamin C., Negroes Daniel and
Beck.   Executor: Robert A. TUCKER.   Witnesses: Robert TUCKER
and Wm. DICKIE and Robert A. TUCKER.   Signed: Joel TUCKER.
Halifax County, Virginia 28 November 1853.   Robert A. TUCKER
refused to act as Executor.   Signed: Wm. S. HOLT, Clerk; Jno.
B. CARRINGTON, Presiding Justice.   Stokes County, North
Carolina, December Term 1853, ordered recorded, Jno. HILL,
Clerk.

Page 287.   4 Apirl 1855.   Will of Adam MITCHELL.   June Term
            1855.   Wife MERCY, 108 acres including Mantion
house her lifetime in lieu her dower; furniture, stock, Bible,
etc.   Eldest daughter Elizabeth WARD (wife of Randolph) and
her children, 156 acres where she lives, bed and furniture,
cow.   Second daughter Mary D. DUNCAN, $250.00 in lieu land
applied a credit on bond her husband, Landon DUNCAN owes;
bed, furniture, cow.   Eldest son James H., 166 acres where
he lives adjoining HAIRSTON; bed, furniture, cow.   Daughter
Margaret S. WARD (wife of Peter), $250.00 in lieu land; bed,
furniture, cow.   Son Adam M., 100 acres known as Butner tract
and 50 acres where he lives adjoining James H. MITCHELL, Wm.
D. WILSON and T.M. SCALES; blacksmith tools, bed, furniture,
cow.   Son Jesse M., part tract where he lives known as Geo.
TAYLOR tract of 215 acres adjoining HAIRSTON and W.A. MIT-
CHELL; blacksmith tools, bed, furniture, cow.   Two sons
Charles A. and Wm. W., 2 tracts, DUGGINS tract, 139½ acres
and John RIED tract 39 acres adjoining W.A. MITCHELL and W.
F. MOORE; bed, furniture, cow and $15.00.   Executors: James
H. MITCHELL, Adam M. MITCHELL and Jesse M. MITCHELL.
Witnesses: Hamilton SCALES and W.A. MITCHELL.   Signed: Adam
MITCHELL.

Page 292.   22 February 1855.   Will of William J. WARD.   June
            Term 1855.   Wife Catharine, 156 acres where I
live and personal estate.   Youngest son Milton, $33.00.
Sons and daughter Randolph, Peter and Ruamer RICHARDSON,
$1.00 each as already received.   Three daughters who now
live with me: Elizabeth, Agnes and Anne WARD, estate equally
divided at death of wife.   Executor: Samuel FULTEN.   Witnesses: Elisha J. EUDAILY and Anderson CARTER.   Signed: Wm. J.
(X) WARD.

Page 294.   20 June 1846.   Will of Thomas JOYCE.   June Term
            1855.   Wife Esther, lifetime estate.   Son Franklin,
$50.00;   Son Andrew $50.00 when comes of age and ½ estate at
wifes death.   To Joshua T. and Elizabeth E. (children of my

143

son Franklin and wife Martha), ½ estate. If Franklin reforms and quits drinking Spirits to excess and becomes sober and steady, then he may have part willed his children. Executors: Son Andrew JOYCE and Hamilton JOYCE. No witnesses. Signed: Thomas JOYCE. Oaths of David B. HATCHER, Samuel H. TAYLOR, Wilson FULTON and John W. BITTING proved will found in said JOYCE'S valuable papers.

Page 296. 8 September 1855. Will of Robert YOUNG. December Term 1855. Wife Mary, 46 acres including Mansion house I live in, bed and years providing. Son E.H. YOUNG, above at wifes death; all remaining land at my death. Daughter Anna, Negro Mariah, aged 44 years. Son Robert F., Negro boy Green, aged 17 years. Daughter Jane FULTON, Negro Patsy mentioned in bill sale to Francis FULTON; also cupboard. Daughter Elizabeth ABBOTT, Negro boy Anderson already received; named in bill of sale to Jacob ABBOTT. Son Josiah, Negro boy William already redd; also girl Lucinda age 8. Son George Henry, Negro girl Vina 9 years; Negro girl Margaret 4 years. Son John, in addition to what I have had to pay for him, residue of my estate not otherwise mentioned. Daughter Mary A. POWERS, Negro girl Marinda as named in bill of sale to B. POWERS. Executors: Sons Josiah and George H. YOUNG. Witnesses: John W. BRANSON and John T.W. DAVIS. Signed: Robert YOUNG.

Page 298. 12 August 1852. Will of Reuben MABE. March Term 1856. Wife Rhoda, lifetime claim land I live on, etc. Children: Anna, James, Reuben, Abner, George, Eddy (Male), Samuel, Frankey (daughter), Rhoda, Lucy, Nancy, Lettitia, Judy, boys horses and girls bed and furniture. Executor: Son James MABE. Witnesses: Wm. C. MOORE and Wm. SHELTON. Signed: Reuben (X) MABE.

Page 300. 27 January 1845. Will of Susannah C. MOORE. March Term 1857. Niece Rachael Ann CARDWELL, Negroes Charlott, Martha and her child James; Rachel to pay niece Lettitia TATUM ½ valuation. Sister Virginia SAWYERS of Tennessee $100.00. Brother Samuel MARTIN of Tennessee $100.00. If sister and brother decease, $200.00 equally divided among nieces Virginia BANNER, Lettitia TATUM (wife of Pryor TATUM), Mary Eliza BANNER, Sarah P. BANNER and Rachael Ann CARDWELL. Nephew Wm. M. MOORE, Negro man Hiram, aged 30. Niece Sarah P. BANNER (wife of Edwin H. BANNER), four Negroes Delphy, Jenny, Mary and Ellin held in trust of Wm. M. MOORE and John BANNER. Executors: Wm. M. MOORE and John BANNER. Witnesses: Erasmus ALLY and J.M. CIX. Signed: Susannah C. (X) MOORE. . . .
CODICIL: 3 April 1850. Have sold Negro Martha and her child James; will niece Lettitia TATUM $250.00. Clause willing sister Va. SAWYERS $100.00 is revoked and only $50.00 to brother Samuel MARTIN. Witnesses: Henry SNOW and James J. HINES. Signed: Susannah C. (X) MOORE.

Page 303. March 1852. Will of Jane CARR, widow of John CARR. March Term 1857. To Dolly Margaret SHACKELFORD and her heirs, estate of every description. Executor: Samuel SHACKELFORD. Witnesses: Robert B. WALL and John A. GILMER.

Signed: Jane (X) CARR.

Page 304.   20 February 1857.   Will of Green L. RICHARDSON.
             March Term 1857.   Four oldest children: Elizabeth,
John, Rachael (wife of Samuel P. RICHARDSON), and Joseph,
27½ acres land each being upper division of my plantation,
also money.   Wife Judith Lad and four youngest children:
Eliza, Richard, Nancy and Green, lower end plantation until
youngest child becomes of age.   Personal property sold and
money divided equally.   Executors: Son Joseph RICHARDSON and
son-in-law Samuel P. RICHARDSON.   Witnesses: John T.W. DAVIS
and Wm. A. LASH.   Signed: Green L. (X) RICHARDSON.

Page 306.   (No date).   Division of land recorded with Green
             L. RICHARDSON'S will-gives degrees-no streams.
Mentions lines of DAVIS, WILLIS and CHAMBERS; surveyed by
Caleb JONES.

Page 307.   10 December 1845.   Will of John W. ASHBY.   Septem-
             ber Term 1857.   Wife Mourning, lifetime estate.
Children: Elizabeth PINNEGAR, Elijah, Jane ALLEY, Nancy
ALLEY, Patsy WOOD, John H., and Pauline ASHBY; daughter
Judah PINNEGAR, deceased, already had her part.   Executors:
Wm. A. MITCHELL and William ALLEY.   Witnesses: William
YOUNG and Simeon (X) WOODALL.   Signed: John W. ASHBY.

Page 308.   7 July 1857.   Will of John SMITH, Senr.   September
             Term 1857.   Son Henry, 27 acres adjoining Anderson
and John WARREN, including dwelling where he lives.   Son
Anderson, 30 acres adjoining tract where he lives, West end
tract willed Henry.   Son John, 43 acres adjoining land he
lives on, adjoining J.B. VAUGHN.   Son Samuel, 50 acres
adjoining Anderson SMITH, widow WARREN and Geo. W. WILSON on
Germanton road; also bed and furniture.   Daughter Mary SMITH,
residue land including dwelling house; $100.00, bed and
furniture and ½ crops.   Sons Larkin, Harrison and Solomon,
$100.00 each.   Daughter Elizabeth (wife of Jordan PARISH),
$300.00.   Executors: John HILL and Samuel B. ALLEN.
Witnesses: James T. GREEN and Geo. W. WILSON.   Signed: John
(X) SMITH, Senr.

Page 310.   1 February 1856.   Will of Joel HILL.   December
             Term 1857.   Wife Milly, live and enjoy profits
of home plantation and all land adjoining on Panther Creek
her lifetime.   Three sons James T., Thomas D., and Lariston
H., above at wifes death.   Sons and daughters: Robert W.,
Joel F., Caleb, James T., Thomas D., Lauriston H., Elizabeth
BLACKBURN and Frances Jane HARDY, equal share residue estate.
Son Robert W., Negroes Albert and Alex; 45 acres I bought of
Samuel B. ALLEN.   Daughter Sally COVINGTON, Negro Lewis and
Let already received.   Son John G., Negro Edmund already
received and no more.   Daughter Martha FULTON, Negroes
Eliza and Stephen.   Son Joel F., Negro Harmon and girl Aley.
Son Caleb, Negro Patric and Ellin; also Ebert and Holland
tracts of land if he make Robt. W. HILL title to 100 acres.
Daughter Elizabeth BLACKBURN, Negro Sukey and her children
Hannah and Mary.   Son Joel F., for benefit of my daughter
Frances Jane who married James M. HARDY, Negroes Sally and

Nathan. Son James T., Negro David and Abram. Son Thomas
D., Negro Doctor. Executors: Sons Joel F. and Caleb HILL.
Witnesses: J.F. REDDICK and Elijah TUTTLE. Signed: Joel HILL.

Page 312. 5 March 1858. Will of John BROWN. June Term 1858.
        Daughters Elizabeth and Ladosha, residue money
from sale of tobacco for payment debts; land on Peters
Creek, 400 acres; also 150 acre tract. Daughter Elizabeth,
Negro Emily, Bird, Lee and Noah. Daughter Ladosha, Negros
Hamp and Amelia, Charles and James. Executors: Daughters
Elizabeth and Ladosha BROWN and Samuel BROWN. Witnesses:
J.L. PEATROP and Andrew J. MARTIN. Signed: John BROWN. . .
CODICIL: Appoints Samuel BROWN guardian of children.

Page 314. 27 April 1858. Will of Massey FRY. June Term
        1858. Seven grandchildren (children of my daugh-
ter Lucinda PETREE): Marion E., Demarius J., Amarah E.,
Jesse F., Gaston M., Wm. D., Francis P., Negro Anthony,
stock, etc. Executor: Son-in-law Wm. W. PETREE. Witnesses:
M.T. BENTON and J.E. BEVEL. Signed: Massey (X) FRY.

Page 315. 14 October 1857. Will of Benjamin ZIGLER. June
        Term 1858. Wife Eleanor C., all estate and she
maintain my sister Polly. Sister Polly ZIGLER who now lives
on my old place on Germanton road, her maintenance and old
Negro Phillis. Specifies he is not appointing Executor,
leaving it to the law to appoint one. Witnesses: J.M.
COVINGTON, L.H. HILL, and Yancy B. DAVIS. Signed: Benjamin
(X) ZIGLAR.

Page 316. 2 July 1856. Will of Maria S. SCHAUB. June Term
        1857. Three daughters (not named) and daughter-
in-law Eliza SCHAUB, wearing apperel. Son William S.,
furniture, silver, etc. Sister Johanna E. FRIES, silver.
Brother-in-law Christopher SCHAUB, spectacles formerly
belonging to his mother and $1.00. Granddaughter Lucretia,
quilt. To Amanda, chest. To Elizabeth S. STRUP (STRUB),
silver. Mentions a note on George NICHOLS. My children:
W.S. SCHAUB, Rebecca SPAINHOUR, Anna Elizabeth CHAFFIN, and
Maria S. WALDRAVEN. Executor: Son Wm. Samuel SCHAUB.
Witnesses: John GRABS and Winbourn B. SCHAUB. Signed: Maria
S. SCHAUB.

Page 317. 15 May 1857. Will of John BOHANNON. June Term
        1858. Wife Frances, all my interest in land
bought of John P. SMITH, adjoining James SHELTON, John P.
SMITH, Wm. SHELTON, Wm. T. SMITH and Charles B. BOLDINGS, all
personal estate, household furniture, etc. Executor: John
P. SMITH. Witnesses: Gabriel H. SHELTON and Hamilton J.
SISK. Signed: John (X) BOHANAN.

Page 319. 19 July 1858. Will of James LYON. September Term
        1858. Grandchildren: Margaret, Mura and Joseph
MARTIN (children of my deceased daughter Christina who married
Joseph MARTIN), $100.00 each. Daughters Sarah W. FLIPPIN
(wife of Joseph F.), Frances F. FLIPPIN (wife of Samuel M.)
and my four grandchildren, Mary, Elizabeth, William and Francis MOORE (children of my deceased daughter Nancy B. late wife

146

of Wm. M. MOORE), land I live on in three tracts South Dan
River, 492 acres divided three equal parts. Daughters Sarah
W., Negro Mary; Frances F., two Negro children of Negro Susan,
Negro Rachel and old blind man Thompson. To MOORE grand-
children, Negro woman Adaline, Ruth and old George. Son
Francis, Negro Alfred. Sons James and William, $1.00 each.
Wife Behetheland, if she survives me, shall have what she
needs of my estate her lifetime. Executor: Son-in-law
Wm. M. MOORE. Witnesses: J.L. PEATROP and C.B. CHRISTIAN.
Signed: James LYON. . . .
CODICIL: 23 July 1858. Executor is allowed 5% commission in
          settlement estate; daughter Sarah W. FLIPPIN benefit
of claim $100.00 due me by Joseph F. FLIPPIN. Witnesses:
J.L. PEATROP and Irvin M. SHELTON. Signed: James LYON.

Page 322. 2 June 1852. Will of Nathan BROWN. September
          Term 1858. Wife Elizabeth, lifetime claim estate.
Children: Bedford T., Sarah Ann Elizabeth, Wilson Davis,
Nancy Amanda, Stephen and Pinkney, above at death of wife.
Executors: Wife Elizabeth BROWN and son Bedford T. BROWN.
Witnesses: Daniel M. LINVILLE and Aaron LINVILLE. Signed:
Natha. (X) BROWN.

Page 324. 21 June 1858. Will of Jacob CLARK of Patrick
          County, Virginia. July term 1858. Mentions
tract of land I live on I purchased of Maj. Clark PENN and
Greensville PENN; also 100 acres bought of Geo. HAIRSTON
"McGruder land" adjoining above; all consisting of 777 acres
together with 250 acres to be cut off tract adjoining above
called "Pennell Place"; balance Pennell Place consisting
of 1,700 acres; 400 acres bought of Perlina SMITH (widow of
John SMITH), land in Stokes County, North Carolina, 600
acres where son George W. CLARK lives; 150 acres near
Elamsville bought of Lewis PEDIGO; 19 acres formerly owned
by Jerry TUGGLE and Geo. W. CLARK; 417 acres in Stokes
County, North Carolina bought of James C. MOIR. Wife Jane,
lifetime claim part land; one dozen slaves (not named) and
$5,000.00. Two youngest sons Wm. H. (land and $500.00 for
school) and Hugh D. (land and $700.00 for school), good
horse and 2 cows each. Son Jacob L., land including where
he lives and Mill on Russel Creek (1/3 of 1,700 acres),
Negro boy Sim and Rebecca and her children, good horse and
two cows. Son James H., part 2/3 1,700 acres; part 400
acres bought of Perlina SMITH, good horse and two cows.
Son Joseph M., part 2/3 1,700 acres; part 400 acres SMITH
land; $400.00 to enable him to attend Medical Lectures; $150.
for one more year in school. Son Thomas J., part 2/3
1,700 acres; part 400 acres SMITH land. Children of son,
George W. CLARK, 600 acres where my son George W. now lives,
to be held by son-in-law Robert F. MOIR in trust. Daughter
Ruth E. FENNEY (wife of Wm. FENNEY), 150 acres near Elamsville
bought of Lewis PEDIGO; also 18 acres formerly owned by
Jerry TUGGLE and Geo. W. CLARK; Negro Justin. Daughter
Serenna J. MOIR (wife of Robert F. MOIR), 417 acres bought
of James C. MOIR in Stokes County, North Carolina; Negro
Betty. Daughter Sarah E. HUBBARD (wife of Joshua HUBBARD),
Negro Abigail and her 3 children Negro girls Mira, Vince and
Absalom; also a Piano already received. Brother Jonathan

147

CLARK, $100.00. Executors: Sons Joseph M. and Thos. J.
CLARK, Son-in-law Robert F. MOIR, Joshua HUBBARD, and Wm.
FENNY. Guardians of two youngest sons: Son Joseph CLARK and
son-in-law Joshua HUBBARD. Witnesses: William FAULKNER,
James M. HUGHS, Jas. T. PEDIGO, and Alfred DOOLY. Signed:
Jacob CLARK. . . .AM. LYBROOK, Stokes County, North Carolina,
December Term 1858; recorded Patrick County, Virginia July
1858; Probated; Taylorsville, Patrick County, Virginia.

Page 330. 20 December 1858. Will of Anderson CARTER. March
        Term 1859. Wife (not named), all property kept
together for her to raise my younger children (not named).
No Executor named. Witnesses: William D. WILSON and James
H. MITCHELL. Signed: Anderson (X) CARTER.

Page 331. 13 November 1858. Will of Elizabeth CARTER.
        March Term 1859. Children: Landon, William,
Mahala VAUGHN, James, Heirs of Benjamin F., deceased, Heirs
of John, deceased, money, negro slaves (not named) from sale
of property. Son William, all property and slaves my
granddaughter Martha Ann BAILEY (wife of Edward L. BAILEY) is
entitled to as legatee through her father John CARTER, in
trust. Executor: Son William CARTER. Witnesses: Samuel S.
WALL and Joseph S. BLACKWELL. Signed: Elizabeth (X) CARTER.
CODICIL: 26 November 1858. Negroes my grandchildren Martha
Ann BAILEY and Sarah E.F. LEMMONS shall inherit to be sold
by my Executor and money equally divided between them.
Witnesses: Samuel S. WALL and Joseph S. BLACKWELL. Signed:
Elizabeth (X) CARTER.

Page 333. 26 October 1855. Will of Anny VAUGHN. March
        Term 1859. Daughter Eliza HOPKINS, furniture.
Grandson Bonaparte HOPKINS, furniture. Daughter Jane
VAUGHN, furniture, cow and calf. Son Jerome B., Negro
Malinda and money in his hands. Executor: Son Jerome B.
VAUGHN. Witnesses: William WITHERS and Joseph TERRY. Signed:
Anny (X) VAUGHN.

Page 334. 24 August 1858. Will of John JOYCE. September
        Term 1859. Brother Robert, my mare and saddle,
stock. Brother Joseph, my interest in land. Executor:
Brother Joseph JOYCE. Witnesses: James D. JONES, Alex.
KING, and Matilda (X) CARTER. Signed: John (X) JOYCE.

Page 335. 29 June 1859. Will of Absalom SCALES, Patrick
        County, Virginia. 28 November 1859. Executors
to sell all land. Daughter Bettie D. SCALES, $1,500 for
clothing, boarding and educating her. Wife Nancy C., 1/9th
part estate. Children: Sarah J., Martha A., Joseph H.,
James R., Fannie E., Nathaniel M., Noah and Bettie D., 1/9th
part estate each. Executor: R.D. HAY. Witnesses: John A.
MARTIN and Wm. B. TAYLOR. Signed: A. SCALES.

Page 377. 15 December 1859. Will of Hampton BYNUM. March
        Term 1861. Grandson John Gray BYNUM, $1,000.00
as his father (not named) in his lifetime had his part.
Six children: Martha, Benjamin, Margaret, Preston, Hampton,
and Harriet (wife of Abram MARTIN), residue of my estate

equally divided. Executors: Tyre GLENN, B.F. BYNUM, W.P. BYNUM. Witnesses: D.G. MONTGOMERY and James M. PLUNKETT. Signed: Hampton BYNUM.

Page 338.   26 December 1856. Will of John WOOD. March Term 1861. Wife Nancy, lifetime claim. Mentions selling land where he lived to James and Wm. TRENT. Children: Asa, Matthew, James, Andrew, Polly (wife of Asa TAYLOR), Henry, Ailsy (wife of Wm. REDMAN), Jinsy, Richard, Jackson, Elizabeth (wife of William YOUNG), John, Edmund L., Martha E. (wife of Ezekial TILLEY) and William, residue of estate equally divided. Executors: Son Asa WOOD and son-in-law Wm. REDMAN. Witnesses: Nathaniel MOODY and T.B. TAYLOR. Signed: John WOOD.

Page 339.   1 November 1859. Will of Isabella RUTLEDGE. March Term 1861. Grandsons Martin and Irvin A., 100 acres where my son, John lives adjoining Benjamin BOLES, deceased, John PEPPER, above grandsons pay heirs of my son Burgiss, deceased. Son John and his wife, Dosha, above grandsons support them their lifetime. Children of my two sons James and Benjamin, 180 acres adjoining Benj. BOLES, deceased and Larkin SMITH (James and Benj. improve land for children under age). Sons William and Irvin, 60 acres land I live on and 50 acres bought of Joseph SIZEMORE, both on waters Neatman Creek adjoining Michael KISER. Son Alexander B. have given him from time to time, so will him nothing. Executors: Sons William and Irvin RUTLEDGE. Witnesses: Joel F. HILL and Hardy R. CARRELL. Signed: Isabella (X) RUTLEDGE.

Page 341.   19 September 1860. Will of Isham OWEN. March Term 1861. Wife (not named), all estate her lifetime; all children (not named), estate equally divided at death of wife except portion to daughters Mary and Rebecca to be placed in hands of Ambrose JESSUP for benefit of their children. Executor: Ambrose JESSUP. Witnesses: John L. SMITH and Edwin Y. PAYNE. Signed: Isham (X) OWEN.

Page 342.   27 October 1845. Will of Henry PELL. March Term 1861. My 19 children: Caty (wife of John FLIPPIN); Nancy; Heirs of daughter Anny, deceased (formerly wife of Jesse McKINNEY); William; Thompson; Cassa; Polly (wife of Martin JESSUP); Richard; Susan; Robert; Sally (wife of David ANDERSON); Martha; Tabitha (wife of Armstead CHILTON); Meredith; Rebecca; Henry; Jane; James; and Lydia, $1.00 each except $30.00 to Henry. Wife Elizabeth, whole remainder of my estate of every kind. Executor: Son William PELL. Witnesses: Jacob CARSON (had left State by 1861) and Ambrose and Eli JESSUP. Signed: Henry (X) PELL.

Page 344.   22 April 1861. Will of William T. JOYCE. June Term 1861. Wife Jane, land where I live, household furniture, etc.; Negro girl Adaline. Two children: Eliza M. BEAZLEY and Wm. S. JOYCE, residue estate. Executor: Peter HUTCHERSON. Witnesses: Wm. B. TAYLOR and John A. MARTIN. Signed: Wm. T. (X) JOYCE.

Page 345.   26 February 1860. Will of John HILL. June Term

1861. Grandsons Isaac H., Wm. F. NELSON, Negroes
Alexander and Jerry BANNER but Jerry BANNER remain in posses-
sion of my wife her lifetime. Son Samuel C., residue of
estate but my wife Julia enjoy it for lifetime. Executor:
Samuel C. HILL. Witnesses: Isaac GOLDING, L.W. HILL and
C. HILL. Signed: Jno. HILL.

Page 347. 9 November 1837. Will of Martha MARTIN. No
probate date. Two sons Edmund L. and John J.,
$1,600 out of Pension money from General Government when
collected by claim now being made. Daughter Martha SCALES,
bedding, clothing and $100.00. To Isabeller and Sarah
Martha, clothing. To Edmund L. MARTIN'S daughters (not
named), balance of my clothing. Grandson Wiley W. MARTIN,
$100.00. Granddaughter Harriet, my wardrobe provided she
does not go live with Rufus SMITH again. Grandson James
MARTIN, silver tumbler. Mentions household property at
Edmund L. MARTINS and John J. MARTINS to remain there for
use of the families. Executors: Sons Edmund L. and John J.
MARTIN. Witnesses: Wm. C. MOORE and John MARTIN. Signed:
Martha MARTIN. (A probate date is carried on page 348, but
not dated).

Page 349. 14 December 1860. Will of Edmond T. MARTIN.
June Term 1861. Son Rufus, 88 acres land where I
live both sides Hollow Road adjoining Solomon SPAINHOUR,
household furniture, stock, etc. but Rufus to support my
wife, Susan MARTIN her lifetime. Executor: Son Rufus MARTIN.
Witnesses: H.C. COE and J.E. SNIDER. Signed: Ed. T. MARTIN.

Page 350. 8 August 1861. Will of Mary S. MATTHEWS. Septem-
ber Term 1861. Daughter Eliza, Negro woman Ruth
and child, Etta, household furniture. Son Calvin J., a child
Negro Ruth might have next, bed and furniture. Son Wm. H.H.,
Negro girl Esther, bed and furniture. Son John T., $5.00.
Children of John T., Negro woman Mariah. Sons James E. and
Hugh M.P., Negro man Jim and my interest in the estate of
my father, George S. STAPLES, deceased. Son George S.,
Negro boy Jim. Executor: R.H. MASSEY. Witnesses: Jesse and
J.D. YOUNG and Richard WILLIAMS. Signed: Mary S. MATTHEWS.

Page 351. 2 April 1862. Will of William M. BROWN. Septem-
ber Term 1862. Wife Nancy, lifetime estate.
Executor: Wife Nancy BROWN. Witnesses: Henry M. BROWN and
R.R. HUTCHERSON. Signed: William M. BROWN.

Page 352. 1 November 1856. Will of Sarah GIBSON. March
Term 1863. Daughter-in-law Elizabeth J. MOODY
(wife of my son Nathaniel MOODY), Negro woman Jincy and her
two children Charles and Cynthia, in trust for lifetime; then
slaves go to Isaac E. GIBSON provided he pay debts of my son,
Nathaniel MOODY. My 6 grandchildren (children of son
Alexander MOODY), Sarah Ann, Mildred, Mary Emaline, Alexander,
Andrew and Emma Elizabeth, Negroes Benjamin and Elizabeth.
Executor: Nathaniel N. PEPPER. Witnesses: H.W. ADKIN and
James RIERSON, Junr. Signed: Sarah GIBSON.

Page 353. 25 August 1862. Will of William C. MOORE. March

Term 1863. Wife Paulina, lifetime estate. Daughter
Sally H. HARRIS (wife of Fletcher A. HARRIS), Negroes Lucy
and Caroline, filly, saddle and bridle, bed and furniture
already received. Daughter Elisa J. (wife of Abraham MARTIN,
Jr.), two girls by name Black Sue and Yellow Sue, furniture,
saddle and bridle. Son Reubin, Negro boy Manuel, horse
bridle and saddle, bed, furniture, land he now lives on
(cannot sell land). Son William J., Negro boy Jack, bed and
furniture already received, Negro Milly at death of my wife.
Son Gabriel B., Negro Patrick, bed and furniture. Daughter
Paulina L. (wife of E.S. HARRIS), Negro girls Grace and
Ellen, bed and furniture already received. Son Gideon A.,
Negro boy Joe, bed and furniture already received; plantation I live on at death of my wife. Daughter Frances F.
(wife of John HAWKINS) and her heirs, Negro girls Martha and
Adaline already received. Daughter Juriah D. (first wife of
Wm. H. HAWKINS) and her heirs, Negro Cricy, bed and furniture
already received; also Negro George. Executors: Sons Wm. J.
and Gabriel B. MOORE. Witnesses: R.D. HAY and G.E. MOORE.
Signed: Wm. C. MOORE.

Page 354. 18 October 1862. Will of John W. CHAMBERS.
March Term 1863. Wife Martha Jane, the six
Negroes received by her in marriage: Green, Stephen and Selena
and her 3 youngest children (not named); also Negros Missouri
and her youngest child Sarah; young woman Margaret; also
household furniture, 1/3 crops and stock; also all money due
me as one of heirs of Hampton BYNUM'S estate; also $2,000.00
Three grandchildren Nancy, John C. and Albert BAILEY (children of Ellen S. BAILEY), Negroes Jinny, Rachel and Agnes;
also $1,000.00 each and appointed their father Benj. BAILEY,
their guardian. Daughter Ellen S. and son-in-law Benj.
BAILEY, residue of my estate. Executor: Son-in-law Benjamin
BAILEY. Witnesses: R.H. MASSEY and Jasper W. DAVIS. Signed:
Jno. W. CHAMBERS.

Page 355. 31 October 1862. Will of Tandy J. HUTCHENS.
March Term 1863. Wife Julia F., different tracts
of land including Mansion house with exception tract adjoining James HAWKINS and Hiram SMITH; Franklin JAMES tract to
be rented by my Executors. My Father David HUTCHENS, house
where he lives. My three children: Sarah Jane, Martha
Frances and John Wesley, all my land, household furniture,
etc. at death of wife. Executors: Edmund BEAZLEY and Stephen
POOR. Witnesses: Thomas HUTCHERSON, Frederick (X) WHITE, and
Stephen POOR. Signed: Tandy J. HUTCHENS.

Page 357. 15 July 1862. Will of Edward H. EDWARDS. March
Term 1863. Son Edward W., land where he lives
East side Yadkin River known as Roll DARNEL land adjoining
Wm. EDWARDS. All my six children: Mary C., Solomon T.,
Nancy P., Edward W., Augustus T. and Lecetamoline, 100 acres
where I now live known as Mike SPAINHOUR land; 100 acres
known as BANNER land and remainder Roll DARNEL land divided
equally; Augustus T. and Lecetamoline designated as youngest
son and daughter and willed money for schooling. Executors:
Sons Solomon T. and Edward W. EDWARDS, and Wm. P. APPERSON.
Witnesses: H.C. COE and J.W. SPAINHOUR. Signed: E.H. EDWARDS.

Page 359.   8 November 1862.   Will of Giles L. SHEPPERD.   June
          Term 1863.   Wife Katharine, 100 acres where I live;
also tract of 53 acres known as Gabe PIKE tract; stock, crops,
household furniture.   Mentions estate to be equally divided
among his children at wifes death, but does not name them.
Executrix: Wife Katharine SHEPPERD.   Witnesses: James HALL
and Thomas and W.H. AYERS.   Signed: Giles L. SHEPPERD.

Page 360.   1 April 1862.   Will of Wilehier HALL.   June Term
          1863.   Wife Mary, my estate unless she marrys then
mirdarter harret to have balance and wife to have a chiTds
part.   No executor.   Witnesses: David and Greenville HALL.
Signed: Wilehier HALL. . . .Proven by oath of David and
Martha HALL.

Page 361.   13 January 1863.   Will of Christina DALTON.
          September Term 1863.   Sons Absalom B. and Isaac,
$1.00 each.   Son David N., note I hold on Dr. W.W. COLE for
$630.20; also Negro man Caleb to be held by Executors until
my son, David N. returns or it is proven he is dead; if he
is dead, Negro Caleb sold and money divided equally between
sons, Thomas H.P., John A.B. and daughter Christina Malissa
COLE.   Son Don F., $1.00 and to his children, Negro Dick and
Susan.   Daughter Christina Malissa COLE, $1.00 and to her
children Negroes Sarah, Mary and William.   Granddaughter
Christina COLE (daughter of C. Malissa), sugar case.   Son
John A.B., Negro girl Lansine and furniture now at his house.
Son Thomas H.P., farm tools, furniture, blacksmith tools,
trunk, Negro boy Jerry, all he owes me ($1,500.00), my
watch and cow.   Grandchildren (children of my son Isaac, not
named), Negro woman Lucretia and her child Lessy.   Requests
sons John A.B. and Thomas H.P. to furnish tombstones for her
grave and that of her daughter Bethenia DALTON, deceased.
Executor: Son John A.B. DALTON.   Witnesses: Wm. A. LASH and
Beverly POWELL.   Signed: Christina DALTON.

Page 362.   9 June 1862.   Will of Ephraim BOULDIN.   June Term
          1863.   Capt. Company H., 22 Regt., North Carolina
Troops of County of Stokes.   My Father Charles B. BOULDIN,
my gold watch worn on my person.   Executor to pay note held
against me by my Mother Mrs. Dorothy T. BOULDIN ($1,111.00)
to invest my money and pay interest to my Mother and Father
anually.   To John Harrison HUNDLEY (a private in Co. H.
22 Regt), principal from above money and in case he dies, to
his widow (not named).   Mentions his lands, 265 acres North
side Madison and Mt. Airy Road adjoining lands of Charles
B. BOULDIN, S.J. LACKEY and wife of Charles R. GRIFFIN; also
land on South side road adjoining Charles B. BOULDIN, Wm. T.
SMITH and Wm. H. RIVERS.   Executor: John P. SMITH, Esq.
Witnesses: C.C. COLE and H.E. CHARLES.   Signed: Ephraim
BOULDIN.

Page 363.   12 September 1863.   Will of Robert JOYCE.   Decem-
          ber Term 1863.   Sister Martha JOYCE, land North
side Double Creek to reside on her lifetime, but she is not
to sell land.   To nephews and nieces (children of Felix G.
JOYCE formerly of Rockingham County, North Carolina), not
named.   Executor: Joel DENNY.   Witnesses: Benj. T. WARD,

Thomas JOYCE and Martin BOYLES.   Signed: Robert (X) JOYCE.

Page 364.   20 March 1842.   Will of Josiah TAYLOR "being of
             advanced age".   December Term 1863.   Wife
Elizabeth, lifetime claim and at her death equally divided
by North and South lines between four single daughters:
Patsy, Sally, Nancy and Ellen, West half land, cow, bed,
and furniture each.   Son Wm. B., East half land.   Son George,
already received.   Daughters Polly VERNON and Jane ALLEY,
already received.   Executor: Wm. B. TAYLOR.   Witnesses:
Lemuel JOYCE, Livingston JOYCE, and Winston EADES.   Signed:
Josiah TAYLOR. . . .John MARTIN proved handwriting of Lemuel
and Livingston JOYCE.

Page 365.   25 March 1859.   Will of David TILLEY.   December
             Term 1863.   Daughter Julia Ann TILLEY, 200 acres
South Double Creek (100 acres known as John DEATHERAGE tract
and bought of Matthew DEATHERAGE), 2nd 100 acres adjoining
Richard COX including where I live; at her death to go to
her two sons, Robert Pink TILLEY and David TILLEY; also
stock, etc.   To Lucinda WATSON and her heirs, $5.00 and no
more.   Grandson David TILLEY (son of my son Hampton B.
TILLEY), horse and bridle and saddle and to Hampton B's
other heirs (not named), $1.00 and no more.   My children:
Reuben D., Nancy (wife of Thomas REDDICK), Alsa, Martha
(wife of Philip McCARTER), Elizabeth (wife of Henry TUTTLE),
Julia Ann, Polly (wife of Alexander RUTLEDGE), and Phebe
(wife of John TUTTLE).   Executors: Nathaniel MOODY and Henry
TUTTLE.   Witnesses: A.M. DURHAM and Major (X) MEADOWS.
Signed: David TILLEY. . . .(Was offered for Probate June
Term 1861; contested and tried September Court 1861; appealed
to Superior Court and tried Fall 1863; came back under a writ
of procendendo and ordered recorded.)

Page 366.   12 July 1862.   Will of Nanm S. KING.   March Term
             1864.   Wife Nancy A., lifetime claim.   Three
children: John Wesley, Mary Ann Florence and Sarah Emily,
above equally divided at death of wife.   Executor: Daniel M.
LINVILLE.   Witnesses: Aaron LINVILLE and Dell LINVILLE.
Signed: Nanm S. KING. . . .Proved by D.M. LINVILLE, Smith
LINVILLE and M.H. LINVILLE.

Page 367.   19 October 1863.   Will of Elijah SAMS.   June Term
             1864.   Wife Carolyne, all estate to wrase the
four children: Thomas R., Henry D., Pinkney A. and Yancy F.M.
and nothing bee wasted.   No Executor.   Witnesses: Samuel
TAYLOR and Joel HILL.   Signed: Elijah SAMS. . . .Proven by
S.H. TAYLOR, Isham F. BOYLES and James SAMS.

Page 368.   23 February 1864.   Will of Joseph P. LINDSAY.
             June Term 1864.   To William Alexander Wallace
RIED when he becomes 21 years old, Negro boy John, horse,
bed and furniture, $100.00 provided he remains with my wife;
Eliza Ann LINDSAY until 21 years and remain dutiful to her;
otherwise, he is to have nothing; also to him at my wifes
death or marriage to have 315 acres including where I live.
To Samuel B. ZIGLAR, Negro boy Green provided he cares for
my wifes business until W.A.W. RIED becomes 21; otherwise he

is to have nothing. To Sarah F. ZIGLAR, Negro girl Frances
provided Sarrah marries to suit my wife; otherwise she is
to have nothing. Wife Eliza Ann, remainder of estate.
Executors: Wife Eliza Ann LINDSAY and Samuel B. ZIGLAR.
Witnesses: John G.H. MITCHELL and Hamilton SCALES. Signed:
J.P. LINDSAY.

Page 369. 3 December 1863. Will of James CUNNINGHAM.
June Term 1864. Wife Martha P., my land including
mansion house; Negroes Juda, Fanny, Ellis, Jo, John and
George RILEY; stock, furniture, etc. Children: Vermillin
Ann (wife of John A. CORN), Betsy Jane (wife of Richard F.
MARTIN), John J. (if he lives to return home from the Army;
if not, to his children), Elviry Davis (wife of Andy J.
FREEMAN), William W. (if he is living). Executor: Stephen
H. POOR. Witnesses: Jeremiah HODGES, Stephen H. POOR, and
Samuel CORN. Signed: James CUNNINGHAM.

Page 370. 21 September 1863. Will of John L. GLIDEWELL.
September Term 1864. Wife Elizabeth, whole of
estate divided equally with my children (not named). Mentions
a guardian being appointed for children if wife dies.
Executrix: Wife Elizabeth GLIDEWELL. Witnesses: W.B. VAUGHN
and Joel F. HILL. Signed: John L. GLIDEWELL.

Page 371. 2 September 1864. Will of John FRANCIS, Senr.
September Term 1864. Wife Nancy R., 438 acres
where I live, household furniture, stock, etc. Son Joel M.,
200 acres North side above. Youngest daughter Augusta G.
FRANCIS, $100.00. Mentions "my children" but names only
two above. Executor: Richard SMITH. Witnesses: R.F. MOIR
and Ep. SIMMONS. Signed: John (X) FRANCIS, Sr.

Page 372. 21 July 1864. Will of Nathaniel MOODY. September
Term 1864. Executors collect all fees due me as
Sheriff of Stokes County; some from Forsyth and other
counties and pay off my debts to: Presley GEORGE, Jr., Jack-
son MOORE, Tyerson LAWSON and Wm. A. LASH. Wife Elizabeth,
remainder above if any left. Executor: Friend and relative
N.M. PEPPER. Witnesses: A.H. JOYCE and John PEPPER. Signed:
Nathaniel MOODY.

Page 373. 13 October 1862. Will of Michael KISER, Jr.
September Term 1864. Wife Elizabeth, land she
lives on; also 1/5 share in 800 acres; also 1/5 share 10
acre Mill tract and Mill, household furniture; all land
bought of Phillip KISER, Senr.; also 33 3/4 acres on
Townfork and at her decease to be divided equally among mine
and her heirs, except her brother, Alexander KISER. Executors: J.B. VAUGHN and M.T. BENTON. Witnesses: Henry KISER,
James HARTGROVE, and Alexander WESTMORELAND. Signed: Michael
KISER.

Page 374. 26 December 1860. Will of Matthew SIMMONS.
December Term 1864. Wife (not named), lifetime
estate; then to my children; wife to name own Executor
(wife or children not named). Witnesses: G.W. ANDREWS and
Peter HUTCHERSON. Signed: Matthew (X) SIMMONS.

Page 375.   16 July 1858.   Will of Prudence M. RIED.   December
            Term 1864.   Granddaughter Julia F. RIED (daughter
of my son Pinkney), Negro girl Ruth; bed, furniture, Julia
to have above my other grandchildren, an extra gift because
I think she deserves it; after above received by Julia,
residue of estate divided two equal parts.   Son William, ½
estate; then to his heirs.   Son Pinkney, ½ estate; then to
his heirs, including Julia.   Executor: Charles DUNCAN.
Witnesses: Hamilton SCALES and Robert WALL.   Signed: Prudence
(X) RIED.

Page 376.   14 December 1864.   Will of Thomas WELCH.   December
            Term 1864.   Sisters Rebecca WELSH and Elizabeth
FLINCHUM.   Niece Minetty M. FLINCHUM, these three to inherit
my estate in common.   No Executor named.   Witnesses: S.B.
TAYLOR and W.M. McCANLESS.   Signed: Thomas (X) WELCH.

END WILL BOOK IV